Designing Web Layouts with Bootstrap 5

Mastering Responsive Web Design with the Open Source CSS Framework

Ajdin Imsirovic

Designing Web Layouts with Bootstrap 5: Mastering Responsive Web Design with the Open Source CSS Framework

Ajdin Imsirovic
Tuzla, Bosnia and Herzegovina

ISBN-13 (pbk): 979-8-8688-1903-2   ISBN-13 (electronic): 979-8-8688-1904-9
https://doi.org/10.1007/979-8-8688-1904-9

Copyright © 2025 by Ajdin Imsirovic

This work is subject to copyright. All rights are reserved by the Publisher, whether the whole or part of the material is concerned, specifically the rights of translation, reprinting, reuse of illustrations, recitation, broadcasting, reproduction on microfilms or in any other physical way, and transmission or information storage and retrieval, electronic adaptation, computer software, or by similar or dissimilar methodology now known or hereafter developed.

Trademarked names, logos, and images may appear in this book. Rather than use a trademark symbol with every occurrence of a trademarked name, logo, or image we use the names, logos, and images only in an editorial fashion and to the benefit of the trademark owner, with no intention of infringement of the trademark.

The use in this publication of trade names, trademarks, service marks, and similar terms, even if they are not identified as such, is not to be taken as an expression of opinion as to whether or not they are subject to proprietary rights.

While the advice and information in this book are believed to be true and accurate at the date of publication, neither the authors nor the editors nor the publisher can accept any legal responsibility for any errors or omissions that may be made. The publisher makes no warranty, express or implied, with respect to the material contained herein.

> Managing Director, Apress Media LLC: Welmoed Spahr
> Acquisitions Editor: James Robinson-Prior
> Coordinating Editor: Gryffin Winkler

Cover image by Placidplace on pixabay.com

Distributed to the book trade worldwide by Springer Science+Business Media New York, 1 New York Plaza, New York, NY 10004. Phone 1-800-SPRINGER, fax (201) 348-4705, e-mail orders-ny@springer-sbm.com, or visit www.springeronline.com. Apress Media, LLC is a Delaware LLC and the sole member (owner) is Springer Science + Business Media Finance Inc (SSBM Finance Inc). SSBM Finance Inc is a **Delaware** corporation.

For information on translations, please e-mail booktranslations@springernature.com; for reprint, paperback, or audio rights, please e-mail bookpermissions@springernature.com.

Apress titles may be purchased in bulk for academic, corporate, or promotional use. eBook versions and licenses are also available for most titles. For more information, reference our Print and eBook Bulk Sales web page at http://www.apress.com/bulk-sales.

Any source code or other supplementary material referenced by the author in this book is available to readers on GitHub (https://github.com/Apress). For more detailed information, please visit https://www.apress.com/gp/services/source-code.

If disposing of this product, please recycle the paper

To my parents. May the Heaven treat you well.

—Ajdin Imsirovic

Table of Contents

About the Author xix

About the Technical Reviewers xxi

Introduction xxiii

Part I: Your First Layout: Portfolio Page 1

Chapter 1: What You Need to Know: Revision of HTML, CSS, and JavaScript 3

   1.1 Understanding File Extensions.. 3

      1.1.1 Exercise 1: Add a New File with the txt Extension, and Then Change It to the Html Extension 4

   1.2 Opening a File with the Html Extension in Your Browser 8

   1.3 Editing a File Using Notepad 9

   1.4 Making Our index.html File Look Better 11

      1.4.1 Exercise 2: Adding Your First Tags 12

   1.5 How Does the Browser Know How to Display Annotated Text? 13

      1.5.1 What Is Whitespace? 14

      1.5.2 Exercise 3: How Does the Browser Deal with Whitespace in html Files?..... 14

      1.5.3 Whitespace Collapsing in HTML 16

   1.6 Heading Tags in HTML.. 18

   1.7 HTML Attributes 19

      1.7.1 The Style Attribute in HTML 20

   1.8 HTML Is for Structure and CSS Is for Display.. 21

   1.9 Multiple Property-Value CSS Pairs in the Style Attribute 22

   1.10 Block vs. Inline Elements 22

   1.11 Making Block Elements Inline and Vice-versa 24

TABLE OF CONTENTS

1.12 Using External Style Sheets in HTML Pages 26
    1.12.1 HTML DOCTYPE and Metadata 27
    1.12.2 Can Browsers Work Without DOCTYPE and Metadata? 29
1.13 Using devtools 29
    1.13.1 Testing If the External Stylesheet Is Properly Linked 30
    1.13.2 The Anatomy of a CSS Declaration 31
1.14 Moving Inline Styles to an External Stylesheet File 31
    1.14.1 Moving the h1 Styles to an External Stylesheet 32
    1.14.2 Moving the p Styles to an External Stylesheet 33
    1.14.3 Moving the Span Styles to an External Stylesheet 33
1.15 CSS Specificity 34
1.16 CSS Class Selectors and CSS id Selectors 35
1.17 Adding an Interactive Button with the Help of JavaScript 37
1.18 Using the Button HTML Element and the Onclick Attribute to Add Interactivity with JS 38
1.19 How Browsers Work with Web Pages 39
1.20 Conclusion 41

Chapter 2: Containers and Rows in Bootstrap 5.3 43

2.1 Introduction 43
2.2 The Box Model 44
2.3 Containers in Bootstrap 5.3 46
2.4 Understanding Breakpoints 46
    2.4.1 What Are Breakpoints? 46
    2.4.2 Why Do We Need Breakpoints? 47
    2.4.3 Bootstrap's Breakpoint System 47
2.5 Understanding Containers 48
    2.5.1 Fixed-Width Container (.container) 48
    2.5.2 Fluid Container (.container-fluid) 48
    2.5.3 Responsive Containers (.container-{breakpoint}) 49
2.6 Rows in Bootstrap 5.3 49
    2.6.1 Key Features of Rows 50
2.7 How to Use Breakpoints in Bootstrap 50

2.8 Bootstrap Contextual Colors 50

    2.8.1 Background Primary (.bg-primary) 51

    2.8.2 Background Success (.bg-success) 51

2.9 Practical Example 51

2.10 Common Pitfalls to Avoid 53

    2.10.1 Container Nesting Rules 53

2.11 Conclusion 55

Chapter 3: Columns, Breakpoints, and the Grid in Bootstrap 5.3 57

3.1 Introduction 57

3.2 Historical Background – What Shaped the Development of Bootstrap? 57

    3.2.1 The Evolution of CSS Display Properties 57

    3.2.2 The First Grid-Based Web Layout System: 960.gs 58

    3.2.3 Early Grid Systems and Bootstrap's Innovation 58

    3.2.4 Another Piece of the Puzzle: The Rise of Responsive Web Design 61

3.3 Understanding the Building Blocks: Flexbox and CSS Grid 62

    3.3.1 Flexbox: The One-Dimensional Layout Model 62

    3.3.2 CSS Grid: The Two-Dimensional Layout Model 63

    3.3.3 One-Dimensional vs. Two-Dimensional Layouts: What's the Difference? 64

    3.3.4 Bootstrap Grid: An Abstraction Layer 68

3.4 Bootstrap's Column System and Breakpoints in Action 70

    3.4.1 The Full Spectrum of Contextual Colors 70

    3.4.2 A Responsive Portfolio Example 71

    3.4.3 How the Layout "Shape-Shifts" 76

3.5 Building with Bootstrap: What We've Learned and What's Next 77

3.6 Summary 78

Chapter 4: Utilities, Typography, Images, and Tables in Bootstrap 5.3 79

4.1 Introduction 79

4.2 Our Starting Website 80

4.3 Understanding Bootstrap's Utility Classes 82

    4.3.1 Utility Classes Already in Our Layout 82

TABLE OF CONTENTS

- 4.4 Enhancing Our Portfolio with Additional Utility Classes 83
  - 4.4.1 Improving the Header 83
  - 4.4.2 Enhancing the Sidebar 84
  - 4.4.3 Improving the Projects Section 85
  - 4.4.4 Enhancing the Footer 87
- 4.5 The Power of Bootstrap's Utility Classes 88
  - 4.5.1 Common Utility Class Categories 89
- 4.6 Typography in Bootstrap 89
  - 4.6.1 Understanding Bootstrap's Typography System 89
  - 4.6.2 Typography Classes in Bootstrap 90
  - 4.6.3 Enhancing Our Portfolio with Typography Classes 90
  - 4.6.4 Bootstrap Typography Classes Reference 94
- 4.7 Images in Bootstrap 95
  - 4.7.1 Bootstrap's Image Classes 95
  - 4.7.2 Enhancing Our Portfolio with Better Images 96
  - 4.7.3 Using Figure and Figure Caption 99
  - 4.7.4 Bootstrap Image Classes Reference 99
- 4.8 Tables in Bootstrap 100
  - 4.8.1 Bootstrap's Table Classes 100
  - 4.8.2 Adding Tables to Our Portfolio 101
  - 4.8.3 Bootstrap Table Classes Reference 107
- 4.9 Conclusion 107

Part II: Your Second Layout: Invoice Maker 109

Chapter 5: Forms in Bootstrap 5.3 111

- 5.1 Introduction 111
- 5.2 HTML Forms: The Foundation 111
  - 5.2.1 The Form Element 111
  - 5.2.2 Form Controls 112
  - 5.2.3 Form Attributes 114
  - 5.2.4 Accessibility with Labels 114

5.3 The Challenges of Styling Forms with CSS	115
5.3.1 Inconsistent Browser Defaults	115
5.3.2 Complex Pseudo-elements	115
5.3.3 Shadow DOM Elements	115
5.3.4 Focus States and Accessibility	116
5.3.5 Responsive Design Challenges	116
5.3.6 Cross-Browser Compatibility	116
5.4 How Bootstrap Simplifies Form Styling	116
5.5 Bootstrap 5.3 Forms in Depth	117
5.5.1 The Overarching Approach	117
5.5.2 BEM Methodology in Bootstrap Forms	117
5.5.3 Form Layout Options	118
5.5.4 Form Controls in Bootstrap	120
5.5.5 Form Validation	121
5.6 Components vs. Form Elements in Bootstrap	122
5.6.1 What are Components?	122
5.6.2 Are Forms Components?	122
5.7 Building the Invoice Maker Project	122
5.7.1 Project Overview	123
5.7.2 HTML Structure	123
5.7.3 Client Information Section	124
5.7.4 Invoice Details Section	124
5.7.5 Item Entry Form	125
5.7.6 Items Table	126
5.7.7 Totals Section	127
5.7.8 The Complete Invoice Maker	128
5.8 What's Next?	128

TABLE OF CONTENTS

Chapter 6: Components in Bootstrap 5.3 131

6.1 Introduction 131

6.2 The Evolution of Web UI Patterns 131

6.3 Component-Based Design 132

6.4 Categorizing Bootstrap Components 133

    6.4.1 Base Components (Primitive Components) 133

    6.4.2 Compound/Dynamic Components 134

6.5 Additional Component Categories 134

    6.5.1 Form Components 135

    6.5.2 Layout Components 135

    6.5.3 Utility Components 135

6.6 Practical Application: Enhancing Our Invoice App 136

6.7 Deep Dive: The Navbar Component 136

    6.7.1 Responsive Behavior 136

    6.7.2 Navbar Architecture 137

    6.7.3 Placement Options 137

    6.7.4 Color Schemes and Customization 138

    6.7.5 Further Accessibility Considerations 138

    6.7.6 Adding a Navbar 139

6.8 Deep Dive: The Card Component 140

    6.8.1 The Anatomy of a Card 140

    6.8.2 Card Variants and Styling 141

    6.8.3 Cards as Content Containers 142

    6.8.4 Card Design Principles 142

    6.8.5 Using Cards for Content Organization 143

    6.8.6 Implementing a Theme Toggle 144

6.9 The Finished Example 145

6.10 The Art of Component Composition 152

    6.10.1 Principles of Effective Component Composition 153

    6.10.2 Common Component Combinations 153

6.10.3 Nested Components in Our Invoice App 155

6.10.4 Advanced Component Composition Techniques 156

6.11 Conclusion 156

Chapter 7: JavaScript-Powered Components in Bootstrap 5.3 159

7.1 Introduction 159

7.2 Implementing Tab Navigation 160

7.2.1 Understanding Bootstrap's Tab Component 160

7.2.2 Adding Tabs to Our Invoice Items Section 161

7.2.3 How the Tab System Works 167

7.2.4 The Card View Layout 167

7.2.5 Making the Tabs Interactive 168

7.2.6 Testing Our Tab Navigation 170

7.3 Implementing a Modal Form 170

7.3.1 Understanding Bootstrap Modals 170

7.3.2 Creating the Add Item Modal 171

7.3.3 Connecting the Modal to Our Buttons 172

7.3.4 Handling Form Submission 173

7.3.5 Form Validation 177

7.3.6 Understanding Dynamic DOM Manipulation 177

7.3.7 Testing the Modal Form 178

7.4 Implementing a Loading Indicator 178

7.4.1 Understanding Bootstrap Spinners 179

7.4.2 Adding the Reset Button 179

7.4.3 Implementing the Loading State 180

7.4.4 Understanding setTimeout 181

7.4.5 The Spinner Component 182

7.4.6 Testing the Loading Indicator 182

7.4.7 Variations of the Spinner Component 183

7.4.8 Best Practices for Loading Indicators 184

TABLE OF CONTENTS

7.5 Calculating and Displaying Invoice Totals 184
####### 7.5.1 Setting Up the Totals Section 185
####### 7.5.2 Implementing the updateTotals Function 186
####### 7.5.3 Understanding the DOM Traversal 188
####### 7.5.4 Calling updateTotals 188
####### 7.5.5 Testing the Totals Calculation 189
####### 7.5.6 Understanding Data Flow 190
####### 7.5.7 Enhancing the User Experience 190
7.6 Conclusion 191

Chapter 8: Sharing Your Invoice Maker App with the World 193
8.1 Introduction 193
8.2 Understanding Git: Your Code's Safety Net 194
####### 8.2.1 What Is Git? 194
####### 8.2.2 Git Basics: The Three-Step Process 194
####### 8.2.3 A Note on Best Practices 195
8.3 GitHub: Your Code's Home in the Cloud 195
####### 8.3.1 What Is GitHub? 195
8.4 Netlify: From Code to Live Website 196
####### 8.4.1 What Is Netlify? 196
8.5 Setting Up Git for Your Invoice Maker App (Optional) 196
####### 8.5.1 What Is Git Again? 197
####### 8.5.2 The Simplest Git Setup 197
####### 8.5.3 Why This Matters 197
8.6 Creating a GitHub Repository 198
####### 8.6.1 Step 1: Create a GitHub Account 198
####### 8.6.2 Step 2: Create a New Repository 198
####### 8.6.3 Step 3: Upload Your Files to GitHub 199
####### 8.6.4 Step 4: Verify Your Repository 200

8.7 Deploying Your App with Netlify 200

    8.7.1 Step 1: Create a Netlify Account 200

    8.7.2 Step 2: Create a New Site from Git 200

    8.7.3 Step 3: Configure Your Build Settings 201

    8.7.4 Step 4: Wait for Deployment 201

    8.7.5 Step 5: Customize Your Site Name (Optional) 201

    8.7.6 Step 6: Visit Your Live Site 202

8.8 Making Updates to Your Live Site 202

8.9 Conclusion 203

Part III: Your Third Layout: Bootstrap 5.3 and React 205

Chapter 9: Modern Front-End Tooling 207

9.1 Introduction 207

9.2 The Evolution of JavaScript: From ES5 to Modern Times 208

9.3 The Module Revolution: Why JavaScript Needed a Better Way to Organize Code 209

9.4 Enter Node.js: JavaScript Beyond the Browser 210

9.5 The Client-Server Model and REST: How Websites Traditionally Work 211

9.6 The Rise of React and the Virtual DOM 212

9.7 npm: The Package Manager That Changed Everything 212

9.8 Installing Node.js and npm 214

    9.8.1 Windows: 214

    9.8.2 macOS: 214

    9.8.3 Ubuntu/Debian Linux: 214

9.9 Modern Project Starters: From Create React App to Vite 215

    9.9.1 The npm create and npx create Commands 215

9.10 CDNs vs. npm: Different Ways to Include Dependencies 216

9.11 Understanding Node Modules and Bundlers 217

9.12 Bringing It All Together: The Modern Front-End Workflow 218

9.13 What This Means for Bootstrap 219

9.14 Conclusion: Staying on the Edge of Competence 220

TABLE OF CONTENTS

Chapter 10: React Concepts You Need to Know to Code Your Layout 221

    10.1 Introduction 221

    10.2 Setting Up Your First React Project 222

        10.2.1 Option 1: Using an Online Code Editor 222

        10.2.2 Option 2: Using Vite Locally 222

        10.2.3 Understanding the Project Structure 223

        10.2.4 Adding Bootstrap to Our Project 224

    10.3 Understanding JSX: React's Special Syntax 224

        10.3.1 What Is JSX? 224

        10.3.2 JSX Rules and Quirks 225

        10.3.3 JSX and HTML Attributes 227

    10.4 Creating Your First React Component 228

        10.4.1 Basic Component Structure 228

        10.4.2 Creating a Header Component 229

        10.4.3 Using the Header Component 230

        10.4.4 Creating a Hero Section Component 231

        10.4.5 Adding the Hero Component to Our App 232

    10.5 Understanding Props: Passing Data to Components 233

        10.5.1 What Are Props? 233

        10.5.2 A Quick Refresher on JavaScript Objects 233

        10.5.3 How Props Work in React 234

        10.5.4 Creating a Reusable PizzaCard Component 234

        10.5.5 Creating a Menu Section Component 235

        10.5.6 Adding the Menu to Our App 238

        10.5.7 Understanding Props in More Detail 238

        10.5.8 Props vs. Hardcoded Values 239

        10.5.9 Props Are Read-Only 240

    10.6 Building a Testimonials Section 240

        10.6.1 Creating a Testimonial Component 240

        10.6.2 Creating a Testimonials Section Component 242

        10.6.3 Adding the Testimonials to Our App 243

10.7 Creating a Footer Component 244

    10.7.1 Adding the Footer to Our App 245

10.8 Importing Assets in React 246

    10.8.1 Adding Images to Your Project 246

    10.8.2 Adding CSS Files 247

10.9 Conclusion: Bringing It All Together 248

    10.9.1 What's Next: Adding Interactivity 249

Chapter 11: Adding Interactivity to Your React Restaurant Website 251

11.1 Introduction 251

11.2 Understanding State in React 251

    11.2.1 Props vs. Internal State 252

11.3 Introducing React Hooks and useState 253

    11.3.1 Understanding Destructuring in JavaScript 253

    11.3.2 Object vs. Array Destructuring: Why React Uses Array Destructuring for useState .. 255

    11.3.3 How useState Works 256

    11.3.4 Using Multiple State Variables 257

    11.3.5 Using Objects with useState 258

11.4 Event Handling in React 258

    11.4.1 Common Events in React 259

    11.4.2 Handling Form Inputs 260

    11.4.3 Adding Interactivity to Our Pizza Paradise Website 261

11.5 Component Hierarchy and State Flow in React 263

    11.5.1 State Lifting 263

    11.5.2 Understanding the Flow of Data 268

    11.5.3 Child-to-Parent Communication 268

    11.5.4 Grandparent-to-Grandchild Communication 269

11.6 Building a Shopping Cart Component 269

11.7 Passing Event Handlers as Props 274

11.8 Conclusion 281

Chapter 12: Improving Your Restaurant Website Using the React-Bootstrap npm Package 283

12.1 Introduction 283

12.2 Understanding React-Bootstrap 284

    12.2.1 What Is React-Bootstrap? 284

    12.2.2 How Does React-Bootstrap Work? 284

    12.2.3 React-Bootstrap vs. Bootstrap 285

    12.2.4 Completeness and Community 286

12.3 Setting Up React-Bootstrap in Our Project 286

    12.3.1 Step 1: Install the Dependencies 286

    12.3.2 Step 2: Import the Bootstrap CSS 286

12.4 Refactoring Our Components with React-Bootstrap 287

    12.4.1 Refactoring the Header Component 287

    12.4.2 Key Changes and Benefits 290

    12.4.3 Refactoring the Hero Component 291

    12.4.4 Refactoring the PizzaCard Component 292

    12.4.5 Refactoring the PizzaCustomizer Component 294

    12.4.6 Refactoring the Menu Component 298

    12.4.7 Refactoring the App Component 299

12.5 Benefits of Using React-Bootstrap 301

    12.5.1 Declarative Component API 302

    12.5.2 Component Composition 302

    12.5.3 Improved Type Safety 303

    12.5.4 Accessibility Improvements 303

    12.5.5 Reduced Bundle Size 303

    12.5.6 Better Integration with React Patterns 303

12.6 Common Pitfalls and How to Avoid Them 303

    12.6.1 Mixing Bootstrap Classes with React-Bootstrap Components 303

    12.6.2 Not Importing the Bootstrap CSS 304

    12.6.3 Using Imperative Code with React-Bootstrap Components 304

12.7 Conclusion 305

12.8 Things That We Didn't Discuss 305
12.8.1 State Management Solutions 306
12.8.2 Type Systems and Tooling 306
12.8.3 Build Tools and Module Bundlers 306
12.8.4 CSS Solutions 307
12.8.5 UI Component Libraries 307
12.8.6 Modern React Patterns 307
12.8.7 State-Driven UI Approaches 308
12.9 Conclusion 308

Index 309

About the Author

Ajdin Imsirovic is a seasoned web developer and passionate educator in the field of programming. He is the creator of UIstate – a modular state management system built on browser primitives.

cssState.js serializes state into CSS custom properties and data attributes, making it visible, introspectable, and directly coupled to styling. eventState.js encapsulates state behind closures and uses DOM events for pub/sub, providing privacy and hierarchical subscriptions.

Both modules are complementary and framework-free. No build tools. No virtual DOM. Just the browser's native capabilities, orchestrated through a modular API you can compose to fit your needs.

About the Technical Reviewers

Mirza Suljic is a Senior Software Development Engineer at ABC TECH Group with extensive experience in software development and technical systems. He holds a bachelor's degree in Computer Software Engineering.

Throughout his career, he has demonstrated expertise in modern web technologies including Angular and JavaScript, with extensive experience in full-stack development, database management (MySQL), and cross-platform application testing.

His professional background spans multiple roles from software development to deployment engineering and technical support, giving him a comprehensive understanding of the software development lifecycle.

Armin Eminagic is a Medior Software Engineer with 4 years of experience in Fullstack Development.

Born in Germany, he currently lives in Bosnia and Herzegovina.

As a software engineer, he has worked across diverse projects and tech stacks, including GoLang, AngularJS, Angular 2+, Python, Java (Servlets), Kotlin, Spring Boot, and GraphQL, with strong integration experience in Kafka, AWS services, and other modern tools.

He is comfortable working in Unix/Linux environments as his primary development platforms. His professional background includes

- Developing server-side web applications for hosting telecommunication software
- Building tools that enable data engineers to generate reports and manage file documentation from multiple data sources

Introduction

Welcome to *Designing Web Layouts with Bootstrap 5*! This book takes you on a comprehensive journey through one of the web's most popular front-end frameworks, equipping you with the knowledge and skills to build beautiful, responsive websites with confidence.

What This Book Is About

In today's fast-paced web development landscape, Bootstrap 5 stands as a reliable framework that allows developers to create professional websites quickly and efficiently. This book demystifies Bootstrap 5.3, teaching you not just how to use it, but how to understand its underlying principles. We go beyond simple copy-paste solutions to provide you with a deep comprehension of how Bootstrap works, enabling you to customize it to your specific needs and integrate it with modern technologies like React.

Who This Book Is For

Whether you're a complete beginner to web development or an experienced developer looking to add Bootstrap to your skill set, this book is designed for you. We start with the fundamentals of HTML, CSS, and JavaScript – ensuring that even those with minimal coding experience can follow along – before progressively advancing to more complex topics.

This approach makes the book ideal for

- Web development beginners who want to learn Bootstrap from the ground up
- Design-focused professionals seeking to implement responsive designs

INTRODUCTION

- Developers transitioning from older Bootstrap versions to version 5.3
- JavaScript developers looking to integrate Bootstrap with React applications

The Structure of This Book

The book follows a carefully structured learning path that builds your knowledge progressively:

1. **Fundamentals First**: We begin with essential HTML, CSS, and JavaScript concepts, ensuring you have a solid foundation.

2. **Core Bootstrap Components**: The middle chapters explore Bootstrap's powerful grid system, containers, components, and utilities.

3. **Advanced Implementation**: Later chapters cover JavaScript integration, deployment strategies, and modern front-end tooling.

4. **React Integration**: The final sections bridge Bootstrap with React, teaching you how to leverage both technologies together.

Chapter Overview

Each chapter in this book serves a specific purpose in your learning journey:

- **Chapter 1**: Establishes the necessary HTML, CSS, and JavaScript knowledge you'll need as a foundation

- **Chapters 2 and 3**: Dive into Bootstrap's layout system with containers, rows, columns, and breakpoints

- **Chapter 4**: Explores Bootstrap's rich utilities for typography, images, and tables

- **Chapter 5**: Masters forms in Bootstrap for effective user input

- **Chapter 6**: Examines Bootstrap's versatile component library

- **Chapter 7**: Integrates JavaScript with Bootstrap for interactive elements
- **Chapter 8**: Takes your projects live with deployment strategies on platforms like Netlify
- **Chapter 9**: Introduces modern front-end tooling to enhance your workflow
- **Chapters 10–12**: Bridge Bootstrap with React, teaching component-based architecture and integrating these powerful technologies

A Practical Approach

What sets this book apart is its practical, hands-on approach. Rather than overwhelming you with theory, we guide you through exercises and real-world examples that reinforce concepts immediately. You'll build progressively more complex projects, starting with simple HTML pages and culminating in a fully functional restaurant website built with React and Bootstrap.

By the end of this journey, you'll have not only mastered Bootstrap 5.3, but you'll also understand how it fits into the broader web development ecosystem – giving you the confidence to tackle various front-end challenges that come your way.

Let's begin this exciting journey together, as we transform you from a Bootstrap novice into a confident web developer capable of creating beautiful, responsive websites with Bootstrap 5.3 and beyond!

PART I

Your First Layout: Portfolio Page

CHAPTER 1

What You Need to Know: Revision of HTML, CSS, and JavaScript

Welcome to the exciting world of Bootstrap 5.3! Before we dive into the intricacies of this powerful front-end framework, it's essential to establish a solid foundation in the fundamental building blocks of web development: HTML, CSS, and JavaScript. In this chapter, we will introduce these technologies, ensuring that you have the necessary skills to understand and effectively use Bootstrap 5.3 in your projects.

Let's begin our journey by jumping right in and creating our very first web page.

Before we can do that, though, we need to build up some understanding of how computers work in general.

We'll start by discussing file extensions.

1.1 Understanding File Extensions

Let's say you have a folder on your desktop, and the folder is named "holiday".

You might have the following files in your "holiday" folder:

- `beach.jpg`
- `map.jpg`
- `itinerary.txt`

Let's imagine that you have saved the image of a beach next to the rental property you want to spend your holiday at, and you're sending this image to your friends so that they can see what a great spot that is. You've saved the file as beach, and the computer likely tacked on the jpg extension while you were saving it. Similarly, you wanted to save a map of the surrounding area; you clicked on the image that was open in your browser, then clicked the "Save as…" command, and typed the name of the file: "map". The computer did the rest; it appended the file extension of jpg to the filename, and the file named map.jpg now ended up in your "holiday" folder.

Let's also say that you prepared the itinerary in a simple text file (whose extension is txt), and thus the computer saved it as itinerary.txt.

This brings us to the first exercise for you.

1.1.1 Exercise 1: Add a New File with the txt Extension, and Then Change It to the Html Extension

In this exercise, you need to make a brand new file and name it "itinerary.txt".

This involves several steps:

1. Make the Desktop visible.
2. Right click on empty area of the Desktop and click on the "New" command.
3. Locate and click on "Text Document" to make a new text file.
4. Name your text file "index.txt".
5. Rename your text file to "index.html".

The first step is to make your Desktop visible. Why would it not be visible? Well, perhaps you have a browser window open, or maybe some other program is open and maximized, obscuring the view of the desktop.

Step 1: Make the Desktop visible

On Windows, you'd do it as follows:

- Press and hold the "Windows" key on the keyboard.
- With the "Windows" key still pressed, press the letter "D" key on the keyboard.

Completing this step will toggle on and off the visibility of the desktop. If you have a program open on your computer, pressing the abovementioned keyboard shortcut will show/hide the visibility of the desktop or the visibility of the program that's open.

Alternatively, if you've got no open programs on your Windows machine, pressing the "WIN D" shortcut key will not do anything.

Step 2: Right-click on the empty area of the Desktop and click on the "New" command

Right-click on the empty area of the Desktop and click on the "New" command.

Figure 1-1. New Command on the Desktop

Step 3: Locate and click on "Text Document" to make a new text file

Locate and click on "Text Document" to make a new text file.

Step 4: Name your text file "index.txt"

Once you've completed Step 3, Windows will readily highlight the "New Document" name and allow you to simply type a new name of the document.

CHAPTER 1   WHAT YOU NEED TO KNOW: REVISION OF HTML, CSS, AND JAVASCRIPT

Figure 1-2. *Creating New Document*

Type in "index.txt".
Step 5: Rename your text file to "index.html"
Now that you have the "index.txt" file on your Desktop, you can hold down the SHIFT key and right-click on it and select the "Rename" command (the second command from the bottom). Now, you can type in the following file name and extension: "index.html".

Figure 1-3. *Renaming File*

Troubleshooting

Sometimes, Windows likes to "simplify" things and hides file extensions from users. In such a case, you need to open the file explorer using the shortcut key of "Win" and "e".

Simply press the "Win" key, hold it down, then press the "e" key, and after that, you can release both keys. You should see the file explorer.

Next, click on the "View" dropdown, then "Show," and finally, ensure that the "File name extensions" option is checked. If it is unchecked, you can check it by clicking on it.

CHAPTER 1   WHAT YOU NEED TO KNOW: REVISION OF HTML, CSS, AND JAVASCRIPT

Figure 1-4. *Changing File Format*

We've successfully changed our file from txt to html.

Your Windows system will likely change the icon of the document from the txt file extension – whose icon is a page with lines of text on it – to the icon for whatever browser is the default browser on your machine. Since Windows comes with the Edge browser as its default browser, you'll see the icon for the Edge browser on your `index.html` file.

Alternatively, if your default browser is Firefox, Chrome, Opera, or some other browser, it's likely that the icon for your `index.html` file will be shown as such.

If you have many icons on your Desktop, understanding that icons are tied to specific file extensions should make it easier to locate your file.

1.2 Opening a File with the Html Extension in Your Browser

Well, if you double-click on the file name, it will open it in a browser.

The browser screen will be empty, because our file is empty.

Since the file is not showing anything in the browser, for now, you can close the browser window, and we'll open it in a piece of software that allows us to change the contents of our `index.html` file – by typing some text into it.

CHAPTER 1 WHAT YOU NEED TO KNOW: REVISION OF HTML, CSS, AND JAVASCRIPT

1.3 Editing a File Using Notepad

Let's now add some content to our `index.html` file so that we can have something shown on the screen once we reopen it in the browser.

To do it, just right-click onto the `index.html` file, locate the "Edit in Notepad" command, and click on it.

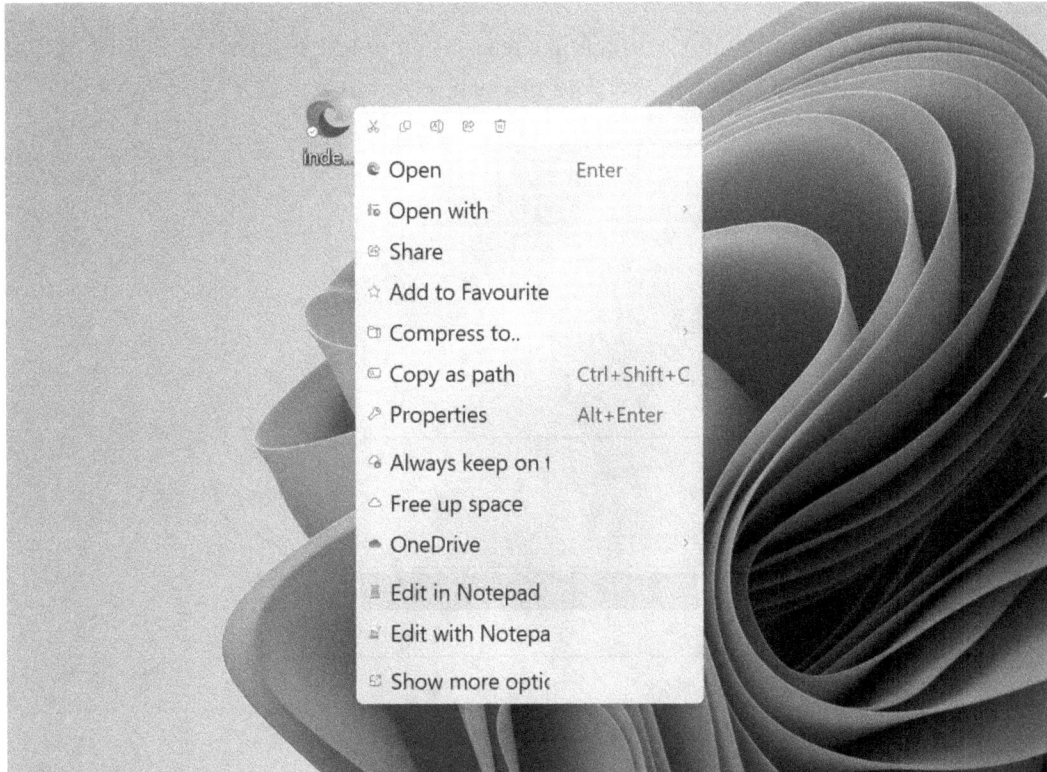

Figure 1-5. *Editing File in Notepad*

You'll be greeted with a very simple interface.

Now, type the following sentence:

```
Welcome to my homepage!
```

CHAPTER 1 WHAT YOU NEED TO KNOW: REVISION OF HTML, CSS, AND JAVASCRIPT

If the text you've typed in is too small, you can change the level of zoom in the Notepad program by

- Holding down the CTRL button and pressing the + button on the numpad (to zoom in)

- Holding down the CTRL button and pressing the – button on the numpad (to zoom out)

In the following screenshot, you'll find the result of holding down the CTRL key and pressing the + button multiple times. It's a pretty large zoom!

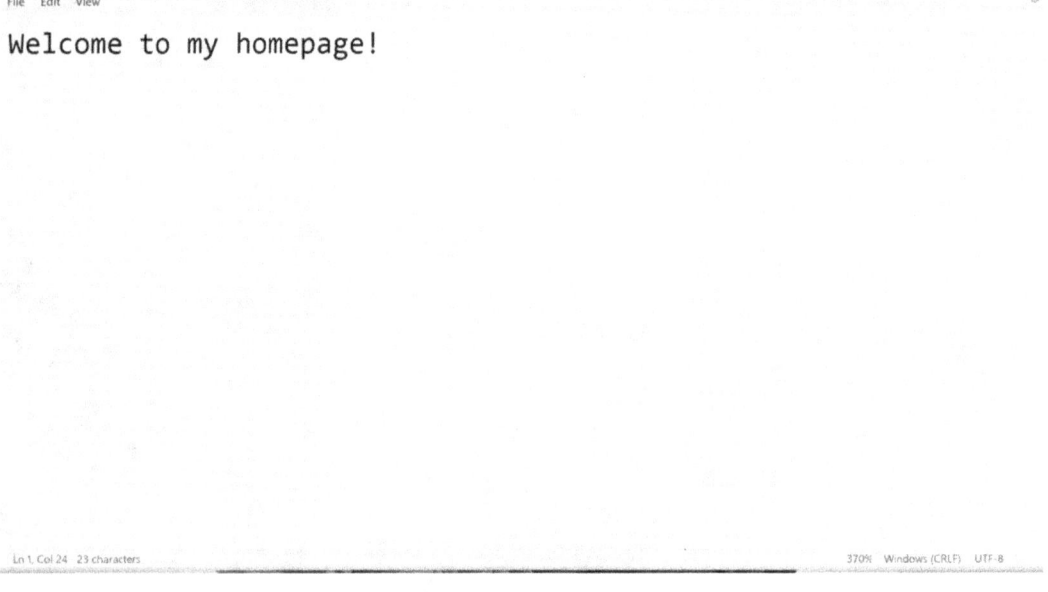

Figure 1-6. *index.html on Notepad*

The point that I'm making here is that you can easily zoom the text in or out to adjust to what works for you and makes it easy for you to read and work with.

Now that you've set the zoom level to your liking, hold down the CTRL key and press the S key on your keyboard to save the update you've just made to your `index.html` file.

Next, close the Notepad program, and locate the `index.html` file again on the desktop.

Open it in your browser again, and you'll see the text you've just written. Your webpage is no longer empty.

As a quick sidenote, just like you zoomed in the text in your Notepad application, you can use the exact same shortcut keys to zoom in on most modern browsers. Hold down the CTRL key and press the + button on the numpad a few times and you'll see the text zoom in.

Here's a screenshot of what that looks like.

Figure 1-7. *Homepage Zoomed In*

As a quick side note, notice how the text it a different font than what you had in Notepad. This is the result of the browser having what's known as "a user agent style sheet" – which simply means it has its own predetermined, internal way of displaying text on the screen in a particular way. We'll come back to this later, but for now, let's continue what we were doing.

If you hold down the CTRL key and then press the 0 button on the numpad, the browser will reset the zoom back to 100% – that is, to the default size of zoom.

Now that we've learned about the basics of opening and closing files in a text editor and in the browser, we can move on to making our `index.html` file look more like a real website.

1.4 Making Our index.html File Look Better

To make our index.html file look better in the browser, we'll use something known as "tags."

A tag is something we use to "annotate" text.

When we annotate text, it's sort of like adding it a special note that the browser will understand and, based on that understanding, will do something.

What is that "something"?

Essentially, it will display our text differently. But not only that – tags also help browsers understand what type of content they are displaying – whether it's a heading, paragraph, or image.

It's best to give you an example.

Let's open the `index.html` file again in Notepad, and let's do another exercise.

1.4.1 Exercise 2: Adding Your First Tags

Currently, we still have the sentence "Welcome to my homepage!" in the `index.html` file.

Now, let's add tags to it. We'll add two "Heading 1" tags by following the steps below:

- Step 1: Add the opening Heading 1 tag
- Step 2: Add the closing Heading 1 tag
- Step 3: Add some more text on the next line
- Step 4: Save the file and open it in the browser

Step 1: Add the opening Heading 1 tag

First, you'll add the following text before the first word ("Welcome"):

```
<h1>
```

This is an example of an opening tag. An opening Heading 1 tag has a less-than character, followed by `h1`, and it ends with a greater-than character.

Step 2: Add the closing Heading 1 tag

Next, after the very last character in your `index.html` file – that is – after the exclamation mark, add the following closing tag:

```
</h1>
```

A closing tag is essentially the same as an opening tag, with the addition of a forward slash character (sometimes referred to just as "slash").

Step 3: Add some more text on the next line

This is an optional step, but an important one.

The reason to add this line is to be able to compare "normal text" in our web page with the text that we've just annotated with the opening and closing `h1` tags.

So, on the second line, let's type anything, for example:

```
The weather is nice today.
```

If you've done everything correctly, your Notepad should look like this.

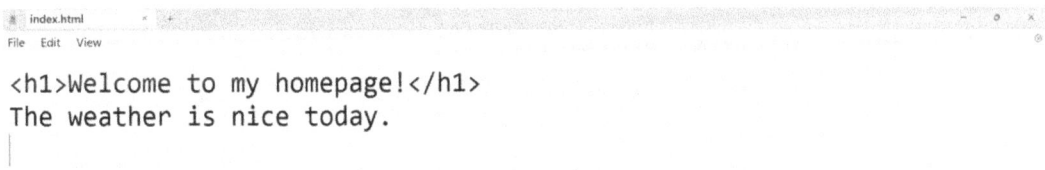

Figure 1-8. *Notepad Results*

Step 4: Save the file and open it in the browser

After saving the file in Notepad and re-opening it in the browser, you'll be greeted with the following screen.

Figure 1-9. *File Opened Up in Browser*

Great, this looks good. One thing you might be wondering is: "How does the browser change the look of the first line of text based on tags?"

This is actually quite interesting. Let's discuss it briefly.

1.5 How Does the Browser Know How to Display Annotated Text?

If we really simplify things, and use a bit of a metaphor, the browser has sort of a "little booklet."

When it tries opening an html document, if that document is formatted correctly (e.g., the tags are written properly), the browser will try to match the tags that it finds in your `index.html` file and it will "look into its little booklet" where it has a set of instructions on how each tag should look like.

So, the browser looks for the `h1` tag and finds that the `h1` tag is supposed to have larger than normal letters, and that those letters should be bold.

Once it understands that this is how an `h1` tag is supposed to be displayed, it then does exactly that.

Obviously, the browser keeps on doing this until the entire file is displayed, or "rendered" on the screen. And that "little booklet" we just discussed? It's what's officially known as a "user agent style sheet." We'll keep coming back to this in various parts of this book, but let's leave it at that for now.

If you are a bit more experienced, you will likely realize that the above explanation is oversimplifying things, but looking at it from the viewpoint of the thing being explained here, this oversimplification is enough. We'll extend our understanding of these concepts as we progress in the book.

Next, let's test out some of our assumptions about how a browser renders your html pages. Specifically, we'll discuss how browser deals with whitespace.

For that, we'll do another exercise.

However, before we can do the exercise, we first need to understand what exactly whitespace is.

1.5.1 What Is Whitespace?

While **whitespace** can mean various things in the world of web development and web design, we are interested in a specific, narrow definition, related to writing code - or, even more precisely, writing html code.

In the strictest sense of writing html code, the term whitespace refers to characters, namely: spaces, line breaks, and tabs in your code.

1.5.2 Exercise 3: How Does the Browser Deal with Whitespace in html Files?

In this exercise, we'll update our `index.html` file in the Notepad app, and inspect what happens with our text, when it's displayed in the browser.

CHAPTER 1   WHAT YOU NEED TO KNOW: REVISION OF HTML, CSS, AND JAVASCRIPT

Here are the steps we'll take:

- Step 1: Update the index.html file by adding multiple spaces between words on the second line
- Step 2: Update the index.html file by adding another line of text and separating the words with tabs
- Step 3: Save the changes and view the updates in the browser

Step 1: Update the index.html file by adding multiple spaces between words on the second line

First, let's reopen our index.html file in Notepad, and update it as follows:

```
<h1>Welcome to my homepage!</h1>
The    weather    is    nice    today.
```

If it's not obvious, instead of having a single space character between words on the second line, I've now added three space characters between each word.

Step 2: Update the index.html file by adding another line of text and separating the words with tabs

Next, let's further change our index.html file by adding another line and separating the words with tabs.

```
<h1>Welcome to my homepage!</h1>
The    weather    is    nice    today.
Whitespace    in    browsers.
```

Again, I've done a similar thing, I've separated each word on line three with two tabs. This is what the index.html file looks like in Notepad after all the changes.

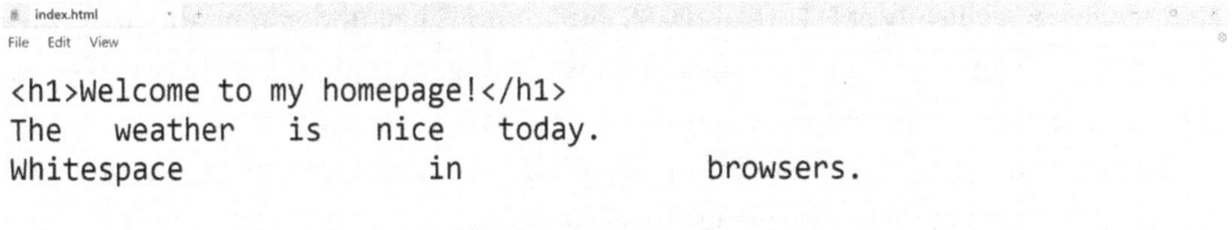

```
<h1>Welcome to my homepage!</h1>
The    weather    is    nice    today.
Whitespace            in              browsers.
```

Figure 1-10. Updated index.html File After Updates

How will this change be displayed in the browser? Let's find out.

Step 3: Save the changes and view the updates in the browser

After saving the changes and re-opening the file in the browser, this is what we get.

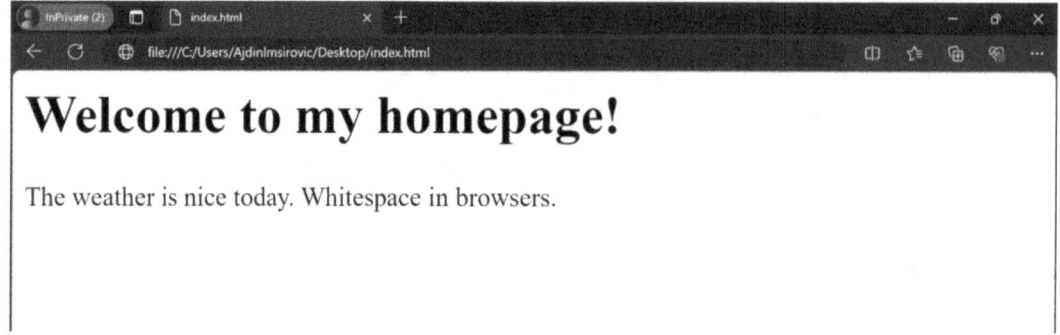

Figure 1-11. *New Homepage*

Notice that the output is different from what we had in the Notepad app?

It's all got to do with something known as "whitespace collapsing" in HTML.

1.5.3 Whitespace Collapsing in HTML

Browsers handle whitespace in HTML in a specific way:

- Multiple consecutive whitespace characters are collapsed into a single space.
- Line breaks and tabs are treated as spaces.

Now that you understand this, you might be wondering exactly how we'll force the browser to display the text exactly as we type it.

The answer to this question will come naturally as you get better at web technologies, specifically at HTML and CSS, but for now, just understand that in most situations, you wouldn't want to do that anyway. Typing multiple spaces between words, or separating words with tabs is usually not the right way of doing things.

If you're still curious and would want to try it out, you can force the browser to not collapse the space characters by using the   code.

1.5.3.1 What Is ?

The   code is one of a number of **HTML entities** – special characters that can sometimes come in handy.

If you really wanted to force your second line to have three spaces between each word, you'd write it like this:

```
The     weather     is
    nice
    today.
```

I could have written this on a single line but it would be very hard to read. Since the browser collapses line breaks anyway, there's no real difference.

Back to the topic of HTML entities, some of them can be a bit more useful, like, for example, the € HTML entity, which prints out the Euro character for currency display.

To see it in action, let's go back to our `index.html` file and update it as follows:

```
<h1>Welcome to my homepage!</h1>
The weather is nice today.
Whitespace in browsers.
<h2>&euro;</h2>
```

If you save the above change and open it in the browser, you'll see three lines of text:

- Welcome to my homepage!
- The weather is nice today. Whitespace in browsers.
- €

Notice that I've surrounded the Euro HTML entity with the h2 opening and closing tags. This is also known as the "Heading 2" tag.

Before we learn more about heading tags in HTML, let's take a very short detour and discuss HTML elements.

1.5.3.2 HTML Elements

An HTML element is simply an opening and closing tag, and whatever there is inside it.

What does that mean in practice?

Let's go back to this line of HTML code:

```
<h1>Welcome to my homepage!</h1>
```

In this line of code, the <h1> is referred to as "the opening h1 tag", the </h1> is referred to as "the closing h1 tag", and the text in between is referred to as "the text node".

Why is this important?

Well, simply put, it's much easier to say "the h1 element" on the page, then it is to say "the opening h1 tag", "the text node", and "the closing h1 tag".

So, to reiterate, an HTML page consists of HTML elements, and these elements consist of

- An opening tag
- A closing tag
- Everything else that's in between an opening and a closing tag

Next, let's discuss heading tags in a bit more detail.

1.6 Heading Tags in HTML

Altogether, there are six heading tags in HTML

- h1
- h2
- h3
- h4
- h5
- h6

The h1 is visually the largest (based on the browser's "little book"), and h6 is the smallest. This is also the case for **importance**: the h1 tag is the most important, and the h6 tag is the least important.

To drive this point home, here's how you can think of each of the tags, using the metaphor of a book:

- h1 is the book's title – a book has only one title, and your HTML page should have a single h1 tag
- h2 is used for separate chapters of the book

- h3, h4, h5, h6 are sections, sub-sections, and sub-sub-sections of the book

Next, let's introduce HTML attributes.

1.7 HTML Attributes

An HTML attribute is a way to add some key-value pairs to our HTML elements.

For example, let's update our h1 element as follows:

```
<h1 align="right">Welcome to my homepage!</h1>
```

If you save your change and open it in the browser, you'll notice that the heading is now right-aligned, rather than left-aligned.

Note that the above example shows code the way it used to be written way, way back – sometimes during the late 1990s. Although browsers still honor this code, it is not considered a best practice, and it hasn't been considered a best practice for a while.

Why did I then show it to you?

Well, I wanted you to understand in a simple and obvious example that HTML attributes are a way to write key-value pairs with the following general formula:

```
key="value"
```

The reason why I showed you the `align="right"` example is that it's a simple pairing, and when you see more complex key-value pairs, you will hopefully not be overwhelmed or confused.

Let's see if it worked.

Instead of using the simple `align="right"` HTML attribute, let's instead update our h1 element to this:

```
<h1  style="text-align: right">
  Welcome to my homepage!
</h1>
```

I've done a couple of things here.

First, I've replaced the previous HTML attribute with `style="text-align: right"`.
Second, I've split my h1 element into three lines – as it was getting a bit too long.
Let's focus on the first update. What is this `style` attribute?

1.7.1 The Style Attribute in HTML

The `style` attribute allows us to "inject" a whole different language into our HTML.

That language is called CSS – Cascading Style Sheets.

No need to get too technical here – CSS is simply a way for you to change the way that a web page is displayed on the screen.

We'll get back to this topic later. For now, let's just briefly discuss the "value" part of the key-value pair for the `style` HTML attribute.

So, the text behind the = sign reads: `text-align: right`.

What is that? That is an actual example of CSS code. To be more precise, it is a CSS declaration. A CSS declaration consists of *properties* and *values*.

In our example, the `text-align` part is the *property*, and the `right` is the *value*.

To simplify things, the property-value syntax is just another example of a key-value pairing that we discussed earlier.

So, to reiterate, this simple example holds two key-value pairs in two languages:

- the word `right` is the value of the key `text-align`
- the `text-align: right` is the value of the key `style`

While the wording here might be a bit convoluted, it would probably help doing another exercise at this point. Understanding how to practically use the `style` HTML attribute in our HTML pages will go a long way in having an easier time understanding the underlying theory.

1.7.1.1 Exercise 4: Practice Using the Style Attribute

In this exercise, we'll go through the following steps:

- Step 1: Replace `text-align: right` with `text-align: center`, and view the result
- Step 2: Replace `text-align: right` with `border: 10px solid green`, and view the result
- Step 3: Replace `border: 1px solid green` with `display: none`, and view the result

Here is each step in detail.

Step 1: Replace `text-align: right` with `text-align: center`, and view the result

In this step, update the first line in your `index.html` file so that it looks as follows:

```
<h1 style="text-align: center">Welcome to my homepage!</h1>
```

The resulting page will now show the h1 element in the center of the screen.

Step 2: Replace `text-align: right` with `border: 1px solid green`, and view the result

Let's now replace the property-value in this CSS declaration completely:

```
<h1 style="border: 1px solid green">Welcome to my homepage!</h1>
```

This update now adds a green border that's 10 pixels wide around our h1 element.

Step 3: Replace `border: 1px solid green` with `display: none`, and view the result

Finally, what will happen if we use the `display` property and set it's value to none?

```
<h1 style="display: none">Welcome to my homepage!</h1>
```

If you open the browser after this change, the h1 element will be completely hidden. What does that tell us?

It tells us that we can control the display of our HTML page with CSS: even though our HTML code is basically the same, by using the `style` attribute and replacing the property-value pairs inside of it, we can change the way that our pages look like, without changing the actual structure of the page.

1.8 HTML Is for Structure and CSS Is for Display

The previous section leads us to a very important conclusion.

We use HTML for content, and we use CSS for changing the display of that content.

In our previous examples, we saw how we can change the way an h1 heading looks with a simple change in the style attribute. It's very important to keep this distinction in mind.

This is why using the `align="right"` HTML attribute is considered a bad practice. It blurs the separation between content and style.

There's another reason why using the `style` HTML attribute is better: you can put multiple property-value pairs inside a single `style` HTML attribute.

1.9 Multiple Property-Value CSS Pairs in the Style Attribute

In this section, let's make our h1 element have:

- a border, which should be `20px dotted orange`
- `text-align` should be `center`
- `display` should be set to `inline`

Here's what that will look like:

```
<h1
  style="border: 20px dotted orange;
         text-align: center;
         display: inline;"
>
  Welcome to my homepage!
</h1>
```

There's a lot going on here; let's go through most relevant updates and conclusions.

First, each single CSS property-value pair is separated using the semi-colon – the `;` character.

Second, notice the weird formatting of HTML? I've tried to make it a bit better by listing CSS property-value pairs one under the other – but still, this just feels *unwieldy*. There is a much better way to do this, and it's known as an *external stylesheet*. We'll come back to this a bit later.

Third, the `display: inline` is changing our heading to not take up the full width of the browser window – instead, it now takes up only as much space as its text is long, and it's followed up immediately with the text node that used to be on the second line. This has to do with different `display` values in your CSS – and the starting point of understanding them is the difference between **block** and **inline**.

1.10 Block vs. Inline Elements

So far, you've only learned about the heading tags in HTML.

However, HTML comes with many other tags.

Here are a few:

- `p` for paragraph
- `span` for tagging sections of text (primarily)
- `img` for displaying images

Here's a new update to our `index.html` page. It's a bit of a bigger update, as you can confirm below.

```
<h1>Hello <span>world</span></h1>
<p>Nice weather <span>today</span>.</p>
<p>Cod<span>ing is fun</span>.</p>
```

Now that we've made this change, let's add borders around each element on this page.

```
<h1 style="border: 10px solid gray">
  Hello <span style="border: 5px solid green">world</span>
</h1>
<p style="border: 10px solid lightgray">
  Nice weather <span style="border: 5px solid purple">today</span>.
</p>
<p style="border: 10px solid lightgray">
  Cod<span style="border: 5px solid orange">ing is fun</span>.
</p>
```

When you open this updated page in the browser, notice that the h1 element has a dark gray border around itself, stretching the entire width of the screen.

Notice also that the same behavior around the paragraphs – only the gray color is lighter, since that's what we specified in their respective `style` attributes.

Finally, notice the green, purple, and orange borders around the three `span` elements. These are not stretching the full width of the page – instead, they are just wrapping the actual text nodes of their respective `span` elements.

Why is this happening?

It's happening because the `h1` and `p` elements are considered "block-level" elements, and the `span` element is considered an inline element.

The browser keeps this information in its "little book." Actually, we no longer need to hold on to the "little book" metaphor – instead, we can say that the browser has some preset CSS styles for each of the elements in HTML. That way, even if there are no style attributes specified for individual HTML elements, the browser knows how to display them regardless.

In other words, each HTML element comes with a number of styles already applied to it *by the browser itself*. These styles are referred to as user-agent styles.

Now that we know about the block-level and inline elements, and that we also know about user-agent styles and the way that HTML elements have the `display` property predefined, we can use the `style` attribute to play around with these settings with the goal of getting a better understanding of how these things fit together.

1.11 Making Block Elements Inline and Vice-versa

Let's update our code so that our h1 and p elements are no longer block-level elements. Instead, we'll set their `display` property to the value of `inline`.

```
<h1
  style="border: 10px solid gray;
         display: inline">
    Hello
    <span style="border: 5px solid green">
      world
    </span>
</h1>
<p
  style="border: 10px solid lightgray;
         display: inline">
    Nice weather
    <span style="border: 5px solid purple">
      today
    </span>.
</p>
```

```
<p
  style="border: 10px solid lightgray; display: inline">
  Cod
  <span style="border: 5px solid orange">
    ing is fun
  </span>.
</p>
```

I've done my best to format this code for readability, but ultimately, while there's nothing inherently wrong with the `style` attribute, there is a much better way to do this, and I'll introduce you to it soon.

For now, however, let's just inspect the updated web page in the browser, and, perhaps not surprisingly, all the items are now inline. You can easily confirm this by inspecting the borders of elements. Indeed, they all now just wrap whatever length each of their respective text nodes is, and they are immediately followed by whatever HTML element comes after.

Again, it's important to note that the actual content of our HTML hasn't changed – these are only "cosmetic" updates – in the sense that we're changing the CSS – the styles, colors, borders, display, etc. – but the underlying HTML structure is unaffected.

Just for fun, let's make another update and further change our `index.html` file by adding the CSS property of `display` to all the `span` elements, and setting all of them to `block`.

```
<h1
  style="border: 10px solid gray;
  display: inline">
    Hello
    <span
      style="border: 5px solid green;
      display: block"
    >
      world
    </span>
</h1>
```

CHAPTER 1   WHAT YOU NEED TO KNOW: REVISION OF HTML, CSS, AND JAVASCRIPT

```
<p
  style="border: 10px solid lightgray;
  display: inline">
    Nice weather
    <span
      style="border: 5px solid purple;
      display: block";
    >
      today
    </span>.
</p>
<p
  style="border: 10px solid lightgray;
  display: inline">
  Cod
  <span
    style="border: 5px solid orange;
    display: block"
  >
    ing is fun
  </span>.
</p>
```

This page now looks really weird – but it does prove the point of the possibility of changing the `display` value in your HTML page. This is important to keep in mind, as the `display` property changing can sometimes come in very handy.

Next, we'll deal with the issue of having too many `style` attributes by using an external style sheet.

1.12 Using External Style Sheets in HTML Pages

An external stylesheet is a separate CSS file that contains your CSS code.

Let's describe the process of moving our `style` attribute values into this separate style sheet.

First, we'll need to make a new file and name it `style.css`.

Next, we'll import it into our HTML file.

To import it, we have to add a few more special elements to our HTML page. Before we do that, we need to make a quick detour and discuss the DOCTYPE definition and the metadata that each HTML page should have.

1.12.1 HTML DOCTYPE and Metadata

Each HTML page has the following structure:

```
<!DOCTYPE html>
<html>
  <head>
    ...metadata goes here...
  </head>
  <body>
    ...our code goes here...
  </body>
</html>
```

The explanation of this compulsory data is as follows:

- The DOCTYPE definition defines the version of HTML – the above example DOCTYPE definition is an example of what's used for HTML5 documents

- The `html` element wraps the entire contents of the `html` page – except for the DOCTYPE definition

- The `head` element contains multiple HTML elements – all of them are the metadata of the page – for example, a link to importing an external stylesheet that's used in the current HTML page

- The `body` element will hold all the code that we've worked on so far

Lots of this metadata is boilerplate code. Many of its sections are not really different from page to page.

However, some are different, and we'll focus on those differences in the context of our web page. Practically, for now, I'll skip some common metadata tags that are likely to be present in all web pages – for the sake of focus on the essentials. Later on in the book, we'll make things more comprehensive - when the time is right.

CHAPTER 1   WHAT YOU NEED TO KNOW: REVISION OF HTML, CSS, AND JAVASCRIPT

To begin, let's discuss the minimal possible update to our current code:

```
<!DOCTYPE html>
<html>
  <head>
    <link rel="stylesheet" href="styles.css">
  </head>
  <body>
    <h1
      style="border: 10px solid gray;
      display: inline">
        Hello
        <span
          style="border: 5px solid green;
          display: block"
        >
          world
        </span>
    </h1>
    <p
      style="border: 10px solid lightgray;
      display: inline">
        Nice weather
        <span
          style="border: 5px solid purple
          display: block";
        >
          today
        </span>.
    </p>
    <p
      style="border: 10px solid lightgray;
      display: inline">
        Cod
        <span
          style="border: 5px solid orange;
```

```
        display: block"
    >
        ing is fun
    </span>.
   </p>
  </body>
</html>
```

This update is essentially the same as our previous page – one major difference is that we are now importing an external stylesheet. This now allows us to slowly move the CSS data from the HTML file into its own separate, dedicated stylesheet file.

So, how come the browser could still read our page even if we didn't write all this additional "boilerplate" code?

1.12.2 Can Browsers Work Without DOCTYPE and Metadata?

The answer to this question is: browsers are very versatile. Even if you give them an incomplete web page, they'll still do their best to display that information. Practically, in our case, that means that they'll dynamically add in the necessary elements that we omitted – the html element, the head, and the body.

To confirm that this is the case, you can make a brand new empty html file, name it, for example, test.html and run it in your browser.

Next, right-click anywhere in the empty area of the page, and click the command "Inspect element".

Your screen will split into two:

- In the left-hand side, you'll see your currently open test.html page
- In the right-hand side, you'll have a special utility in the browser. This utility is referred to as Developer Tools, or devtools for short.

1.13 Using devtools

Devtools is there to help you interact with your webpage more like a web developer – hence the name.

It come with a host of separate pieces of functionality.

For now, let's focus on the "Elements" tab.

The "Elements" tab lists the HTML structure of your currently loaded HTML file.

While your HTML file is a static text file with the `html` extension, the devtools contains a dynamic *representation* of that file in the browser's memory.

What does that mean?

It means that you can inspect various aspects of this dynamic representation of your static file, you can add elements, delete them, update the styles – and do all of these actions *non-destructively* – meaning: you cannot save the changes you've made in your browser's in-memory representation of your file, to the actual `test.html` file sitting on your desktop.

For now, that's all that you should know about devtools. Later on, we'll revisit it briefly when we're discussing JavaScript. For now, however, let's bring our focus back to our external stylesheet.

We'll begin by testing if the external stylesheet is properly linked to our `index.html` page.

1.13.1 Testing If the External Stylesheet Is Properly Linked

To test if the stylesheet is linked, open your `styles.css` file, and add the following code to it:

```css
body {
  background-color: orange;
}
```

Save the file, and reopen the browser.

You should see that the entire page's background is now orange.

What happened here?

Essentially, what we did is as if we added the following `style` attibute to the `body` element in our HTML code:

```html
<body style="background-color: orange">
   ... etc ...
</body>
```

So, one possible way to add external styles to our HTML pages is by

1. Finding an element – in the above example, the body element
2. Opening a pair of curly brackets – { }
3. In between these curly brackets, copy-paste the value of the HTML `style` attribute – in our example: `background-color: orange`

That's all there is to it! Being a completely different language, you'll probably agree that the syntax of CSS is quite minimal.

1.13.2 The Anatomy of a CSS Declaration

The code that we've just added is referred to as a "CSS declaration."

The "formula" for it is as follows:

```
selector {
  property: value;
  property: value;
}
```

The `selector` in the above pseudo-code hints at its purpose: to select a part of the HTML page. In our example with setting the body element's background to `orange`, it's obvious that the body element is the selector.

Thus, we can conclude that **any valid HTML element can be used as a selector** in a style sheet.

Next, between the curly braces, add as many `property: value` pairs as you need. There can be one or multiple – just like we had it in the `style` attribute in HTML.

1.14 Moving Inline Styles to an External Stylesheet File

In this section, we'll start updating the `styles.css` external stylesheet file.

We'll do it as follows:

1. We'll extract a style from our current `index.html` page and move it to the `styles.css` file.

2. We'll reload our page in the browser to make sure that the changes are working properly.

3. We'll repeat steps 1 and 2.

Let's get started!

1.14.1 Moving the h1 Styles to an External Stylesheet

Locate this line of code:

```
<h1 style="border: 10px solid gray; display: inline"></h1>
```

Update it to the following:

```
<h1></h1>
```

Back in the `styles.css` file, add this code:

```
h1 {
  border: 10px dashed black;
  /* display: block; */
}
```

Notice the `display: block` line, surrounded with /* and */? These are CSS comments.

Any code that's commented out will be ignored by the browser. Which is ok, since all h1 elements are by default defined to have the `display` property set to `block` in the user agent stylesheet (i.e., in the default browser styles that a browser comes "pre-packaged" with).

Notice also that I've set the border to be `10px dashed black`. It's a simple way for me to test that my updates have worked. Had I left the same code as I've had in the `style` attribute, I'd have no quick way to confirm whether or not my updates were made properly and if the "took hold" in my HTML page in the browser.

1.14.2 Moving the p Styles to an External Stylesheet

Let's update the styling for paragraphs.

Update each paragraph's opening tag so that it's as plain as this:

```
<p></p>
```

Back in `styles.css`, add the following CSS:

```
p {
  border: 10px dashed lightgray;
}
```

Again, we don't have to specify the `display` property as we'll just let the browser implement its predefined settings specified in the user agent stylesheet.

1.14.3 Moving the Span Styles to an External Stylesheet

We'll now be updating the `span` tags.

However, we have a slight issue here. If we extract each individual span's opening tag, we'll get the following:

```
<span style="border: 5px solid green; display: block">
  <span style="border: 5px solid purple; display: block">
    <span style="border: 5px solid orange; display: block"></span></span>
  /span>
```

Since we don't want to change the `display` behavior of the `span` element, we have some redundant code above, namely the `display: block` property-value pairs.

So let's again inspect a simplified list of the opening `span` tags:

```
<span style="border: 5px solid green">
  <span style="border: 5px solid purple">
    <span style="border: 5px solid orange"></span></span>
  /span>
```

Now that we're sure what styles we need to move, let's start doing it.

In `styles.css`, add the following code:

```
span {
  border: 5px dashed green;
}
```

This should work; I've even added the `dashed` value to ensure that once I've saved everything, it's obvious that the update was made correctly.

If I save it now and run my code, the update will… well, it will not be made.

What is the cause of this?

It's all to do with CSS specificity.

1.15 CSS Specificity

CSS specificity is a reconciliation mechanism. In other words, it's a set of rules for the browser to determine *exactly* which styles it will use to render an HTML page in the browser.

There are multiple rules to handle this decision-making process, but for now let's just mention the one rule that pertains to our current example.

Let's first reiterate what is happening here.

In our HTML, we have the `style` attribute specifying the CSS properties to use on a given `span` element. For example:

```
<span style="border: 5px solid green; display: block"> world </span>
```

However, in our external CSS, we have the following:

```
span {
  border: 5px dashed green;
}
```

So which one will it be? Will the border be dashed or solid?

This is where specificity comes in.

In our example, the rule that affects the output is:

- Inline `style` attribute takes precedence over an external stylesheet

In other words, it's as if we didn't write anything in our CSS file regarding `span` elements in our HTML. The `style` attribute on a given element takes precedence.

However, this is not the only issue that we have here. The second issue can be described as follows.

Since we are planning to remove the style attribute from all spans, how do we keep the different border colors? In our HTML, each border currently has a different color, but the span selector in our CSS doesn't allow us that kind of flexibility.

The solution exists, and it comes in two varieties: class selectors and id selectors.

1.16 CSS Class Selectors and CSS id Selectors

These two kinds of CSS selectors allow us to have a different way to select elements on an HTML page.

The id selector can be thought of like a person's id card. It's unique, and there should be only one per page – similar to how each person should have a unique id card.

The class selector allows us to classify groups of elements.

Let's update our HTML to give you a practical example:

```
<!DOCTYPE html>
<html>
  <head>
    <link rel="stylesheet" href="styles.css" />
  </head>
  <body>
    <h1 class="purple-border">
      Hello
      <span class="green-border"> world </span>
    </h1>
    <p>
      Nice weather
      <span class="purple-border"> today </span>.
    </p>
    <p>
      Cod
      <span class="orange-border"> ing is fun </span>.
    </p>
  </body>
</html>
```

And here's the final CSS:

```css
body {
  background-color: orange;
}

h1 {
  border: 10px dashed black;
  /* display: block; */
}

p {
  border: 10px solid lightgray;
}
.green-border {
  border: 5px dashed green;
}
.purple-border {
  border: 5px dashed purple;
}
.orange-border {
  border: 5px dashed orange;
}
```

Notice that we're using the class of `purple-border` on two elements in our HTML: on the second `span` element, and on the `h1` element above. We're doing this so as to show that the same class can be used on multiple elements in your HTML.

Finally, one quick note about the syntax. To use the CSS class selectors, we follow this rule:

- in HTML, we use the `class` attribute and assign to it a value, such as `green-border`
- in CSS, we specify that we're targeting all HTML elements whose class attribute is set to `green-border` by placing a `.` (dot) in front of the class name. The rest of the code works the same way as it does for element selectors – we can add one or more property-value pairs to specify as many CSS properties and their values as we need to

Now that we've had a quick revision of HTML and CSS basics, it's time to go back to devtools and write some JavaScript too.

Don't worry if you haven't used JavaScript before; we'll keep things light and to the point by adding an interactive button to our HTML page.

1.17 Adding an Interactive Button with the Help of JavaScript

To begin improving our HTML page, open your `index.html` file and scroll to the bottom.

The last couple of lines of code should look like this:

```
  </body>
</html>
```

Just above the closing body tag, we'll add a special element, the `script` element. Here's the relevant section of our `index.html` file, after the update.

```
    <script>
        function clearIt() {
            document.body.innerHTML = "You've clicked the button";
        }
    </script>
  </body>
</html>
```

Next, a bit higher up in our html, we'll add a button element. It doesn't really matter where, but to keep things simple and straightforward, let's place it right after the opening body tag, so that it ends up at the very top of the page (above the first `h1` element).

Here's our update:

```
<body>
  <button onclick="clearIt()">Clear all</button>
  ... etc
</body>
```

After this simple update, when you refresh your browser, you'll see a button added to the page. When you click the button, what will happen?

Give it a try.

Indeed, the button worked. All the contents of the page are cleared, and you only have the text of "You've clicked the button" on the screen, together with the orange background on the entire web page.

Don't worry, though. You can just refresh the page and everything will be "back to normal."

This brings us to several conclusions:

1. The JS is non-destructive – just like the devtools in the Elements tab

2. Even if we remove most of the HTML structure, the CSS selectors will work fine, for as long as they have an HTML element that they can style – in this case, the body element

3. It's not very hard to add some simple interactivity to our HTML pages using JavaScript

Let's now discuss in a bit more detail what happened with our JavaScript code and why did it work the way it did.

First, let's look at the button element.

1.18 Using the Button HTML Element and the Onclick Attribute to Add Interactivity with JS

The button HTML element can have the onclick attribute. The onclick attribute is an event-handling attribute. The event in this case is a click event. There are all sorts of events in the browser, but the onclick is usually triggered (ran) by the user – the person visiting and using our web page.

In our example, the onclick attribute's value is a piece of JS code:

```
<button onclick="clearIt()">Clear all</button>
```

Specifically, the JS code is inserted as a value of the onclick attribute – that is, the JS code is everything in between the double quotes in the snippet above.

So, how does this clearIt() piece of code work?

Well, the clearIt itself is a name of a JavaScript function. The behavior of the clearIt function is defined in its function definition.

The function definition begins with the keyword `function`, followed by the function's name – in this case, `clearIt`.

The parentheses after the name of the function – the (and) characters – are there to instruct the function if it will have some input to deal with. In our case, there is no input, so we'll skip this part for now. The body of the function is everything between the curly braces - that is, between the { and } characters:

`document.body.innerHTML = "You've clicked the button";`

To understand what is happening here, we'll need to again discuss the browser's "in-memory representation of our web page."

1.19 How Browsers Work with Web Pages

In this section, we'll discuss at a high level what happens when a user tries to open a web page, for example, `google.com`.

Notice that a lot of things here are glossed over or simplified, so as to focus on the point of the discussion.

If you type this web address into your browser's address bar, the following sequence of things will happen:

1. The browser will reach out to the server on this address.
2. The server will send a response, usually in some form of html.
3. The html page will be sent to your browser.
4. Your browser will read the html page and render it on your screen.

This is essentially what is happening when you visit any web page.

So what's this got to do with this *in-memory representation of the web page* – in this case, google.com?

Well, your browser doesn't just read this page in. It actually creates an object that represents the webpage that you've downloaded.

Without getting too technical, the browser takes this raw, static text of the HTML file and converts it to something that the JavaScript language can work with.

That something is a JavaScript object.

What is a JavaScript object?

It's just a grouping of property-value pairs.

CHAPTER 1   WHAT YOU NEED TO KNOW: REVISION OF HTML, CSS, AND JAVASCRIPT

Just like in CSS, you have a property, and you have a value.

In the case of our webpage in-memory representation, this object is known as "the document".

Whatever web page you visit online, you have access to this document object in your devtools.

So, right-click on your `index.html` file that's currently open in your browser, and click on the "Inspect" command.

Once the devtools are open, either press the ESC key on your keyboard to have a "Console" tray open or, alternatively, locate the "Console" tab (by default, usually next to the "Elements" tab).

If you see a bunch of output in the Console, you can clear it in various ways:

- By clicking into the console to make sure it's active, and then holding down the CTRL key and then pressing the L key.

- By clicking on the icon that looks like a crossed-out circle – some people say it reminds them of an icon of a pill

There are other ways to clear the Console, but these two are the most common ones. Once you've cleared the console, type the following into it:

`document`

If you follow it up with a . (dot), you'll get a contextual menu with various entries. Ignore it for now. Instead, continue typing:

`document.body`

All of a sudden, the browser will now highlight all the text (content) of the page.

If you've been following along, that means that it will highlight the text that reads: "You've clicked the button".

Next, type another dot (.).

`document.body.`

Again, you'll be greeted with tens of entries offered. Again, ignore them all, and simply type:

`document.body.innerHTML`

Pay attention to capitalization – it's important.

Finally, type the = sign, and after that, the following: `"Hello there"`.

Once you've done all of this, you can press the ENTER key to run this command. The text will change to "Hello there."

That's it for now. We will not dive too deep into JavaScript at this point.

The important thing is, you understand the interactive nature of the in-memory representation of any HTML page you open in your browser, and this is a great starting point for further exploration.

1.20 Conclusion

In this chapter, we've reviewed the basics of HTML, CSS, and JavaScript.

We've discussed the bare basics – the minimum that you need to know to be able to work with Bootstrap in the following chapters. Still, if needed, we'll also add some additional background info from time to time.

In the next chapter, we'll learn about Bootstrap and we'll start using it in our HTML pages.

CHAPTER 2

Containers and Rows in Bootstrap 5.3

2.1 Introduction

As a quick reminder of what we discussed in Chapter 1, recall that a website is essentially a collection of HTML elements. These elements are added to the page similar to how you read a regular piece of English text, but with an important distinction: HTML elements follow different display behaviors. Some elements, like <span> or <a>, are inline elements that flow within the text and only occupy as much width as necessary for their content. Others, like <div>, <p>, or <h1>, are block elements that create distinct "blocks" on the page, automatically starting on a new line and stretching to fill the full width of their parent container – the parent container being either the <body> element itself, or any nested element like a wrapping <div> for example.

Understanding this distinction between inline elements and block elements is crucial for effective layout design, especially when working with Bootstrap's container and row system.

Now, before we even start discussing containers and rows in Bootstrap 5.3, there is one additional piece of the puzzle that was left out on purpose. That missing piece is the box model in CSS. And the reason why it wasn't discussed before is because of how closely related it is to containers and rows in Bootstrap.

CHAPTER 2   CONTAINERS AND ROWS IN BOOTSTRAP 5.3

2.2 The Box Model

The CSS box model is fundamental to understanding how elements are sized and positioned on a webpage. Every HTML element is essentially a box that consists of four layers:

1. **Content**: The innermost layer where text, images, or other media appears
2. **Padding**: The space between the content and the border
3. **Border**: A line that surrounds the padding
4. **Margin**: The outermost layer that creates space between elements

Modern browsers are very helpful in dynamically showing you this box model for every single element on the page, like in the example below.

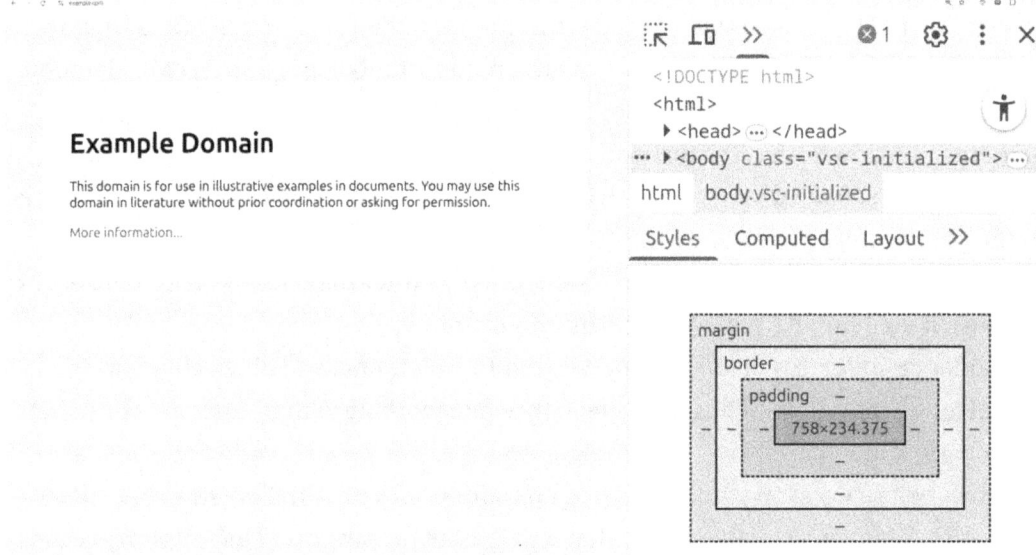

Figure 2-1. *The Box Model*

The image above is a screenshot of the example.com homepage, available on the world wide web (www) – aka, the internet.

You can get to the same display by navigating your browser to the said website, then in the elements panel, left-clicking on the body elements to highlight it, and finally, scrolling down to the bottom of the styles element – and that's where this multi-colored box can be found.

The blue (innermost area) is the content, and the green area is the padding – and the browser helpfully labels them as such.

Going further to the outer boxes, there are also the border (light orange) and margin (dark orange background).

To better grasp the box model, let's use another suitable metaphor.

Imagine you're putting a picture in a frame. The picture is your content, the space between the picture and the frame is padding, the frame itself is the border, and the space between the frame and other object(s) on the wall is the margin.

Understanding the box model is crucial because it affects how we calculate the total width and height of an element. By default, when you set a width or height in CSS, you're only setting the content area's dimensions. The total space an element occupies also includes its padding, border, and margin.

```
.box {
  width: 300px;
  padding: 20px;
  border: 1px solid black;
  margin: 10px;
}
```

In the example above, the total width the element occupies is: 300px (content) + 40px (padding: 20px on each side) + 2px (border: 1px on each side) + 20px (margin: 10px on each side) = 362px

However, modern CSS provides the box-sizing property to change this behavior:

```
.box2 {
  box-sizing: border-box;
  width: 300px;
  padding: 20px;
  border: 1px solid black;
  margin: 10px;
}
```

With box-sizing: border-box, the width and height properties include content, padding, and border. So the content area automatically shrinks to accommodate the padding and border. The total width the element occupies is now: 300px (content + padding + border) + 20px (margin) = 320px

Bootstrap 5.3 applies box-sizing: border-box to all elements by default, making size calculations more intuitive.

2.3 Containers in Bootstrap 5.3

Containers are the most basic layout element in Bootstrap and are required when using the grid system. They're used to contain, pad, and (sometimes) center the content within them.

Bootstrap 5.3 offers three different container types:

1. **.container**: A responsive fixed-width container
2. **.container-fluid**: A full-width container that spans the entire viewport
3. **.container-{breakpoint}**: Width is 100% until the specified breakpoint

Before we can examine each type in detail, we need to discuss breakpoints.

2.4 Understanding Breakpoints

Breakpoints are one of the most important concepts in responsive web design, especially when using a framework like Bootstrap. Let's explore what they are and how they work.

2.4.1 What Are Breakpoints?

Breakpoints are specific screen widths that determine when your website's layout should change to provide the optimal viewing experience. Think of them as "breaking points" where your layout "breaks" from one form to another to better fit different screen sizes.

2.4.2 Why Do We Need Breakpoints?

Imagine trying to view a desktop website on a small mobile phone – the text would be tiny, and you'd have to constantly zoom and scroll horizontally. Breakpoints solve this problem by allowing your website to adapt to different screen sizes automatically.

2.4.3 Bootstrap's Breakpoint System

Bootstrap 5.3 gives us six standard breakpoints to work with. Each one represents a screen width where your layout might need to change.

The smallest is the extra small breakpoint, which doesn't even have a special class infix – it's just the default. This covers most mobile phones with screens narrower than 576 pixels.

Next comes the small breakpoint (sm), which kicks in at 576 pixels and covers larger phones and small tablets. Medium (md) starts at 768 pixels, which is perfect for tablets and small laptops.

For regular laptops and desktop computers, we have the large breakpoint (lg) at 992 pixels. If you're working with larger monitors, the extra large (xl) breakpoint at 1200 pixels has you covered. And for those massive screens, there's the extra extra large (xxl) breakpoint at 1400 pixels and up.

Here's a quick reference table I put together.

Table 2-1. *Breakpoint Reference Table*

Breakpoint	Class infix	Width threshold
Extra small	(none)	$< 576px$
Small	sm	$\geq 576px$
Medium	md	$\geq 768px$
Large	lg	$\geq 992px$
Extra large	xl	$\geq 1200px$
Extra extra large	xxl	$\geq 1400px$

Now that we understand breakpoints, we're ready to look at the three different types of containers in Bootstrap.

2.5 Understanding Containers

As mentioned earlier, there are three different types of containers in Bootstrap 5.3. You've got your standard .container, the full-width .container-fluid, and the responsive .container-{breakpoint} that adapts based on screen size. Let's take a closer look at each one.

2.5.1 Fixed-Width Container (.container)

The .container class sets a max-width at each responsive breakpoint.

Table 2-2. *Container Breakpoint*

Breakpoint	Class infix	Dimensions
Extra small	None	100%
Small	sm	540px
Medium	md	720px
Large	lg	960px
Extra large	xl	1140px
Extra extra large	xxl	1320px

Sample code snippet:

```
<div class="container">
  <!-- Content here -->
</div>
```

This container type is perfect for most websites where you want content to be centered and have a reasonable width on all devices.

2.5.2 Fluid Container (.container-fluid)

The .container-fluid class creates a full-width container that spans the entire width of the viewport:

```
<div class="container-fluid">
  <!-- Content here -->
</div>
```

This is useful for layouts where you want to utilize the full screen width, such as dashboards, maps, or hero sections.

2.5.3 Responsive Containers (.container-{breakpoint})

Responsive containers expand to full width until the specified breakpoint is reached, after which they adopt fixed widths like .container for better readability on large screens:

```
<div class="container-md">
  <!-- 100% wide until medium breakpoint, then like a container -->
</div>
```

Available classes include:

- .container-sm (100% wide until 576px)
- .container-md (100% wide until 768px)
- .container-lg (100% wide until 992px)
- .container-xl (100% wide until 1200px)
- .container-xxl (100% wide until 1400px)

This flexibility allows you to choose exactly when your fluid-width container should start behaving like a fixed-width container.

2.6 Rows in Bootstrap 5.3

Rows are horizontal wrappers for columns. Each row contains 12 column units, and you can use as many of these units as needed for each column.

```
<div class="container">
  <div class="row">
    <!-- Row content will go here (we'll add columns in future
    chapters) -->
  </div>
</div>
```

This basic structure forms the foundation of all Bootstrap layouts that use the Bootstrap grid.

2.6.1 Key Features of Rows

Rows in Bootstrap are horizontal containers that help organize content. They're designed to hold columns (which we'll cover in a future chapter), but for now, just think of them as horizontal sections within your container.

Rows have some special properties that make them work well with Bootstrap's layout system. They help ensure proper spacing and alignment of content, making your layouts look clean and professional.

2.7 How to Use Breakpoints in Bootstrap

For now, the main way you'll use breakpoints is with container classes. As we saw earlier, you can create responsive containers that change their behavior at specific screen widths:

```
<div class="container-md">
  <!-- Content here -->
</div>
```

This creates a container that is 100% wide (full width) until it reaches the medium breakpoint (768px), after which it becomes a fixed-width container surrounded by whitespace on either horizontal side, making the container itself centered on the page.

In future chapters, we'll explore how breakpoints can be used with columns and other Bootstrap components to create fully responsive layouts.

A caveat: we said that the container, when it becomes fixed width, is centered on the page. That doesn't mean the contents of that container are centered or not centered; those options are set elsewhere, and we'll discuss it in due course.

2.8 Bootstrap Contextual Colors

Bootstrap provides a set of contextual color classes that can be applied to various elements. For now, we'll focus on just two background color classes:

2.8.1 Background Primary (.bg-primary)

The .bg-primary class applies the primary color of your Bootstrap theme (typically blue by default) as the background color of an element:

```
<div class="container bg-primary">
  This container has a primary background color
</div>
```

2.8.2 Background Success (.bg-success)

The .bg-success class applies a success color (typically green by default) as the background color of an element:

```
<div class="container bg-success">
  This container has a success background color
</div>
```

2.9 Practical Example

Let's put everything together in a simple example that uses containers, rows, and our two contextual colors.

Here's the end result that we'll achieve.

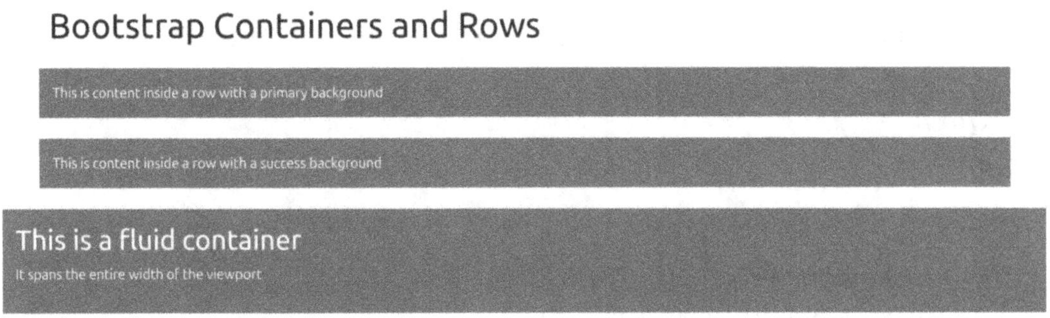

Figure 2-2. A Simple Webpage with Containers, Rows, and Contextual Background Colors

And this is the code for it (you can ignore the head element for now – the focus is on containers in the body element):

CHAPTER 2   CONTAINERS AND ROWS IN BOOTSTRAP 5.3

```html
<!DOCTYPE html>
<html lang="en">
<head>
  <meta charset="UTF-8">
  <meta name="viewport" content="width=device-width, initial-scale=1.0">
  <title>Bootstrap Containers and Rows</title>
  <link href="https://cdn.jsdelivr.net/npm/bootstrap@5.3.0/dist/css/
  bootstrap.min.css" rel="stylesheet">
</head>
<body>
  <!-- Fixed-width container -->
  <div class="container">
    <h1 class="my-4">Bootstrap Containers and Rows</h1>

    <!-- A row with primary background -->
    <div class="row mb-4">
      <div class="bg-primary p-3 text-white">
        This is content inside a row with a primary background
      </div>
    </div>

    <!-- Another row with success background -->
    <div class="row mb-4">
      <div class="bg-success p-3 text-white">
        This is content inside a row with a success background
      </div>
    </div>
  </div>

  <!-- Fluid container -->
  <div class="container-fluid mt-4 bg-primary p-3 text-white">
    <h2>This is a fluid container</h2>
    <p>It spans the entire width of the viewport</p>
  </div>

</body>
</html>
```

Let's start discussing the above example by clarifying that there's a piece of the puzzle that's currently missing from the above code. Specifically, it is technically correct to add Bootstrap grid system's column classes inside an element with a row – we're not doing that here because we're going to properly introduce Bootstrap's grid system in the next chapter. So, for now, let's just focus on the above code as is, and we'll extend it further and correct this little wrinkle soon enough.

In the example above, I've set up a fixed-width .container with two different rows. Each row has content with one of our contextual background colors – .bg-primary for the blue background and .bg-success for the green one. I've also added some padding and text color adjustments with the .p-3 and .text-white classes.

At the bottom, there's a .container-fluid that stretches all the way across the viewport, showing how different it looks compared to the fixed-width container above it.

Now that we've discussed the main point of this section, let's go back to explaining just what this viewport thing here exactly is:

```
<meta name="viewport" content="width=device-width, initial-scale=1.0">
```

To explain it very briefly, the meta tag with the name attribute set to viewport ensures proper scaling and layout on mobile devices. The specifics are saved as a value inside the content HTML attribute.

2.10 Common Pitfalls to Avoid

When working with Bootstrap's layout system, there are a couple of mistakes I see beginners make all the time.

First, never nest one container inside another container. This creates weird spacing issues and defeats the purpose of the container system.

However, there are caveats.

2.10.1 Container Nesting Rules

The primary reason for avoiding container nesting is that each container has its own padding and responsive behavior. Nesting them can create:

- Unexpected padding (doubled padding)
- Inconsistent responsive behavior
- Layout issues where margins compound

2.10.1.1 The Container-Fluid Exception

Using a .container-fluid with a .container inside it is actually a recognized pattern in some Bootstrap implementations. This combination can be useful when you want:

1. **Full-width background-colored sections with centered content**: The outer .container-fluid can have a background color that spans the full viewport, while the inner .container centers the content with appropriate padding.

2. **Two-tier responsive behavior**: The outer fluid container responds differently from the inner fixed-width container.

2.10.1.2 Bootstrap's Official Position

Bootstrap's documentation doesn't explicitly prohibit this pattern. The advice against nesting is more about avoiding nesting identical containers (.container inside .container or .container-fluid inside another .container-fluid).

2.10.1.3 Practical Recommendation

In practice, the .container-fluid + .container pattern is widely used and works well for creating full-width sections with centered content.

While it technically violates the "no nesting" guideline, it's a pragmatic exception that many Bootstrap developers (including those building themes and templates) regularly employ.

If you're building a complex layout system or a design system where consistency is paramount, you might want to create your own utility classes to handle this pattern more explicitly. Otherwise, this pattern is generally acceptable despite the guideline.

Another common mistake is putting a row directly in the <body> without a container. Remember, rows are designed to work inside containers – they need that parent element to function properly.

2.11 Conclusion

In this chapter, we've covered the fundamentals of Bootstrap's layout system: containers and rows. We've also introduced two contextual background colors: .bg-primary and .bg-success. These basic building blocks will allow you to create simple, responsive layouts for your web projects.

Just to recap what we've covered: containers give you either a nice, centered layout with .container or a full-width layout with .container-fluid. Inside these containers, you'll place rows that organize your content. And don't forget those handy background colors like .bg-primary and .bg-success – they're great for adding visual hierarchy to your layouts.

In the next chapter, we'll build on this foundation and explore more Bootstrap components and utilities to enhance your layouts.

CHAPTER 3

Columns, Breakpoints, and the Grid in Bootstrap 5.3

3.1 Introduction

In the previous chapter, we explored containers and rows in Bootstrap 5.3, along with an introduction to breakpoints. Now it's time to dive deeper into columns, understand how breakpoints work with them, and master Bootstrap's powerful grid system.

Before we jump into the technical details, it's worth understanding the historical context that led to the development of Bootstrap's grid system. This background will help you appreciate why Bootstrap works the way it does and why it has become such a fundamental tool for web developers.

3.2 Historical Background – What Shaped the Development of Bootstrap?

3.2.1 The Evolution of CSS Display Properties

When the web first began, layout options were extremely limited. In the early days of CSS, we primarily had two display values to work with: block and inline. As we discussed in Chapter 2, block elements would take up the full width of their container and start on a new line, while inline elements would flow within the text and only take up as much space as needed.

This binary approach was quite limiting for creating complex layouts. Developers needed more flexibility, which led to the introduction of additional display values like inline-block (combining features of both inline and block elements) and various table-related display properties.

During this era, creating multi-column layouts was particularly challenging. Developers often resorted to using "float-based" layouts, where elements would be floated left or right, with various clearfix hacks to prevent layout issues. If you've ever had to use clear: both in your CSS, you've experienced the pain of float-based layouts. However, since this was used about 20 years ago, it's likely that you've either not heard of it or not used it.

It took the web development industry nearly a decade to develop better solutions. Eventually, two powerful layout modes emerged: Flexbox (officially called CSS Flexible Box Layout) and CSS Grid. These modern layout systems finally gave developers the tools they needed to create complex, responsive layouts without resorting to hacks and workarounds.

What we have in modern browsers today is the result of this long evolution – powerful, purpose-built layout tools that make creating complex designs much more straightforward.

3.2.2 The First Grid-Based Web Layout System: 960.gs

In 2008, a new concept in laying out website content came about. It used a simple 12-column grid to lay out a site on a static, 960-pixel-wide screen. This improvement was invented before the proliferation of cell phones, tablets, and ultra-wide screens, but it was crucial for the brewing responsive design revolution.

Let's discuss the innovation behind 960.gs first, as that will allow us to bridge the gap between its innovation and how it became a natural source for RWD (responsive web design).

3.2.3 Early Grid Systems and Bootstrap's Innovation

The 960 grid system – aka 960.gs – provided a framework for creating layouts based on a 12-column or 16-column grid within a 960-pixel width "container." While not fully responsive by today's standards, it introduced the concept of thinking about layouts in terms of grid columns.

Interestingly, the website is still around, after almost 20 years! Here's the link if you're curious: https://960.gs/.

The 960 Grid System represented a watershed moment in web design history. Created by Nathan Smith in 2008, it addressed a fundamental challenge that web designers faced: how to create consistent, well-structured layouts across different browsers and screen resolutions. The system was named after the most common screen width at the time – 960 pixels – which worked well on the then-standard 1024×768 pixel monitors, leaving room for browser scrollbars and margins.

What made 960.gs truly innovative was its systematic approach to layout design. Rather than treating each webpage as a unique design challenge, it introduced a mathematical framework based on a grid of either 12 or 16 columns. The 12-column version divided the 960-pixel width into 12 equal columns of 60 pixels each (with 20-pixel gutters between them), while the 16-column version created 16 columns of 40 pixels each (with 20-pixel gutters). This standardization made design decisions more straightforward – elements could span 3 columns, 6 columns, 9 columns, and so on.

The system came with pre-built CSS files and templates that developers could use immediately. This was revolutionary at a time when CSS frameworks were not yet commonplace. Designers could download the 960.gs package, which included not only the CSS but also printable sketch sheets and design templates for various graphics programs. This comprehensive approach helped bridge the gap between design and development, making it easier for teams to collaborate.

One of the most significant aspects of 960.gs was how it influenced the mental model of web designers. Before grid systems became popular, many designers approached web layouts in a more freeform manner, often leading to inconsistent results and difficult-to-maintain code. The 960 Grid System encouraged designers to think in terms of a structured grid, considering how elements would align and relate to each other within that framework. This shift in thinking laid the groundwork for the responsive design revolution that would follow.

The class naming convention in 960.gs also proved influential. It used simple, logical class names like .grid_1, .grid_2, etc., to indicate how many columns an element should span. This approach to semantic class naming influenced many subsequent CSS frameworks, including Bootstrap. The system also introduced helper classes like .alpha and .omega for the first and last elements in a row, addressing the specific challenges of the float-based layout technique it employed.

Despite its fixed-width limitation, 960.gs was remarkably versatile. Designers used it to create everything from corporate websites to blogs, e-commerce platforms, and web applications. Its popularity stemmed partly from this versatility – the same framework could be adapted to widely different design aesthetics while maintaining structural integrity. The system didn't dictate visual style, only layout structure, giving designers creative freedom within a consistent framework.

The documentation and community around 960.gs also contributed significantly to its success. Smith created clear, accessible documentation and examples that made the system approachable even for designers with limited coding experience. A community of users emerged, sharing templates, extensions, and implementations. This community aspect became a model for later frameworks, demonstrating the importance of documentation and user support in the adoption of web technologies.

While 960.gs wasn't the first grid system for the web (it was preceded by systems like YUI Grids), it achieved widespread adoption due to its simplicity and timing. It arrived just as CSS was maturing, and designers were seeking more structured approaches to web layout. Its straightforward implementation and clear benefits made it accessible to a broad audience of web professionals, helping to mainstream the concept of grid-based web design.

The limitations of 960.gs – particularly its fixed width – eventually became apparent as mobile devices gained popularity. The system wasn't designed to adapt to different screen sizes, which became increasingly problematic as smartphones and tablets proliferated. However, these limitations sparked innovation, leading directly to the development of responsive grid systems like Bootstrap. In this way, 960.gs served as both a solution for its time and a catalyst for the responsive design approaches that would follow.

The legacy of 960.gs extends far beyond its actual usage. Many of today's web designers and developers have never used it directly, yet they work with concepts and approaches that evolved from it. The 12-column grid structure has become a standard in web design, appearing in frameworks like Bootstrap, Foundation, and many others. Even as CSS Grid and Flexbox have provided native solutions for grid-based layouts, the conceptual framework that 960.gs helped establish – thinking of layouts in terms of a structured grid system – remains fundamental to modern web design practice.

3.2.4 Another Piece of the Puzzle: The Rise of Responsive Web Design

Parallel to the evolution of CSS display properties and the invention of the original 960 grid system, there was another significant development: the need for responsive web design.

In the early 2000s, websites were typically designed for desktop screens only. The concept of a website adapting to different screen sizes wasn't necessary because most people accessed the web through desktop computers with relatively similar screen sizes. Websites were static and designed for a fixed width - usually around 960 pixels, which worked well on the common screen resolutions of the time.

Then came the revolution: smartphones and tablets entered the mainstream. Suddenly, websites were being viewed on screens of all sizes – from tiny phone displays to large desktop monitors. The old fixed-width approach no longer worked. A website designed for a desktop would be frustratingly difficult to use on a mobile phone, requiring constant zooming and horizontal scrolling.

This new reality demanded a new approach to web design. As Bruce Lee famously said, "You pour water into a cup, it becomes the cup." Websites needed to be like water – adapting fluidly to whatever container (screen) they were viewed on.

In 2011 (just two years after 960.gs invention), the first version of the Bootstrap framework came out. Back then, it was called Twitter Bootstrap, as it was built by two then-Twitter employees: Mark Otto (@mdo) and Jacob Thornton (@fat).

Twitter Bootstrap revolutionized how developers approached responsive web design. Building on the foundation laid by earlier grid systems, and eventually shedding the "Twitter" part of its name, Bootstrap introduced several key innovations:

1. **A truly responsive grid**: Unlike its predecessors, Bootstrap's grid was designed from the ground up to be responsive, with breakpoints that allowed layouts to adapt to different screen sizes.

2. **Mobile-first approach**: Bootstrap encouraged developers to design for mobile devices first, then progressively enhance the experience for larger screens.

3. **Consistent component library**: Beyond just a grid system, Bootstrap provided a comprehensive set of UI components that worked seamlessly with the grid.

4. **Standardized approach**: Bootstrap established conventions that helped teams work more consistently and efficiently.

Bootstrap wasn't the first grid system, but it was the one that successfully brought responsive design into the mainstream of web development. Its approach was so influential that many of its concepts have become standard practice, even for developers who don't use Bootstrap directly.

In the rest of this chapter, we'll explore how Bootstrap's grid system works in detail, focusing on columns and how they interact with breakpoints to create responsive layouts. We'll build on the foundation of containers and rows that we established in Chapter 2, completing our understanding of Bootstrap's core layout system.

Note We mentioned mobile-first development in the context of responsive web design. We'll come back to this in a later chapter.

3.3 Understanding the Building Blocks: Flexbox and CSS Grid

Now that we understand the historical context that led to Bootstrap's development, let's examine the underlying technologies that power Bootstrap's grid system: Flexbox and CSS Grid. Understanding these technologies will give you deeper insight into how Bootstrap works under the hood.

3.3.1 Flexbox: The One-Dimensional Layout Model

Flexbox, formally known as the CSS Flexible Box Layout Module, was designed to provide a more efficient way to lay out, align, and distribute space among items in a container, even when their size is unknown or dynamic.

The key concept behind Flexbox is that it's a **one-dimensional layout model**. What does this mean? It means that Flexbox deals with layout in one dimension at a time – either as a row or as a column. When you apply display: flex to an element, you're essentially telling the browser, "I want to arrange the children of this element along a single axis."

Here's a simple example of Flexbox in action:

```
.ducks-in-a-row {
  display: flex;
  justify-content: space-between;
}
```

With just these two lines of CSS, we've created a flex wrapping element where its children will be arranged in a row (the default direction), with space distributed evenly between them. No floats, no clearfix hacks, no complex calculations.

Flexbox gives us powerful control over

- The direction items are laid out (row, row-reverse, column, column-reverse)
- How items align along the main axis (justify-content)
- How items align along the cross axis (align-items)
- How items wrap when they run out of space (flex-wrap)
- How space is distributed among items (flex-grow, flex-shrink, flex-basis)

These capabilities make Flexbox particularly well-suited for components of an application's UI, or small-scale layouts. However, for more complex, two-dimensional layouts, we need something more powerful.

3.3.2 CSS Grid: The Two-Dimensional Layout Model

CSS Grid Layout is a two-dimensional layout system designed specifically for more complex layouts. Unlike Flexbox, which operates in one dimension, CSS grid allows you to control layout in both rows and columns simultaneously.

When you apply display: grid to an element, it's like flipping a switch: you've just made the element and all its children a part of a CSS grid display. You can then define the columns and rows of the grid, and place items precisely within these grid cells.

Here's a basic example of CSS Grid:

```
.container {
  display: grid;
  grid-template-columns: 1fr 2fr 1fr;
  grid-template-rows: auto auto;
  gap: 20px;
  background: wheat;
}
```

This CSS creates a grid with three columns (the middle one being twice as wide as the others) and two rows that automatically size to their content, with a 20-pixel gap between all grid items. The fr unit stands for "fraction" as in "fraction of the full width of the columns."

CSS Grid provides control over

- The exact dimensions of grid tracks (rows and columns)
- The placement of items in specific grid cells
- The alignment of items within their grid cells
- The spacing between grid tracks
- The creation of named grid areas for more intuitive item placement

The power of Grid becomes apparent when you need to create complex layouts that align both horizontally and vertically, such as entire page layouts or complex dashboard interfaces.

3.3.3 One-Dimensional vs. Two-Dimensional Layouts: What's the Difference?

To understand the difference between one-dimensional and two-dimensional layouts, consider the following analogies.

Imagine a security guard in charge of ensuring people in a queue at the post office are lined up properly and grouped according to a rule. The guard can only arrange people along a single line but can control spacing between individuals and groups. That's **flexbox** – managing layout along a single axis at a time.

In contrast, imagine having a city zoning map where the map itself is divided into 1-by-1-mile squares. Zones can't overlap with one another, and each zone can be at minimum 1-by-1 square in size, up to an X-by-X square in size. City planners can precisely control which zones go where in both dimensions simultaneously. That, in essence, is **CSS grid** – controlling layout in both rows and columns at the same time.

Additionally, note that with flexbox you can build a "fake CSS grid" by nesting flex containers. While this works for simple layouts, it quickly becomes unwieldy for complex ones – similar to how you could technically build a skyscraper with wood, but steel and concrete would be more appropriate materials.

Here's a simple example showing how you could create a fake CSS-grid-like layout with two sidebars and a main content area that has three stacked elements using **nested flexbox**:

```
<!-- HTML Structure -->
<div class="layout">
  <div class="sidebar-left">Left Sidebar</div>
  <div class="main-content">
    <div class="main-item">Main Content Item 1</div>
    <div class="main-item">Main Content Item 2</div>
    <div class="main-item">Main Content Item 3</div>
  </div>
  <div class="sidebar-right">Right Sidebar</div>
</div>
 /* CSS for nested flexbox approach */
.layout {
  display: flex;
  min-height: 300px;
}

.sidebar-left, .sidebar-right {
  background-color: #f0f0f0;
```

CHAPTER 3   COLUMNS, BREAKPOINTS, AND THE GRID IN BOOTSTRAP 5.3

```css
  padding: 20px;
  width: 200px;
}

.main-content {
  display: flex;
  flex-direction: column;
  flex: 1;
}

.main-item {
  background-color: #e0e0e0;
  margin: 10px;
  padding: 20px;
  flex: 1;
}
```

The same layout could be achieved more elegantly with CSS Grid:

```html
<!DOCTYPE html>
<html lang="en">
<head>
    <meta charset="UTF-8">
    <meta name="viewport" content="width=device-width, initial-scale=1.0">
    <title>3.3.2 CSS Grid: The Two-Dimensional Layout Model</title>
    <style>
        /* CSS Grid approach */
        .layout {
            display: grid;
            grid-template-columns: 200px 1fr 200px;
            grid-template-areas:
                "left main right"
                "left main right"
                "left main right";
            min-height: 300px;
            gap: 10px;
        }
```

```css
        .sidebar-left {
            grid-area: left;
            background-color: #f0f0f0;
        }

        .sidebar-right {
            grid-area: right;
            background-color: #f0f0f0;
        }

        .main-item {
            grid-column: 2;
            background-color: #e0e0e0;
        }
    </style>
</head>
<body>
    <!-- HTML Structure -->
    <div class="layout">
        <div class="sidebar-left">Left Sidebar</div>
        <div class="main-item">Main Content Item 1</div>
        <div class="main-item">Main Content Item 2</div>
        <div class="main-item">Main Content Item 3</div>
        <div class="sidebar-right">Right Sidebar</div>
    </div>
</body>
</html>
```

The CSS Grid approach is not only more concise but also gives you more precise control over the layout in both dimensions. You could easily make the main content span multiple columns or make one of the sidebars span multiple rows - something that would be much more complex with nested flexbox.

In web layout terms:

- **One-dimensional (Flexbox)**: You're primarily concerned with laying out items in a row OR a column. While Flexbox can create wrapping rows or columns, it doesn't provide direct control over the alignment of items across multiple rows or columns simultaneously.

- **Two-dimensional (Grid)**: You're concerned with laying out items in rows *and* columns, with precise control over both dimensions simultaneously. Grid allows you to create a layout where items can span multiple rows and columns, and where alignment can be controlled in both directions at once.

Both models have their strengths, and they're often used together in modern web development. Flexbox is excellent for component-level layouts and one-dimensional alignment needs, while Grid excels at page-level layouts and complex two-dimensional structures.

3.3.4 Bootstrap Grid: An Abstraction Layer

Now that we understand Flexbox and CSS Grid, we can appreciate what Bootstrap's grid system actually is: an **abstraction** built on top of these CSS layout technologies.

But what exactly is an abstraction in this context?

In software development, an abstraction is a way of hiding complex implementation details behind a simpler interface. It's like driving a car – you don't need to understand how the engine works internally to operate the vehicle; you just need to know how to use the steering wheel, pedals, and other controls.

Bootstrap's grid system is an abstraction because it provides a simplified, standardized way to create layouts without requiring you to write complex Flexbox or Grid CSS yourself. Instead of writing display: flex or display: grid and configuring all the associated properties, you can use Bootstrap's predefined classes like .container, .row, and .col-* to achieve similar results.

Under the hood, Bootstrap 5.3 primarily uses Flexbox for its grid system, with some aspects of its layout system leveraging CSS Grid. But as a user of Bootstrap, you don't need to worry about these implementation details – you just need to understand Bootstrap's own system of containers, rows, and columns.

It's worth noting that the term "abstraction" has a slightly different meaning when we talk about JavaScript. In JavaScript, abstractions often refer to higher-level functions or objects that encapsulate and simplify more complex operations or data structures. The principle is similar – hiding complexity behind a simpler interface – but the context and implementation are different.

How does this abstraction actually work?

It's very simple. We have a number of predefined CSS classes, using the following pattern:

`.col-{breakpoint}-{number}`

In the above pattern, you can think of the .col- as the "group identifier," meaning that *any* CSS class whose name begins with col- is what we use when we want to define any specific Bootstrap grid layout.

The second part of this naming pattern is the breakpoint. This adheres to the Bootstrap breakpoint system we discussed before.

The number simply determines the width (in columns) of a given element.

This is much easier to understand given an example:

```
<div class="col-1">...</div>
<section class="col-1 col-md-2">...</section>
<article class="col-sm-6 col-lg-3 col-xl-8">...</article>
```

Looking at the above examples, we can conclude that:

- We can use Bootstrap's grid classes on any HTML element (there's no limitations here ons here other than the need to have them wrapped in an element that has the row CSS class)
- We can use one or more Bootstrap grid classes *on the same element*
- In some cases, we can omit the {breakpoint} part of the pattern

Why can we use more than one Bootstrap grid class? And why can we sometimes omit the breakpoint part of the pattern?

We can use more than one grid class on the same element because each class is tied to a different breakpoint. This allows us to define how the same element should behave at different screen sizes. For example, by combining col-sm-6 and col-lg-3, we're telling Bootstrap: "On small devices, take up half the row, but on large devices, shrink down to a quarter of the row." The multiple classes don't conflict; instead, Bootstrap applies whichever one is relevant to the current screen width.

As for omitting the breakpoint, if we simply write something like col-4, that class applies to all screen sizes, from the smallest to the largest. It's essentially the "default" rule. Then, if we add breakpoint-specific classes alongside it (e.g., col-md-6), those rules only kick in once the screen passes the given breakpoint. This way, we can set a baseline layout (col-4) and then adjust it step by step for larger screens.

Finally, one important rule to remember is: higher-width breakpoints "override" the previous layout once the width of the screen gets wide enough. In other words, let's say we have the following setup.

```
<div class="col-md-9 col-lg-3">...</div>
```

Here's what the above example will do. On resolutions up to md, the div will span the full width of the row. Between the md and lg breakpoints, the div will take up 9 of the available 12 columns in that row. And finally, on the widths of lg and above, that same div will take up 3 of the available 12 columns of that row, on lg resolution and above.

3.4 Bootstrap's Column System and Breakpoints in Action

Now that we understand the theoretical underpinnings of Bootstrap's grid system, let's see how columns and breakpoints work together in practice. We'll create a simple but realistic example that demonstrates how columns can "shape-shift" based on screen size.

3.4.1 The Full Spectrum of Contextual Colors

Before we dive into our example, let's expand our color palette. In Chapter 2, we introduced two contextual background colors: .bg-primary and .bg-success. Bootstrap actually provides a full spectrum of contextual colors that you can use to convey meaning through color:

- **.bg-primary**: Blue – represents primary actions or information
- **.bg-secondary**: Gray – represents secondary actions or information
- **.bg-success**: Green – represents successful or positive actions
- **.bg-danger**: Red – represents dangerous or negative actions
- **.bg-warning**: Yellow – represents warnings or cautions
- **.bg-info**: Light blue – represents informational content
- **.bg-light**: Very light gray – useful for light backgrounds
- **.bg-dark**: Dark gray/black – useful for dark backgrounds

These same color contexts are available for text (.text-*), buttons (.btn-*), and other components.

3.4.2 A Responsive Portfolio Example

Let's create a simple portfolio page that demonstrates how Bootstrap's columns and breakpoints work together. Our page will have a header, a main section with a sidebar and a content area, and a footer. We'll use different column configurations at different breakpoints to ensure the layout works well on all devices.

Here's the HTML for our example:

```html
<!DOCTYPE html>
<html lang="en">
<head>
  <meta charset="UTF-8">
  <meta name="viewport" content="width=device-width, initial-scale=1.0">
  <title>My Portfolio</title>
  <link href="https://cdn.jsdelivr.net/npm/bootstrap@5.3.0/dist/css/
  bootstrap.min.css" rel="stylesheet">
</head>
<body>
  <!-- Header - Full width on all devices -->
  <header class="container-fluid bg-dark text-white py-4 mb-4">
    <div class="container">
      <h1>Jane Developer</h1>
      <p class="lead">Web Developer & Designer</p>
    </div>
  </header>

  <!-- Main content area -->
  <main class="container mb-4">
    <div class="row">
      <!-- Sidebar - Full width on mobile, 4 columns on larger screens -->
      <div class="col-12 col-md-4 mb-4">
        <div class="bg-light p-4">
          <h2 class="text-primary">About Me</h2>
```

```html
      <img src="https://via.placeholder.com/150" alt="Profile photo"
      class="img-fluid rounded-circle mb-3">
      <p>I'm a passionate web developer with expertise in HTML, CSS,
      JavaScript, and modern frameworks.</p>
      <div class="bg-info p-3 mb-3">
        <h3 class="h5">Contact</h3>
        <p class="mb-0">email@example.com</p>
      </div>
      <div class="bg-secondary text-white p-3">
        <h3 class="h5">Skills</h3>
        <p class="mb-0">HTML, CSS, JavaScript, Bootstrap</p>
      </div>
    </div>
</div>

<!-- Main content - Full width on mobile, 8 columns on larger
screens -->
<div class="col-12 col-md-8">
  <h2 class="text-primary mb-4">My Projects</h2>

  <!-- Projects - Each project takes full width on mobile, half width
  on medium screens, one-third on large screens -->
  <div class="row">
    <div class="col-12 col-md-6 col-lg-4 mb-4">
      <div class="bg-success text-white p-3 h-100">
        <h3 class="h4">E-commerce Site</h3>
        <p>A responsive online store built with Bootstrap and
        JavaScript.</p>
      </div>
    </div>
    <div class="col-12 col-md-6 col-lg-4 mb-4">
      <div class="bg-warning p-3 h-100">
        <h3 class="h4">Portfolio Template</h3>
        <p>A customizable portfolio template for creative
        professionals.</p>
      </div>
    </div>
```

```html
      <div class="col-12 col-md-6 col-lg-4 mb-4">
        <div class="bg-danger text-white p-3 h-100">
          <h3 class="h4">Weather App</h3>
          <p>A simple weather application using a third-party API.</p>
        </div>
      </div>
    </div>

    <!-- Testimonials section -->
    <div class="bg-primary text-white p-4 mt-2">
      <h2>Testimonials</h2>
      <p>"Jane is an exceptional developer who delivers high-quality
      work on time." - Client Name</p>
    </div>
   </div>
  </div>
 </main>

 <!-- Footer - Full width on all devices -->
 <footer class="container-fluid bg-dark text-white py-4">
  <div class="container">
    <p class="mb-0">&copy; 2025 Jane Developer. All rights reserved.</p>
  </div>
 </footer>
</body>
</html>
```

Here's what this code will end up looking like in the browser.

CHAPTER 3   COLUMNS, BREAKPOINTS, AND THE GRID IN BOOTSTRAP 5.3

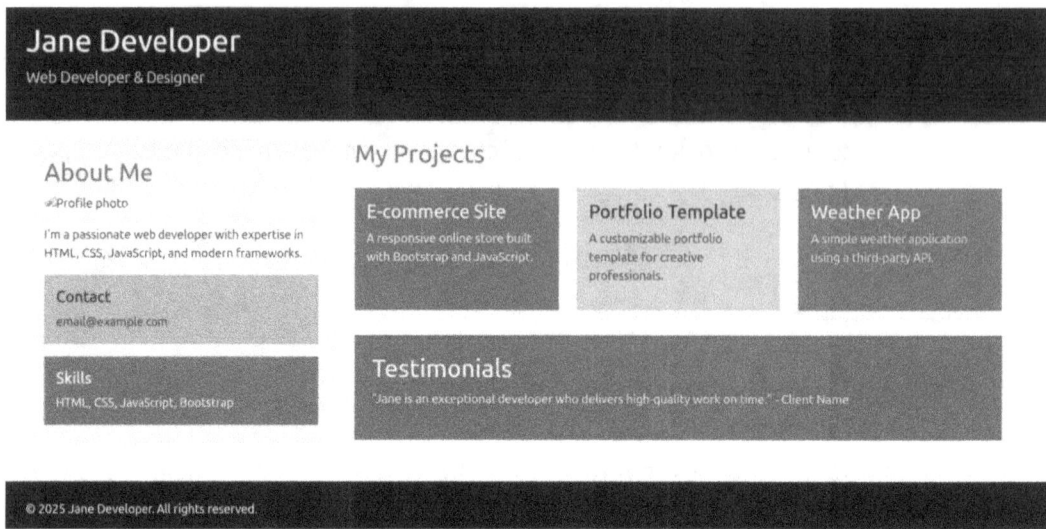

Figure 3-1. *Result in the Browser*

Note that there are some chrome extensions that allow you to visualize a Bootstrap grid on any Bootstrap-powered website. Here's what that looks like for the current example.

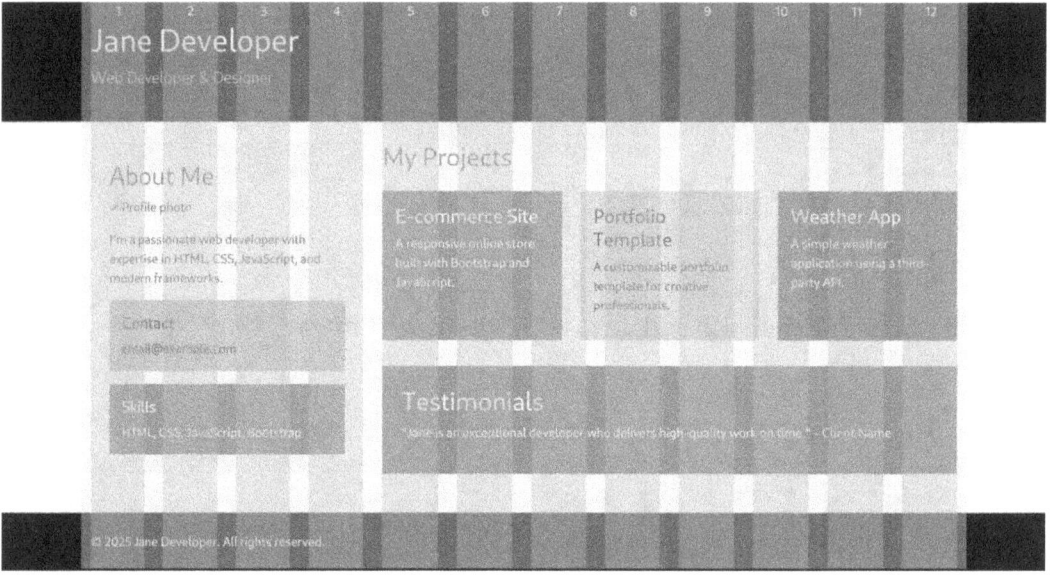

Figure 3-2. *Bootstrap Grid*

If you're curious to try this yourself, you can use the *Bootstrap Grid Viewer* or the *Bootstrap Grid Overlay* Chrome extensions.

Let's break down what's happening in this example's code:

1. **Header and Footer**: We're using .container-fluid for full-width sections with a nested .container to keep the content at a reasonable width.

2. **Main Layout**: We have a two-column layout using .col-12 col-md-4 for the sidebar and .col-12 col-md-8 for the main content area.

    a. On mobile (< 768px), both sections take up the full width (.col-12), stacking vertically.

    b. On medium screens and up (≥ 768px), they sit side by side, with the sidebar taking 4 columns and the main content taking 8 columns.

3. **Project Cards**: Inside the main content, we have project cards that also respond to different screen sizes:

    a. On mobile (< 768px), each card takes the full width (.col-12).

    b. On medium screens (≥ 768px), they take half the width (.col-md-6), creating two columns.

    c. On large screens (≥ 992px), they take one-third of the width (.col-lg-4), creating three columns.

4. **Contextual Colors**: We're using various background colors (.bg-*) and text colors (.text-*) to add visual interest and convey meaning.

This example demonstrates the power of Bootstrap's grid system and breakpoints. With just a few classes, we've created a layout that adapts beautifully to different screen sizes without writing any custom CSS.

3.4.3 How the Layout "Shape-Shifts"

Let's visualize how our portfolio example changes across different screen sizes:

On Mobile (< 768px):

Section	Layout
Header	Full Width
Sidebar	Full Width
Main Content	Full Width
Project 1	Full Width
Project 2	Full Width
Project 3	Full Width
Testimonials	Full Width
Footer	Full Width

On Medium Screens (≥ 768px):

Section	Layout
Header	Full Width
Sidebar	25% Width, Full Height
Main Content	75% Width
Projects	2 per row (Project 1, 2) and 1 per row (Project 3)
Testimonials	75% Width (next to Sidebar)
Footer	Full Width

On Large Screens (≥ 992px):

Section	Layout
Header	Full Width
Sidebar	20% Width, Full Height
Main Content	80% Width
Projects	3 per row (Project 1, 2, 3)
Testimonials	80% Width (next to Sidebar)
Footer	Full Width

This "shape-shifting" behavior is the essence of responsive design with Bootstrap. The layout automatically adapts to provide the best user experience on whatever device is being used.

3.5 Building with Bootstrap: What We've Learned and What's Next

With what we've covered so far – containers, rows, columns, breakpoints, and contextual colors – you now have enough knowledge to build simple, responsive layouts using Bootstrap. Our portfolio example demonstrates how these basic building blocks can be combined to create a functional, responsive webpage.

However, you might have noticed that our example still feels somewhat basic. While it's responsive and functional, it lacks the polished, professional look of many modern websites. That's because we haven't yet explored Bootstrap's rich component library.

Imagine if we wanted to add:

- A navigation menu with dropdowns
- Image carousels for project showcases
- Modal dialogs for detailed project information
- Forms for contact information
- Cards with consistent styling for projects
- Tooltips and popovers for additional information

Implementing these features from scratch would require significant custom CSS and JavaScript. This is where Bootstrap's component system comes in – it provides pre-built, customizable components that handle all of this functionality for you.

In the coming chapters, we'll explore Bootstrap's component library and learn how to leverage these powerful tools to create more sophisticated, interactive websites with minimal custom code. We'll also dive deeper into Bootstrap's utility classes, which provide fine-grained control over spacing, typography, borders, and more.

For now, practice working with the grid system and breakpoints. Try modifying our portfolio example to experiment with different column configurations and breakpoints. The more you work with these fundamental concepts, the more intuitive responsive design will become.

3.6 Summary

In this chapter, we've explored the historical context that led to Bootstrap's development, from the early days of CSS display properties to the rise of grid systems and responsive design. We've examined the underlying technologies that power Bootstrap's grid system – Flexbox and CSS Grid – and understood how Bootstrap provides an abstraction layer that simplifies these complex technologies.

We've also put theory into practice by building a responsive portfolio page that demonstrates how columns and breakpoints work together to create layouts that adapt to different screen sizes. Along the way, we've expanded our color palette with Bootstrap's full range of contextual colors.

In the next chapter, we'll begin exploring Bootstrap's component library, starting with navigation components that will allow us to create professional, responsive navigation menus for our websites.

CHAPTER 4

Utilities, Typography, Images, and Tables in Bootstrap 5.3

4.1 Introduction

In the previous chapter, we successfully combined containers, rows, columns, breakpoints, and the Bootstrap grid to build a simple but functional and fully responsive developer portfolio site.

In this chapter, we'll discuss how to work with various additional built-in CSS classes that are provided by Bootstrap.

Specifically

- Utility classes (such as pre-set margin values, padding values, visibility, etc.)
- Typography classes (controlling the alignment, sizing, decoration, and other aspects of text)
- Image-related CSS classes in Bootstrap
- Tables-related CSS class in Bootstrap

We'll explore all these various built-in CSS classes in the Bootstrap framework with a hands-on approach – by further improving the developer portfolio we started building in the previous chapter.

CHAPTER 4   UTILITIES, TYPOGRAPHY, IMAGES, AND TABLES IN BOOTSTRAP 5.3

4.2 Our Starting Website

Let's revisit the portfolio web page as we left it in Chapter 3.

```
<!DOCTYPE html>
<html lang="en">
<head>
  <meta charset="UTF-8">
  <meta name="viewport" content="width=device-width, initial-scale=1.0">
  <title>My Portfolio</title>
  <link href="https://cdn.jsdelivr.net/npm/bootstrap@5.3.0/dist/css/
  bootstrap.min.css" rel="stylesheet">
</head>
<body>
  <!-- Header - Full width on all devices -->
  <header class="container-fluid bg-dark text-white py-4 mb-4">
    <div class="container">
      <h1>Jane Developer</h1>
      <p class="lead">Web Developer & Designer</p>
    </div>
  </header>

  <!-- Main content area -->
  <main class="container mb-4">
    <div class="row">
      <!-- Sidebar - Full width on mobile, 4 columns on larger screens -->
      <div class="col-12 col-md-4 mb-4">
        <div class="bg-light p-4">
          <h2 class="text-primary">About Me</h2>
          <img src="https://via.placeholder.com/150" alt="Profile photo"
          class="img-fluid rounded-circle mb-3">
          <p>I'm a passionate web developer with expertise in HTML, CSS,
          JavaScript, and modern frameworks.</p>
          <div class="bg-info p-3 mb-3">
            <h3 class="h5">Contact</h3>
            <p class="mb-0">email@example.com</p>
          </div>
```

```html
    <div class="bg-secondary text-white p-3">
      <h3 class="h5">Skills</h3>
      <p class="mb-0">HTML, CSS, JavaScript, Bootstrap</p>
    </div>
  </div>
</div>

<!-- Main content - Full width on mobile, 8 columns on larger screens -->
<div class="col-12 col-md-8">
  <h2 class="text-primary mb-4">My Projects</h2>

  <!-- Projects - Each project takes full width on mobile, half width
  on medium screens, one-third on large screens -->
  <div class="row">
    <div class="col-12 col-md-6 col-lg-4 mb-4">
      <div class="bg-success text-white p-3 h-100">
        <h3 class="h4">E-commerce Site</h3>
        <p>A responsive online store built with Bootstrap and
        JavaScript.</p>
      </div>
    </div>
    <div class="col-12 col-md-6 col-lg-4 mb-4">
      <div class="bg-warning p-3 h-100">
        <h3 class="h4">Portfolio Template</h3>
        <p>A customizable portfolio template for creative
        professionals.</p>
      </div>
    </div>
    <div class="col-12 col-md-6 col-lg-4 mb-4">
      <div class="bg-danger text-white p-3 h-100">
        <h3 class="h4">Weather App</h3>
        <p>A simple weather application using a third-party API.</p>
      </div>
    </div>
  </div>
```

```
      <!-- Testimonials section -->
      <div class="bg-primary text-white p-4 mt-2">
        <h2>Testimonials</h2>
        <p>"Jane is an exceptional developer who delivers high-quality
        work on time." - Client Name</p>
      </div>
    </div>
  </div>
</main>

<!-- Footer - Full width on all devices -->
<footer class="container-fluid bg-dark text-white py-4">
  <div class="container">
    <p class="mb-0">&copy; 2025 Jane Developer. All rights reserved.</p>
  </div>
</footer>
</body>
</html>
```

4.3 Understanding Bootstrap's Utility Classes

Before we start enhancing our portfolio, let's understand what utility classes are and why they're so valuable. Bootstrap's utility classes follow a consistent naming pattern and allow you to apply styles directly in your HTML without writing custom CSS.

4.3.1 Utility Classes Already in Our Layout

Our portfolio already uses several utility classes:

1. **Spacing utilities**: py-4, mb-4, p-4, p-3, mb-3, mb-0, mt-2

    a. These control padding (p) and margin (m) with directional indicators (y for top and bottom) and size values (0-5)

    b. For example, py-4 adds padding to the top and bottom, while mb-4 adds margin to the bottom

2. **Color utilities**: bg-dark, text-white, bg-light, text-primary, etc.

    a. These apply background colors (bg-*) and colors to text (text-*)

    b. Bootstrap includes a range of contextual colors (primary, secondary, success, danger, warning, info, light, dark)

3. **Display and sizing utilities:** img-fluid, h-100

    a. img-fluid makes images responsive by setting max-width: 100% and height: auto

    b. h-100 sets height to 100% of the parent container

4. **Text utilities:** lead

    a. Makes text stand out as an introduction or leading paragraph

4.4 Enhancing Our Portfolio with Additional Utility Classes

Now let's improve our portfolio by adding more utility classes. We'll go section by section, explaining each enhancement.

4.4.1 Improving the Header

Let's make our header more visually appealing with these additions:

```
<header class="container-fluid bg-dark text-white py-4 mb-4 shadow-sm">
  <div class="container">
    <h1 class="display-4 fw-bold">Jane Developer</h1>
    <p class="lead text-light opacity-75 mb-0">Web Developer & Designer</p>
  </div>
</header>
```

What we added:

- shadow-sm: Adds a subtle shadow for depth and visual separation
- display-4: Makes the heading larger and more prominent (part of Bootstrap's display headings)

- fw-bold: Makes the text bold (font-weight utility)
- text-light: A slightly different shade of white for subtle contrast
- opacity-75: Makes the text slightly transparent (75% opacity)
- mb-0: Removes bottom margin from the paragraph

4.4.2 Enhancing the Sidebar

Let's improve the sidebar with these changes:

```html
<div class="col-12 col-md-4 mb-4">
  <div class="bg-light p-4 rounded shadow-sm border">
    <h2 class="text-primary border-bottom pb-2 mb-3">About Me</h2>
    <img src="https://via.placeholder.com/150" alt="Profile photo"
    class="img-fluid rounded-circle mb-3 d-block mx-auto shadow">
    <p class="text-muted">I'm a passionate web developer with expertise in
    HTML, CSS, JavaScript, and modern frameworks.</p>
    <div class="bg-info p-3 mb-3 rounded-3 bg-opacity-25">
      <h3 class="h5 text-info">Contact</h3>
      <p class="mb-0 d-flex align-items-center">
        <span class="me-2">✉</span> email@example.com
      </p>
    </div>
    <div class="bg-secondary p-3 rounded-3 bg-opacity-25 text-dark">
      <h3 class="h5 text-secondary">Skills</h3>
      <p class="mb-0 d-flex flex-wrap gap-2">
        <span class="badge bg-primary">HTML</span>
        <span class="badge bg-primary">CSS</span>
        <span class="badge bg-primary">JavaScript</span>
        <span class="badge bg-primary">Bootstrap</span>
      </p>
    </div>
  </div>
</div>
```

What we added:

- rounded, rounded-3: Adds border radius for rounded corners
- shadow-sm, shadow: Adds shadows for depth
- border, border-bottom: Adds borders for visual separation
- pb-2: Padding at the bottom (size 2)
- d-block mx-auto: Centers the image (display block with auto margins on left and right)
- text-muted: Subtly colored text for better hierarchy
- bg-opacity-25: Makes background colors more subtle (25% opacity)
- d-flex align-items-center: Aligns items vertically in a flex container
- me-2: Margin on the right side (end margin)
- d-flex flex-wrap gap-2: Creates a flexible container with wrapping and gaps
- badge: Creates badge-style elements for skills

4.4.3 Improving the Projects Section

Let's enhance the projects section:

```
<div class="col-12 col-md-8">
  <h2 class="text-primary mb-4 border-bottom pb-2">My Projects</h2>

  <div class="row g-4">  <!-- Added g-4 for gutters -->
    <div class="col-12 col-md-6 col-lg-4">
      <div class="bg-success bg-opacity-75 text-white p-3 h-100 rounded
      shadow-sm position-relative overflow-hidden">
        <div class="position-absolute top-0 end-0 p-2 badge bg-dark bg-
        opacity-50">2023</div>
        <h3 class="h4">E-commerce Site</h3>
        <p>A responsive online store built with Bootstrap and
        JavaScript.</p>
```

```html
      <a href="#" class="btn btn-light btn-sm mt-auto d-block">View
      Project</a>
    </div>
  </div>
  <!-- Apply similar changes to other project cards -->
  <div class="col-12 col-md-6 col-lg-4">
    <div class="bg-warning bg-opacity-75 p-3 h-100 rounded shadow-sm
    position-relative overflow-hidden">
      <div class="position-absolute top-0 end-0 p-2 badge bg-dark bg-
      opacity-50">2024</div>
      <h3 class="h4 text-dark">Portfolio Template</h3>
      <p class="text-dark">A customizable portfolio template for creative
      professionals.</p>
      <a href="#" class="btn btn-dark btn-sm mt-auto d-block">View
      Project</a>
    </div>
  </div>
  <div class="col-12 col-md-6 col-lg-4">
    <div class="bg-danger bg-opacity-75 text-white p-3 h-100 rounded
    shadow-sm position-relative overflow-hidden">
      <div class="position-absolute top-0 end-0 p-2 badge bg-dark bg-
      opacity-50">2024</div>
      <h3 class="h4">Weather App</h3>
      <p>A simple weather application using a third-party API.</p>
      <a href="#" class="btn btn-light btn-sm mt-auto d-block">View
      Project</a>
    </div>
  </div>
</div>

<div class="bg-primary bg-opacity-75 text-white p-4 mt-4 rounded
shadow-sm">
  <h2 class="border-bottom border-light border-opacity-25
  pb-2">Testimonials</h2>
```

```
    <p class="fst-italic">"Jane is an exceptional developer who delivers
    high-quality work on time." <span class="d-block text-end">- Client
    Name</span></p>
  </div>
</div>
```

What we added:

- g-4: Controls the gutter (spacing) between grid items
- bg-opacity-75: Makes background colors less intense
- rounded: Adds rounded corners
- shadow-sm: Adds subtle shadow
- position-relative, position-absolute, top-0, end-0: Positioning utilities for the year badge
- overflow-hidden: Prevents content from spilling out
- badge: Creates a badge-style element
- btn, btn-light, btn-sm: Button styling
- mt-auto: Pushes the button to the bottom of the card
- d-block: Makes the button full width
- border-light, border-opacity-25: Subtle border
- fst-italic: Italic text for the testimonial ("font-style: italic" in regular CSS)
- text-end: Right-aligned text for the client name

4.4.4 Enhancing the Footer

Finally, let's improve the footer:

```
<footer class="container-fluid bg-dark text-white py-4 mt-5">
  <div class="container">
    <div class="d-flex justify-content-between align-items-center flex-wrap">
      <p class="mb-0">&copy; 2025 Jane Developer. All rights reserved.</p>
```

```
    <div class="d-flex gap-3">
      <a href="#" class="text-white text-decoration-none">GitHub</a>
      <a href="#" class="text-white text-decoration-none">LinkedIn</a>
      <a href="#" class="text-white text-decoration-none">Twitter</a>
    </div>
   </div>
  </div>
</footer>
```

What we added:

- mt-5: Adds larger margin at the top
- d-flex justify-content-between align-items-center flex-wrap: Creates a flexible container with items justified between and aligned vertically
- gap-3: Adds spacing between flex items
- text-decoration-none: Removes underlines from links

4.5 The Power of Bootstrap's Utility Classes

As you can see, we've significantly improved the visual appeal of our portfolio without writing a single line of custom CSS. This is the power of Bootstrap's utility classes:

1. **Speed of Development**: Apply styles instantly without switching between HTML and CSS files
2. **Consistency**: Predefined values ensure consistent spacing, colors, and typography
3. **Responsive Design**: Many utilities work with responsive breakpoints (e.g., d-md-none)
4. **Reduced CSS Bloat**: No need to write custom CSS for common styling needs

4.5.1 Common Utility Class Categories

Here's a quick reference of the most commonly used utility categories:

Table 4-1. Utility Categories

Category	Prefix	Examples	Purpose
Spacing	m-, p-	mt-3, pb-2, my-4	Control margins and padding
Colors	bg-, text-	bg-primary, text-danger	Set background and text colors
Opacity	opacity-, bg-opacity-	opacity-75, bg-opacity-25	Control element transparency
Display	d-	d-flex, d-none, d-md-block	Control how elements display
Flex	flex-, justify-content-	flex-column, justify-content-between	Control flex layout behaviors
Position	position-, top-, start-	position-relative, top-0	Control element positioning
Borders	border, rounded	border-top, rounded-circle	Add and style borders and border-radius
Shadows	shadow	shadow-sm, shadow-lg	Add drop shadows
Text	text-, fw-, fs-	text-center, fw-bold, fs-5	Control text styling

4.6 Typography in Bootstrap

Typography is a crucial aspect of web design that affects readability, visual hierarchy, and overall user experience. Bootstrap provides a comprehensive set of typography classes that allow you to control how text appears on your website without writing custom CSS.

Let's explore Bootstrap's typography system and apply it to our portfolio website.

4.6.1 Understanding Bootstrap's Typography System

Bootstrap's typography is built on a few key principles:

1. **Responsive Font Sizes**: Text scales appropriately across different screen sizes
2. **Consistent Spacing**: Headings and paragraphs have standardized margins

3. **Clear Hierarchy**: Different text elements have distinct visual weights

4. **Native Font Stack**: Bootstrap uses the system's default fonts for better performance

4.6.2 Typography Classes in Bootstrap

Here are the main categories of typography-related classes in Bootstrap:

1. **Heading Styles**: h1 through h6 and their class equivalents .h1 through .h6

2. **Display Headings**: .display-1 through .display-6 for larger, more dramatic headings

3. **Text Utilities**: Classes for alignment, wrapping, weight, and style

4. **Lists**: Styling for ordered, unordered, and description lists

5. **Inline Text Elements**: Styling for highlighting, quoting, and emphasizing text

4.6.3 Enhancing Our Portfolio with Typography Classes

Let's improve the typography in our portfolio to make it more visually appealing and readable. We'll focus on applying appropriate typography classes to different sections.

4.6.3.1 Improving Text in the Header

We've already made some typography improvements to the header with the display-4 and fw-bold classes. Let's enhance it further:

```
<header class="container-fluid bg-dark text-white py-4 mb-4 shadow-sm">
  <div class="container">
    <h1 class="display-4 fw-bold text-uppercase">Jane Developer</h1>
    <p class="lead text-light opacity-75 mb-0 fs-4">Web Developer & Designer</p>
  </div>
</header>
```

What we added:

- text-uppercase: Transforms text to uppercase for a stronger visual impact
- fs-4: Increases the font size of the lead text

4.6.3.2 Enhancing Typography in the Sidebar

Let's improve the text in the sidebar section:

```html
<div class="bg-light p-4 rounded shadow-sm border">
  <h2 class="text-primary border-bottom pb-2 mb-3 fw-bold">About Me</h2>
  <img src="https://via.placeholder.com/150" alt="Profile photo"
  class="img-fluid rounded-circle mb-3 d-block mx-auto shadow">
  <p class="text-muted lh-lg">I'm a passionate web developer with expertise
  in HTML, CSS, JavaScript, and modern frameworks.</p>
  <div class="bg-info p-3 mb-3 rounded-3 bg-opacity-25">
    <h3 class="h5 text-info fw-bold">Contact</h3>
    <p class="mb-0 d-flex align-items-center">
      <span class="me-2">✉</span> <a href="mailto:email@example.com"
      class="text-decoration-none">email@example.com</a>
    </p>
  </div>
  <div class="bg-secondary p-3 rounded-3 bg-opacity-25 text-dark">
    <h3 class="h5 text-secondary fw-bold">Skills</h3>
    <p class="mb-0 d-flex flex-wrap gap-2">
      <span class="badge bg-primary">HTML</span>
      <span class="badge bg-primary">CSS</span>
      <span class="badge bg-primary">JavaScript</span>
      <span class="badge bg-primary">Bootstrap</span>
    </p>
  </div>
</div>
```

What we added:

- fw-bold: Makes headings bold for better emphasis
- lh-lg: Increases line height for better readability of paragraph text
- text-decoration-none: Removes the underline from the email link

4.6.3.3 Improving Typography in the Projects Section

Let's enhance the text in the projects section:

```
<div class="col-12 col-md-8">
  <h2 class="text-primary mb-4 border-bottom pb-2 fw-bold">My Projects</h2>

  <div class="row g-4">  <!-- Added g-4 for gutters -->
    <div class="col-12 col-md-6 col-lg-4">
      <div class="bg-success bg-opacity-75 text-white p-3 h-100 rounded
      shadow-sm position-relative overflow-hidden">
        <div class="position-absolute top-0 end-0 p-2 badge bg-dark bg-
        opacity-50">2023</div>
        <h3 class="h4 fw-bold">E-commerce Site</h3>
        <p class="lh-sm small">A responsive online store built with
        Bootstrap and JavaScript.</p>
        <a href="#" class="btn btn-light btn-sm mt-auto d-block">View
        Project</a>
      </div>
    </div>
    <div class="col-12 col-md-6 col-lg-4">
      <div class="bg-warning bg-opacity-75 p-3 h-100 rounded shadow-sm
      position-relative overflow-hidden">
        <div class="position-absolute top-0 end-0 p-2 badge bg-dark bg-
        opacity-50">2024</div>
        <h3 class="h4 text-dark fw-bold">Portfolio Template</h3>
        <p class="text-dark lh-sm small">A customizable portfolio template
        for creative professionals.</p>
        <a href="#" class="btn btn-dark btn-sm mt-auto d-block">View
        Project</a>
```

```
      </div>
    </div>
    <div class="col-12 col-md-6 col-lg-4">
      <div class="bg-danger bg-opacity-75 text-white p-3 h-100 rounded
      shadow-sm position-relative overflow-hidden">
        <div class="position-absolute top-0 end-0 p-2 badge bg-dark bg-
        opacity-50">2024</div>
        <h3 class="h4 fw-bold">Weather App</h3>
        <p class="lh-sm small">A simple weather application using a third-
        party API.</p>
        <a href="#" class="btn btn-light btn-sm mt-auto d-block">View
        Project</a>
      </div>
    </div>
  </div>

  <div class="bg-primary bg-opacity-75 text-white p-4 mt-4 rounded
  shadow-sm">
    <h2 class="border-bottom border-light border-opacity-25 pb-2 fw-
    bold">Testimonials</h2>
    <blockquote class="blockquote">
      <p class="fst-italic lh-lg">"Jane is an exceptional developer who
      delivers high-quality work on time."</p>
      <footer class="blockquote-footer text-white-50">Client Name, <cite
      title="Company">Tech Company</cite></footer>
    </blockquote>
  </div>
</div>
```

What we added:

- fw-bold: Makes all headings bold for better emphasis
- lh-sm and small: Reduces line height and font size for project descriptions to fit more content
- blockquote and blockquote-footer: Proper semantic markup for testimonials

CHAPTER 4 UTILITIES, TYPOGRAPHY, IMAGES, AND TABLES IN BOOTSTRAP 5.3

- cite: Semantic element for the source of a quote
- text-white-50: Makes the citation slightly transparent

4.6.3.4 Improving Typography in the Footer

Let's enhance the text in the footer:

```
<footer class="container-fluid bg-dark text-white py-4 mt-5">
  <div class="container">
    <div class="d-flex justify-content-between align-items-center
    flex-wrap">
      <p class="mb-0 small text-white-50">&copy; 2025 Jane Developer. All
      rights reserved.</p>
      <div class="d-flex gap-3">
        <a href="#" class="text-white text-decoration-none fw-bold">
        GitHub</a>
        <a href="#" class="text-white text-decoration-none fw-bold">
        LinkedIn</a>
        <a href="#" class="text-white text-decoration-none fw-bold">
        Twitter</a>
      </div>
    </div>
  </div>
</footer>
```

What we added:

- small and text-white-50: Makes copyright text smaller and slightly transparent
- fw-bold: Makes links bold for better visibility

4.6.4 Bootstrap Typography Classes Reference

Here's a quick reference of Bootstrap's typography classes:

Table 4-2. *Typography Classes*

Category	Classes	Purpose
Headings	h1-h6, .h1-.h6	Define heading hierarchy
Display headings	display-1 to display-6	Larger, more dramatic headings
Lead	lead	Makes a paragraph stand out
Text alignment	text-start, text-center, text-end	Control text alignment
Text wrapping	text-wrap, text-nowrap	Control text wrapping
Text transform	text-lowercase, text-uppercase, text-capitalize	Change text case
Font weight	fw-bold, fw-normal, fw-light	Control text weight
Font style	fst-italic, fst-normal	Control text style
Line height	lh-1, lh-sm, lh-base, lh-lg	Control line spacing
Monospace	font-monospace	Use monospace font
Reset color	text-reset	Reset text color to inherit
Text decoration	text-decoration-none, text-decoration-underline	Control underlines

4.7 Images in Bootstrap

Images are a crucial part of web design, especially for a portfolio site. Bootstrap provides several classes to make working with images easier and more consistent across different devices and screen sizes.

4.7.1 Bootstrap's Image Classes

Bootstrap offers several key classes for working with images:

1. **Responsive Images**: img-fluid makes images responsive by setting max-width: 100% and height: auto
2. **Image Shapes**: rounded, rounded-circle, img-thumbnail for different styling options

3. **Alignment**: Using utility classes like float-start, float-end, or mx-auto d-block

4. **Picture Element Support**: Bootstrap's responsive utilities work well with the HTML5 <picture> element

4.7.2 Enhancing Our Portfolio with Better Images

Let's improve the images in our portfolio site. We'll replace the placeholder image with a more professional-looking one from Lorem Picsum, which provides random professional stock photos.

4.7.2.1 Updating the Profile Image

First, let's update the profile image in the sidebar:

```
<div class="col-12 col-md-4 mb-4">
  <div class="bg-light p-4 rounded shadow-sm border">
    <h2 class="text-primary border-bottom pb-2 mb-3 fw-bold">About Me</h2>

    <!-- Updated profile image -->
    <img src="https://picsum.photos/id/1012/150/150"
        alt="Jane Developer"
        class="img-fluid rounded-circle mb-3 d-block mx-auto shadow border
        border-3 border-white">

    <p class="text-muted lh-lg">I'm a passionate web developer with
    expertise in HTML, CSS, JavaScript, and modern frameworks.</p>
    <!-- Rest of the sidebar content -->
  </div>
</div>
```

What we changed:

- Replaced the placeholder with a specific Lorem Picsum image (ID 1012)

- Added border border-3 border-white to create a white border around the image

- Improved the alt text for better accessibility

4.7.2.2 Adding Project Images

Let's enhance our project cards with relevant images:

```
<div class="col-12 col-md-6 col-lg-4">
  <div class="bg-success bg-opacity-75 text-white p-3 h-100 rounded shadow-sm position-relative overflow-hidden">
    <div class="position-absolute top-0 end-0 p-2 badge bg-dark bg-opacity-50">2023</div>

    <!-- Added project image -->
    <img src="https://picsum.photos/id/3/300/150"
         alt="E-commerce Project Screenshot"
         class="img-fluid rounded mb-2 w-100 object-fit-cover"
         style="height: 120px;">

    <h3 class="h4 fw-bold">E-commerce Site</h3>
    <p class="lh-sm small">A responsive online store built with Bootstrap and JavaScript.</p>
    <a href="#" class="btn btn-light btn-sm mt-auto d-block">View Project</a>
  </div>
</div>
```

What we added:

- A relevant image from Lorem Picsum that could represent an e-commerce project
- object-fit-cover to ensure the image fills the space without distortion
- A fixed height using inline style (we'd normally use a CSS class for this, but for simplicity we're using an inline style attribute)

4.7.2.3 Demonstrating Different Image Shapes

Let's add a section to showcase Bootstrap's different image shape options:

```
<div class="col-12 mt-4">
  <h2 class="text-primary mb-4 border-bottom pb-2 fw-bold">My
  Photography</h2>
  <div class="row g-4 text-center">
    <div class="col-6 col-md-3">
      <img src="https://picsum.photos/id/1005/200/200" alt="Portrait"
      class="img-fluid mb-2">
      <p class="small text-muted">Default</p>
    </div>
    <div class="col-6 col-md-3">
      <img src="https://picsum.photos/id/1005/200/200" alt="Portrait"
      class="img-fluid rounded mb-2">
      <p class="small text-muted">Rounded</p>
    </div>
    <div class="col-6 col-md-3">
      <img src="https://picsum.photos/id/1005/200/200" alt="Portrait"
      class="img-fluid rounded-circle mb-2">
      <p class="small text-muted">Circle</p>
    </div>
    <div class="col-6 col-md-3">
      <img src="https://picsum.photos/id/1005/200/200" alt="Portrait"
      class="img-fluid img-thumbnail mb-2">
      <p class="small text-muted">Thumbnail</p>
    </div>
  </div>
</div>
```

What we created:

- A new section that demonstrates the four main image styles in Bootstrap
- Each image uses the same source but different Bootstrap classes
- Simple captions explain each style

4.7.3 Using Figure and Figure Caption

Bootstrap also provides styling for the semantic <figure> and <figcaption> elements. Let's add an example:

```
<div class="col-12 mt-4">
  <h2 class="text-primary mb-4 border-bottom pb-2 fw-bold">Featured
  Work</h2>
  <figure class="figure">
    <img src="https://picsum.photos/id/0/800/400" alt="Laptop with code"
    class="figure-img img-fluid rounded shadow-sm">
    <figcaption class="figure-caption text-center">A screenshot of my
    latest project, showcasing responsive design and modern UI.
    </figcaption>
  </figure>
</div>
```

What we used:

- figure and figcaption for semantic HTML
- figure-img and figure-caption Bootstrap classes for styling
- A random image that serves the purpose of being a placeholder

4.7.4 Bootstrap Image Classes Reference

Here's a quick reference of Bootstrap's image-related classes:

Table 4-3. Image-Related Classes

Class	Purpose
img-fluid	Makes images responsive (max-width: 100%, height: auto)
rounded	Adds border-radius to create rounded corners
rounded-circle	Makes the image a circle (requires square dimensions for perfect circles)
img-thumbnail	Adds padding and a border for a thumbnail effect
figure	Container for figure and caption
figure-img	Applies margin-bottom to images inside figures
figure-caption	Styles for image captions

4.8 Tables in Bootstrap

Tables are essential for displaying structured data in a readable format. Bootstrap provides several classes to enhance the appearance and functionality of HTML tables without requiring custom CSS.

4.8.1 Bootstrap's Table Classes

Bootstrap offers several key classes for working with tables:

1. **Basic Styling**: table provides basic styling with horizontal dividers
2. **Variants**: table-striped, table-bordered, table-hover for different visual styles
3. **Contextual Classes**: table-primary, table-success, etc. for colored backgrounds
4. **Responsive Tables**: table-responsive makes tables scroll horizontally on small devices
5. **Size Variants**: table-sm for more compact tables

4.8.2 Adding Tables to Our Portfolio

Let's add some relevant tables to our portfolio site to showcase different types of data a developer might want to present.

4.8.2.1 Skills and Proficiency Table

First, let's add a table that shows skill proficiency levels:

```
<div class="col-12 mt-4">
  <h2 class="text-primary mb-4 border-bottom pb-2 fw-bold">Skills
  Assessment</h2>

  <div class="table-responsive">
    <table class="table table-striped table-hover">
      <thead class="table-dark">
        <tr>
          <th scope="col">Skill</th>
          <th scope="col">Proficiency</th>
          <th scope="col">Years Experience</th>
          <th scope="col">Last Used</th>
        </tr>
      </thead>
      <tbody>
        <tr>
          <td>HTML/CSS</td>
          <td>
            <div class="progress" style="height: 20px;">
              <div class="progress-bar bg-success" role="progressbar"
                style="width: 90%" aria-valuenow="90" aria-valuemin="0"
                aria-valuemax="100">90%</div>
            </div>
          </td>
          <td>5</td>
          <td>Current</td>
        </tr>
```

```html
<tr>
  <td>JavaScript</td>
  <td>
    <div class="progress" style="height: 20px;">
      <div class="progress-bar bg-success" role="progressbar"
        style="width: 85%" aria-valuenow="85" aria-valuemin="0"
        aria-valuemax="100">85%</div>
    </div>
  </td>
  <td>4</td>
  <td>Current</td>
</tr>
<tr>
  <td>Bootstrap</td>
  <td>
    <div class="progress" style="height: 20px;">
      <div class="progress-bar bg-success" role="progressbar"
        style="width: 80%" aria-valuenow="80" aria-valuemin="0"
        aria-valuemax="100">80%</div>
    </div>
  </td>
  <td>3</td>
  <td>Current</td>
</tr>
<tr>
  <td>React</td>
  <td>
    <div class="progress" style="height: 20px;">
      <div class="progress-bar bg-warning" role="progressbar"
        style="width: 65%" aria-valuenow="65" aria-valuemin="0"
        aria-valuemax="100">65%</div>
    </div>
  </td>
  <td>2</td>
  <td>Current</td>
</tr>
```

```
      <tr>
        <td>Node.js</td>
        <td>
          <div class="progress" style="height: 20px;">
            <div class="progress-bar bg-warning" role="progressbar"
              style="width: 60%" aria-valuenow="60" aria-valuemin="0"
              aria-valuemax="100">60%</div>
          </div>
        </td>
        <td>2</td>
        <td>Current</td>
      </tr>
    </tbody>
  </table>
 </div>
</div>
```

What we used:

- table for basic styling
- table-striped for alternating row colors
- table-hover to highlight rows on hover
- table-dark for the dark header
- table-responsive to make the table scroll horizontally on small screens
- Progress bars to visually represent skill proficiency

4.8.2.2 Project Timeline Table

Next, let's add a table showing a project timeline:

```
<div class="col-12 mt-4">
  <h2 class="text-primary mb-4 border-bottom pb-2 fw-bold">Project
  Timeline</h2>
```

```html
<div class="table-responsive">
  <table class="table table-bordered table-sm">
    <thead>
      <tr class="table-primary">
        <th scope="col">Project</th>
        <th scope="col">Client</th>
        <th scope="col">Start Date</th>
        <th scope="col">End Date</th>
        <th scope="col">Status</th>
      </tr>
    </thead>
    <tbody>
      <tr>
        <td>E-commerce Redesign</td>
        <td>Fashion Boutique</td>
        <td>Jan 2023</td>
        <td>Mar 2023</td>
        <td><span class="badge bg-success">Completed</span></td>
      </tr>
      <tr>
        <td>Portfolio Template</td>
        <td>Creative Agency</td>
        <td>Apr 2023</td>
        <td>May 2023</td>
        <td><span class="badge bg-success">Completed</span></td>
      </tr>
      <tr class="table-active">
        <td>Weather App</td>
        <td>Tech Startup</td>
        <td>Jun 2023</td>
        <td>Aug 2023</td>
        <td><span class="badge bg-success">Completed</span></td>
      </tr>
      <tr>
        <td>CRM Dashboard</td>
```

```
          <td>Marketing Firm</td>
          <td>Sep 2023</td>
          <td>Dec 2023</td>
          <td><span class="badge bg-success">Completed</span></td>
        </tr>
        <tr>
          <td>Mobile App</td>
          <td>Health & Fitness</td>
          <td>Jan 2024</td>
          <td>Present</td>
          <td><span class="badge bg-warning">In Progress</span></td>
        </tr>
      </tbody>
    </table>
  </div>
</div>
```

What we used:

- table-bordered to add borders to all cells
- table-sm for a more compact table
- table-primary for the header background
- table-active to highlight a specific row
- Badges to show status

4.8.2.3 Education and Certifications Table

Finally, let's add a table for education and certifications:

```
<div class="col-12 mt-4 mb-5">
  <h2 class="text-primary mb-4 border-bottom pb-2 fw-bold">Education & Certifications</h2>

  <table class="table">    <thead>
      <tr>
        <th scope="col">Degree/Certification</th>
```

```html
          <th scope="col">Institution</th>
          <th scope="col">Year</th>
        </tr>
      </thead>
      <tbody>
        <tr>
          <td>BSc Computer Science</td>
          <td>University of Technology</td>
          <td>2018</td>
        </tr>
        <tr class="table-light">
          <th scope="row" colspan="3" class="text-center">Certifications</th>
        </tr>
        <tr>
          <td>Front-End Web Development</td>
          <td>Udacity</td>
          <td>2019</td>
        </tr>
        <tr>
          <td>React Developer</td>
          <td>Meta</td>
          <td>2021</td>
        </tr>
        <tr>
          <td>AWS Cloud Practitioner</td>
          <td>Amazon Web Services</td>
          <td>2022</td>
        </tr>
      </tbody>
    </table>
</div>
```

What we used:

- Basic table styling without additional variants
- table-light for a section header row

- colspan="3" to make a header span multiple columns
- scope="row" for proper accessibility

4.8.3 Bootstrap Table Classes Reference

Here's a quick reference of Bootstrap's table-related classes:

Table 4-4. *Table-Related Classes*

Class	Purpose
table	Basic styling with horizontal dividers
table-striped	Adds zebra-striping to rows
table-bordered	Adds borders on all sides of table and cells
table-hover	Enables hover state on rows
table-sm	Makes tables more compact by cutting cell padding in half
table-responsive	Makes tables scroll horizontally on small devices
table-responsive-sm/md/lg/xl/xxl	Responsive breakpoint-specific variants
table-primary/secondary/success/danger/warning/info/light/dark	Contextual classes for row or cell background colors
table-active	Applies the hover color to a row or cell

4.9 Conclusion

In this chapter, we've explored Bootstrap's utility classes, typography system, image styling, and table formatting. By applying these classes to our portfolio website, we've significantly improved its appearance and functionality without writing custom CSS.

We've learned how to:

1. Use utility classes for spacing, colors, display, and positioning
2. Apply typography classes to improve text readability and hierarchy

3. Enhance images with responsive behavior and various shape options

4. Create well-structured tables for presenting different types of data

These Bootstrap features allow us to build professional-looking websites quickly and consistently. In the next chapter, we'll explore Bootstrap's form styling features.

PART II

Your Second Layout: Invoice Maker

CHAPTER 5

Forms in Bootstrap 5.3

5.1 Introduction

Forms are essential components of web applications, allowing users to input data and interact with websites. However, creating well-designed, accessible, and responsive forms can be challenging. Bootstrap 5.3 provides a comprehensive set of tools and classes to simplify form creation and styling.

In this chapter, we'll explore how Bootstrap handles forms, from basic inputs to complex layouts. We'll build on our knowledge from previous chapters to create a practical project: an Invoice Maker application. This project will demonstrate how to implement various form elements while maintaining a clean, professional design.

5.2 HTML Forms: The Foundation

Before diving into Bootstrap's form features, let's review the basics of HTML forms.

5.2.1 The Form Element

The <form> element is the container for all form controls. It has several important attributes:

```
<form action="/submit-form" method="POST" enctype="multipart/form-data">
  <!-- Form controls go here -->
</form>
```

- **action**: Specifies where to send the form data when submitted
- **method**: Defines the HTTP method to use (GET or POST)

- **enctype**: Specifies how form data should be encoded (important for file uploads)
- **novalidate**: Disables browser's built-in validation
- **autocomplete**: Controls browser autocomplete functionality

Note that if we add only this form element to a web page, without any form controls, it will not be visible. Think of the form element as a web form's "invisible container" that nonetheless serves important purposes of specifying various meta-information about the form, as mentioned above.

5.2.2 Form Controls

HTML provides various form controls for different types of data input, as follows.

5.2.2.1 Text Inputs

The most common form control is the text input:

```
<input type="text" name="username" id="username" placeholder="Enter username">
```

The type attribute can be changed to create different input types:

- **text**: Basic text input
- **password**: Masked text input for sensitive information
- **email**: Input with email validation
- **number**: Input for numerical values
- **tel**: Input for telephone numbers
- **url**: Input for web addresses
- **search**: Input for search queries
- **date**, **time**, **datetime-local**: Inputs for date and time values
- **color**: Color picker
- **range**: Slider control

5.2.2.2 Selection Controls

For selecting from predefined options:

```
<!-- Dropdown select -->
<select name="country" id="country">
  <option value="us">United States</option>
  <option value="ca">Canada</option>
  <option value="uk">United Kingdom</option>
</select>

<!-- Radio buttons -->
<input type="radio" name="gender" id="male" value="male">
<label for="male">Male</label>
<input type="radio" name="gender" id="female" value="female">
<label for="female">Female</label>

<!-- Checkboxes -->
<input type="checkbox" name="interests" id="sports" value="sports">
<label for="sports">Sports</label>
<input type="checkbox" name="interests" id="music" value="music">
<label for="music">Music</label>
```

5.2.2.3 Buttons

Buttons trigger actions within forms:

```
<button type="submit">Submit Form</button>
<button type="reset">Reset Form</button>
<button type="button">Regular Button</button>
```

5.2.2.4 Other Form Elements

```
<!-- Multi-line text input -->
<textarea name="message" id="message" rows="4" cols="50"></textarea>

<!-- File upload -->
<input type="file" name="document" id="document">
```

```
<!-- Hidden input -->
<input type="hidden" name="user_id" value="123">
```

5.2.3 Form Attributes

Form controls have several important attributes:

- **name**: Identifies the control in form submissions
- **id**: Unique identifier for the element (used with labels)
- **value**: Specifies the initial value
- **placeholder**: Provides a hint about the expected value
- **required**: Makes the field mandatory
- **disabled**: Makes the field non-interactive
- **readonly**: Makes the field non-editable but still submittable
- **min**, **max**, **step**: For numerical inputs
- **pattern**: Regex pattern for validation
- **autofocus**: Automatically focuses the control when page loads

5.2.4 Accessibility with Labels

Labels are crucial for accessibility, helping screen readers identify form controls:

```
<!-- Explicit labeling (preferred) -->
<label for="email">Email Address:</label>
<input type="email" id="email" name="email">

<!-- Implicit labeling -->
<label>
  Email Address:
  <input type="email" name="email">
</label>
```

5.3 The Challenges of Styling Forms with CSS

Styling forms with vanilla CSS presents several challenges:

5.3.1 Inconsistent Browser Defaults

Browsers apply their own default styles to form elements, resulting in inconsistent appearances across different browsers. For example, a <select> element looks different in Chrome, Firefox, and Safari.

5.3.2 Complex Pseudo-elements

Some form controls use pseudo-elements that are difficult to style. For instance, styling a file input button or a dropdown arrow requires complex CSS workarounds.

```css
/* Example of complex styling for a custom file input */
input[type="file"] {
  opacity: 0;
  position: absolute;
  z-index: -1;
}

.file-label {
  display: inline-block;
  padding: 8px 12px;
  background-color: #f0f0f0;
  border: 1px solid #ccc;
  cursor: pointer;
}
```

5.3.3 Shadow DOM Elements

Some form controls like date pickers and color inputs use Shadow DOM, which encapsulates their internal structure and makes them difficult to style with regular CSS.

5.3.4 Focus States and Accessibility

Properly styling focus states for accessibility requires careful attention to ensure they remain visible and clear for keyboard navigation.

```css
/* Basic focus state styling */
input:focus {
  outline: 2px solid blue;
  outline-offset: 2px;
}
```

5.3.5 Responsive Design Challenges

Creating responsive forms that work well on all devices requires complex media queries and layout adjustments.

5.3.6 Cross-Browser Compatibility

Ensuring consistent form styling across all browsers often requires vendor prefixes and browser-specific hacks.

5.4 How Bootstrap Simplifies Form Styling

Bootstrap 5.3 addresses these challenges by providing:

1. **Normalized Styling**: Bootstrap normalizes form elements across browsers for consistent appearance
2. **Responsive Form Layouts**: Built-in responsive classes for form layouts
3. **Accessible Controls**: Pre-styled form controls with proper focus states and accessibility features
4. **Validation States**: Visual feedback for form validation
5. **Custom Form Controls**: Consistent styling for complex controls like file inputs and selects

Bootstrap's excellent handling of forms is one of the many strengths that has made it remain so popular among developers.

In the next sections, we'll explore Bootstrap's form system in depth and use it to build our Invoice Maker application.

5.5 Bootstrap 5.3 Forms in Depth

5.5.1 The Overarching Approach

Bootstrap's approach to forms is built on a few key principles:

1. **Consistency**: Forms should look and behave consistently across browsers and devices
2. **Accessibility**: Forms should be accessible to all users, including those using screen readers
3. **Flexibility**: The system should support various form layouts and configurations
4. **Feedback**: Users should receive clear feedback about their input

Bootstrap achieves these goals through a system of classes that can be applied to standard HTML form elements.

5.5.2 BEM Methodology in Bootstrap Forms

Bootstrap adopts aspects of the Block Element Modifier (BEM) methodology in its CSS architecture, though it applies it pragmatically rather than strictly.

What is BEM?

BEM is a naming convention for CSS classes that helps create reusable components:

- **Block**: A standalone entity (e.g., form-control)
- **Element**: A part of a block (e.g., form-label)
- **Modifier**: A flag on a block or element (e.g., form-control-lg)

In pure BEM, these would be written as:

- Block: form
- Element: form__label
- Modifier: form--large or form__label--required

Bootstrap's Pragmatic BEM

Bootstrap uses a simplified version of BEM. For example:

- Block: form-control
- Related element: form-label
- Modifier: form-control-lg

This approach maintains the organizational benefits of BEM while using more concise class names.

Bootstrap uses a utility-first naming convention inspired by BEM but does not strictly follow BEM syntax.

5.5.3 Form Layout Options

Bootstrap offers several layout options for forms:

5.5.3.1 Default Stacked Form

The default layout stacks form controls vertically:

```
<form>
  <div class="mb-3">
    <label for="email" class="form-label">Email address</label>
    <input type="email" class="form-control" id="email">
  </div>
  <div class="mb-3">
    <label for="password" class="form-label">Password</label>
    <input type="password" class="form-control" id="password">
  </div>
  <button type="submit" class="btn btn-primary">Submit</button>
</form>
```

5.5.3.2 Horizontal Form

Horizontal forms place labels and controls side-by-side using the grid system:

```
<form>
  <div class="row mb-3">
    <label for="email" class="col-sm-2 col-form-label">Email</label>
    <div class="col-sm-10">
      <input type="email" class="form-control" id="email">
    </div>
  </div>
  <div class="row mb-3">
    <label for="password" class="col-sm-2 col-form-label">Password</label>
    <div class="col-sm-10">
      <input type="password" class="form-control" id="password">
    </div>
  </div>
  <button type="submit" class="btn btn-primary">Submit</button>
</form>
```

5.5.3.3 Inline Form

Inline forms display controls in a single horizontal row, useful for compact layouts:

```
<form class="row row-cols-lg-auto g-3 align-items-center">
  <div class="col-12">
    <label class="visually-hidden" for="email">Email</label>
    <input type="email" class="form-control" id="email"
    placeholder="Email">
  </div>
  <div class="col-12">
    <label class="visually-hidden" for="password">Password</label>
    <input type="password" class="form-control" id="password"
    placeholder="Password">
  </div>
```

```html
  <div class="col-12">
    <button type="submit" class="btn btn-primary">Submit</button>
  </div>
</form>
```

5.5.4 Form Controls in Bootstrap

Bootstrap provides styling for all standard form controls:

5.5.4.1 Text Inputs

```html
<input type="text" class="form-control" placeholder="Standard text input">
<input type="text" class="form-control form-control-lg" placeholder="Large input">
<input type="text" class="form-control form-control-sm" placeholder="Small input">
```

5.5.4.2 Select Dropdowns

```html
<select class="form-select">
  <option selected>Choose an option</option>
  <option value="1">Option 1</option>
  <option value="2">Option 2</option>
  <option value="3">Option 3</option>
</select>
```

5.5.4.3 Checkboxes and Radio Buttons

```html
<!-- Checkbox -->
<div class="form-check">
  <input class="form-check-input" type="checkbox" id="checkbox1">
  <label class="form-check-label" for="checkbox1">Default checkbox</label>
</div>

<!-- Radio button -->
<div class="form-check">
```

```
<input class="form-check-input" type="radio" name="radioGroup"
  id="radio1">
<label class="form-check-label" for="radio1">Default radio</label>
</div>
```

5.5.4.4 Input Groups

Input groups allow you to add text, buttons, or other elements directly adjacent to form controls:

```
<div class="input-group mb-3">
  <span class="input-group-text">$</span>
  <input type="text" class="form-control" aria-label="Amount">
  <span class="input-group-text">.00</span>
</div>
```

5.5.4.5 Floating Labels

Floating labels provide a clean, modern look where the label floats above the input when it contains content:

```
<div class="form-floating mb-3">
  <input type="email" class="form-control" id="floatingEmail"
  placeholder="name@example.com">
  <label for="floatingEmail">Email address</label>
</div>
```

5.5.5 Form Validation

Bootstrap includes styles for form validation feedback:

```
<div class="mb-3">
  <label for="validationInput" class="form-label">Username</label>
  <input type="text" class="form-control is-invalid" id="validationInput">
  <div class="invalid-feedback">
    Please choose a username.
  </div>
</div>
```

5.6 Components vs. Form Elements in Bootstrap

5.6.1 What are Components?

In Bootstrap, components are reusable UI elements that combine HTML structure, CSS styling, and sometimes JavaScript functionality. They're designed to be modular and customizable.

Examples of Bootstrap components include

- Navbars
- Cards
- Modals
- Carousels
- Alerts

5.6.2 Are Forms Components?

In Bootstrap's architecture, forms occupy a middle ground:

- **Basic form controls** (inputs, selects, etc.) are considered foundational elements, similar to typography or the grid system.
- **Complex form arrangements** like input groups, floating labels, and custom selects have component-like behavior but are still part of the forms system.

This distinction is important because it affects how we use and customize these elements. Form controls are designed to work within any component, while components have more specific use cases.

5.7 Building the Invoice Maker Project

Now, let's apply what we've learned to create an Invoice Maker application. This will be a static version for now, focusing on the form layout and styling.

5.7.1 Project Overview

Our Invoice Maker will include:

1. Client information section
2. Invoice details section
3. Item entry form
4. Items table
5. Totals calculation section

5.7.2 HTML Structure

Let's start with the basic HTML structure:

```
<!DOCTYPE html>
<html lang="en">
<head>
  <meta charset="UTF-8">
  <meta name="viewport" content="width=device-width, initial-scale=1.0">
  <title>Invoice Maker</title>
  <link href="https://cdn.jsdelivr.net/npm/bootstrap@5.3.0/dist/css/
  bootstrap.min.css" rel="stylesheet">
</head>
<body class="bg-light">
  <div class="container py-5">
    <div class="row justify-content-center">
      <div class="col-lg-10">
        <div class="card shadow-sm">
          <div class="card-body p-4">
            <h1 class="text-center mb-4">Invoice Maker</h1>

            <!-- Invoice Form will go here -->

          </div>
        </div>
      </div>
```

```
      </div>
    </div>
  </body>
</html>
```

5.7.3 Client Information Section

Let's add the client information section:

```
<section class="mb-4">
  <h2 class="h4 mb-3 border-bottom pb-2">Client Information</h2>
  <div class="row g-3">
    <div class="col-md-6">
      <label for="clientName" class="form-label">Client Name</label>
      <input type="text" class="form-control" id="clientName">
    </div>
    <div class="col-md-6">
      <label for="clientEmail" class="form-label">Client Email</label>
      <input type="email" class="form-control" id="clientEmail">
    </div>
    <div class="col-md-12">
      <label for="clientAddress" class="form-label">Client Address</label>
      <textarea class="form-control" id="clientAddress" rows="2">
      </textarea>
    </div>
  </div>
</section>
```

5.7.4 Invoice Details Section

Next, let's add the invoice details:

```
<section class="mb-4">
  <h2 class="h4 mb-3 border-bottom pb-2">Invoice Details</h2>
  <div class="row g-3">
    <div class="col-md-4">
```

CHAPTER 5 FORMS IN BOOTSTRAP 5.3

```
      <label for="invoiceNumber" class="form-label">Invoice #</label>
      <input type="text" class="form-control" id="invoiceNumber">
    </div>
    <div class="col-md-4">
      <label for="invoiceDate" class="form-label">Date</label>
      <input type="date" class="form-control" id="invoiceDate">
    </div>
    <div class="col-md-4">
      <label for="dueDate" class="form-label">Due Date</label>
      <input type="date" class="form-control" id="dueDate">
    </div>
  </div>
</section>
```

5.7.5 Item Entry Form

Now, let's create the form for adding invoice items:

```
<section class="mb-4">
  <h2 class="h4 mb-3 border-bottom pb-2">Add Items</h2>
  <div class="row g-3 align-items-end">
    <div class="col-md-5">
      <label for="itemDescription" class="form-label">Description</label>
      <input type="text" class="form-control" id="itemDescription">
    </div>
    <div class="col-md-2">
      <label for="itemQuantity" class="form-label">Quantity</label>
      <input type="number" class="form-control" id="itemQuantity" min="1"
        value="1" step="1" >
    </div>
    <div class="col-md-2">
      <label for="itemPrice" class="form-label">Price</label>
      <div class="input-group">
        <span class="input-group-text">$</span>
        <input type="number" class="form-control" id="itemPrice"
          step="0.01" min="0">
```

CHAPTER 5 FORMS IN BOOTSTRAP 5.3

```
      </div>
    </div>
    <div class="col-md-2">
      <label for="itemTax" class="form-label">Tax (%)</label>
      <input type="number" class="form-control" id="itemTax" min="0"
      value="0">
    </div>
    <div class="col-md-1">
      <button type="button" class="btn btn-primary w-100">Add</button>
    </div>
  </div>
</section>
```

5.7.6 Items Table

Let's add a table to display the invoice items:

```
<section class="mb-4">
  <h2 class="h4 mb-3 border-bottom pb-2">Invoice Items</h2>
  <div class="table-responsive">
    <table class="table table-striped table-bordered">
      <thead class="table-light">
        <tr>
          <th>Description</th>
          <th>Quantity</th>
          <th>Price</th>
          <th>Tax</th>
          <th>Total</th>
          <th>Actions</th>
        </tr>
      </thead>
      <tbody>
        <tr>
          <td>Web Design Services</td>
          <td>1</td>
          <td>$500.00</td>
```

```
          <td>10%</td>
          <td>$550.00</td>
          <td>
            <button type="button" class="btn btn-sm btn-danger">
            Remove</button>
          </td>
        </tr>
        <tr>
          <td>Logo Design</td>
          <td>1</td>
          <td>$200.00</td>
          <td>10%</td>
          <td>$220.00</td>
          <td>
            <button type="button" class="btn btn-sm btn-danger">
            Remove</button>
          </td>
        </tr>
      </tbody>
    </table>
  </div>
</section>
```

5.7.7 Totals Section

Finally, let's add the totals section. Notice that the values have been hardcoded here for demonstration. Hardcoded is a word that describes that we have used some "literal" values like $700.00 in the code below, rather than making it dynamic with the help of JavaScript.

```
<section class="mb-4">
  <div class="row justify-content-end">
    <div class="col-md-5">
      <div class="card">
        <div class="card-body">
          <div class="d-flex justify-content-between mb-2">
```

```html
          <span>Subtotal:</span>
          <span>$700.00</span>
        </div>
        <div class="d-flex justify-content-between mb-2">
          <span>Tax:</span>
          <span>$70.00</span>
        </div>
        <div class="d-flex justify-content-between border-top pt-2 
        fw-bold">
          <span>Total:</span>
          <span>$770.00</span>
        </div>
      </div>
    </div>
  </div>
</div>
</section>

<div class="d-flex justify-content-between mt-4">
  <button type="button" class="btn btn-outline-secondary">Reset</button>
  <button type="button" class="btn btn-success">Generate Invoice</button>
</div>
```

5.7.8 The Complete Invoice Maker

Putting it all together, we have a functional invoice form with multiple sections, various form controls, and a clean layout.

5.8 What's Next?

In this chapter, we've explored HTML forms, the challenges of styling them with vanilla CSS, and how Bootstrap simplifies form creation. We've also built a static version of our Invoice Maker application using Bootstrap's form classes.

In the next chapters, we'll continue enhancing our Invoice Maker:

- **Chapter 6**: We'll add Bootstrap components like a navbar, modals, and tooltips to improve the user interface.

- **Chapter 7**: We'll introduce JavaScript to add interactivity, allowing users to add/remove items, calculate totals, and generate a printable invoice.

- **Chapter 8**: We'll deploy our application to Netlify, making it accessible online.

By the end of this section, you'll have built and deployed a complete web application's design using Bootstrap and JavaScript, demonstrating how these technologies work together to create functional, responsive user interfaces.

CHAPTER 6

Components in Bootstrap 5.3

6.1 Introduction

In this chapter, we'll dive deeper into components in Bootstrap 5.3. So far in the book, we've managed to avoid tackling them head-on. There was a very practical reason for this approach: using components in Bootstrap without properly understanding the underlying history, techniques, and principles would lead to a very shallow and superficial understanding. This would hamper your ability to design truly professional web layouts with Bootstrap 5, which is the goal of this book.

That being said, we've finally reached a point where we can discuss components in Bootstrap from an already well-informed viewpoint. That should make this relatively complex topic a lot easier to tackle.

Let's begin by understanding how components came to be and what that means for us in the context of the Bootstrap framework.

6.2 The Evolution of Web UI Patterns

The early days of the web were a bit like the Wild West of design. If you look back at websites from the late 1990s and early 2000s, you'll notice that layouts, navigation systems, and interactive elements varied wildly from site to site. Users had to learn how to navigate each website individually, as there were few established conventions.

As the web matured, certain design patterns began to crystallize. This wasn't by accident or decree – it was through a natural process of evolution. Designers and developers discovered, through trial and error, what worked best for users. Patterns that proved intuitive and effective were adopted more widely, while confusing or cumbersome approaches fell by the wayside.

Take the humble navigation bar, for example. Early websites experimented with navigation placed in various positions - left sidebars, right sidebars, bottom footers, scattered throughout the content, or hidden behind cryptic icons. Over time, the top horizontal navbar emerged as a dominant pattern, especially for primary navigation. Why? Because it's immediately visible, it doesn't consume too much valuable screen real estate, and aligns with how we naturally scan content (from top to bottom).

That's not to say alternative approaches disappeared entirely. Side navigation remains common for applications with deep hierarchies or many options, and we often see hybrid approaches that combine top navigation with side menus for secondary options. But the point is that these patterns became recognizable and expected. Users developed mental models about how websites should work, and deviating too far from these expectations often resulted in poor user experiences.

As these UI patterns solidified, designers and developers recognized the efficiency of packaging these recurring elements into reusable components. Why reinvent the navbar, card, or modal dialog for every project when the core functionality remains consistent? This realization led to the development of component-based design systems, of which Bootstrap is one of the most successful examples.

6.3 Component-Based Design

Component-based design is more than just a development convenience – it represents a fundamental shift in how we think about web interfaces. Instead of viewing a webpage as a monolithic entity, we now see it as a composition of discrete, reusable building blocks.

This approach offers several advantages:

1. **Consistency**: Using standardized components ensures visual and behavioral consistency across an application.

2. **Efficiency**: Developers don't need to reinvent solutions to common problems.

3. **Maintainability**: Updates to a component automatically propagate to all instances.

4. **Collaboration**: Designers and developers can speak a common language about UI elements.

Bootstrap embraced this component-based philosophy early on, which partly explains its enduring popularity. The framework provides a comprehensive library of components that address nearly every common UI need, from simple buttons to complex interactive elements.

6.4 Categorizing Bootstrap Components

While Bootstrap's documentation doesn't explicitly categorize components this way, it's helpful to think of them in terms of complexity and behavior. For our purposes, we can divide Bootstrap components into two broad categories:

6.4.1 Base Components (Primitive Components)

These are the fundamental building blocks of a Bootstrap interface – relatively simple, usually static elements that serve as the foundation for more complex components. They're analogous to primitive data types in programming languages: basic, essential, and used to build more complex structures.

In this unofficial categorization, base components include:

- **Alerts**: Contextual feedback messages for typical user actions
- **Badges**: Small count and labeling components
- **Breadcrumbs**: Navigational hierarchy indicators
- **Buttons**: Action triggers in various styles and sizes
- **Button Groups**: Sets of buttons arranged in a group
- **Cards**: Flexible content containers with header/footer options
- **List Groups**: Versatile components for displaying lists of content
- **Progress Bars**: Visual indicators of a process completion
- **Spinners**: Loading indicators

These components generally don't have complex behaviors or state changes. They render in a particular way and stay that way, though they may respond to basic interactions like hover states.

6.4.2 Compound/Dynamic Components

These more sophisticated components typically combine multiple elements and include JavaScript-powered behaviors like toggling, animation, or state management. They often respond to user interactions in complex ways.

Compound/dynamic components include:

- **Accordion**: Collapsible content panels
- **Carousel**: Slideshow for cycling through elements
- **Collapse**: Toggle content visibility
- **Dropdowns**: Toggleable, contextual overlays for displaying lists
- **Modal**: Dialog boxes/popups
- **Navbar**: Responsive navigation header
- **Navs and Tabs**: Navigational components with tabbed interfaces
- **Offcanvas**: Hidden sidebars for navigation or other content
- **Pagination**: Indicators for navigating through multi-page content
- **Popovers**: Rich content tooltips
- **Scrollspy**: Automatically update navigation based on scroll position
- **Toasts**: Lightweight notifications
- **Tooltips**: Small informational popups

These components often require JavaScript to function properly and may maintain internal state (like whether a dropdown is open or closed).

6.5 Additional Component Categories

Beyond these two main categories, Bootstrap also provides:

6.5.1 Form Components

- **Form Controls**: Textual inputs, checkboxes, radios, etc.
- **Form Selects**: Custom select menus
- **Input Groups**: Form controls with text or buttons
- **Floating Labels**: Compact form styling with animated labels
- **Form Validation**: Visual feedback for form validation states

6.5.2 Layout Components

- **Close Button**: Universal close trigger for dismissible components
- **Placeholders**: Loading placeholders for content
- **Figures**: Image with optional caption

6.5.3 Utility Components

- **Stretched Link**: Make any element clickable by stretching a nested link
- **Ratio**: Responsive media aspect ratios

It's worth noting that this categorization is unofficial and meant to help conceptualize the components rather than representing Bootstrap's official organization. The official documentation (`https://getbootstrap.com/docs/5.3/components/`) remains the definitive reference for all components and their usage.

This book isn't intended to replace that reference. Instead, it's meant to provide a structured curriculum to help you understand these components in context, with practical examples of how they work together in real-world applications. The official documentation tells you what each component does; this book shows you how to use them effectively in your projects.

6.6 Practical Application: Enhancing Our Invoice App

Now that we understand the component landscape in Bootstrap, let's apply this knowledge to enhance our invoice application. We'll add three key components:

1. A responsive navbar for navigation
2. Cards to better organize our content
3. A theme toggle for light/dark mode switching

6.7 Deep Dive: The Navbar Component

Before we implement our navbar, let's take a closer look at how this essential component works in Bootstrap 5.3. Understanding its architecture will help you customize it more effectively for your own projects.

6.7.1 Responsive Behavior

The navbar in Bootstrap is designed with a "mobile-first" approach. By default, it starts in a collapsed state and expands at specified breakpoints using the navbar-expand-{breakpoint} classes:

- navbar-expand-sm: Expands at the small breakpoint (≥576px)
- navbar-expand-md: Expands at the medium breakpoint (≥768px)
- navbar-expand-lg: Expands at the large breakpoint (≥992px)
- navbar-expand-xl: Expands at the extra-large breakpoint (≥1200px)
- navbar-expand-xxl: Expands at the extra-extra-large breakpoint (≥1400px)

When the viewport width is below the specified breakpoint, the navbar collapses into a hamburger menu. When it's at or above the breakpoint, it displays horizontally.

This responsive behavior is achieved through a combination of CSS and JavaScript:

1. The .navbar-toggler button is visible only on smaller screens (controlled by CSS)

2. The .collapse.navbar-collapse container is hidden by default on smaller screens

3. When the toggler is clicked, Bootstrap's JavaScript toggles the .show class on the collapse container

6.7.2 Navbar Architecture

A typical Bootstrap navbar consists of several key components:

1. **Container**: Controls the width and padding of the navbar content

2. **Brand**: Your site's logo or name, usually the first element

3. **Toggler**: The button that appears on small screens to toggle the collapsed content

4. **Collapse Container**: Wraps the content that will be collapsed on small screens

5. **Navigation Items**: The actual links, typically in an unordered list

The relationship between these elements is crucial. The toggler targets the collapse container via the data-bs-target attribute, which must match the ID of the collapse container.

6.7.3 Placement Options

Bootstrap offers several placement options for navbars:

- **Default**: Standard positioning within the document flow
- **Fixed top** (.fixed-top): Navbar stays at the top of the viewport, even when scrolling

- **Fixed bottom** (.fixed-bottom): Navbar stays at the bottom of the viewport
- **Sticky top** (.sticky-top): Navbar scrolls with the page until it reaches the top, then sticks

When using fixed positioning, remember to add appropriate padding to your <body> element to prevent content from hiding behind the navbar.

6.7.4 Color Schemes and Customization

Bootstrap's navbar comes with two base color schemes:

- .navbar-light: For use with light background colors
- .navbar-dark: For use with dark background colors

These classes control the color of text and icons within the navbar, but they do not set the background color themselves. To set the background, pair them with Bootstrap's background utility classes (.bg-*). Correctly combining these classes allows us to improve the text contrast and thus the accessibility of the navbar component.

For example:

- .navbar-dark.bg-dark: Dark background with light text
- .navbar-light.bg-light: Light background with dark text
- .navbar-dark.bg-primary: Primary color background with light text

6.7.5 Further Accessibility Considerations

To ensure your navbar is accessible to all users, pay attention to these details:

- Include aria-controls on the toggler button, pointing to the ID of the collapsible content
- Set aria-expanded="false" initially on the toggler button, which JavaScript will update
- Add aria-label="Toggle navigation" to the toggler button
- Use aria-current="page" on the active navigation link

These attributes help screen readers understand the structure and state of your navigation.

6.7.6 Adding a Navbar

Let's start by adding a responsive navbar to our invoice application. The navbar will provide navigation and branding for our app:

```
<nav class="navbar navbar-expand-lg navbar-light bg-light">
  <div class="container-fluid">
    <a class="navbar-brand" href="#">Invoice Maker</a>
    <button class="navbar-toggler" type="button" data-bs-toggle="collapse"
    data-bs-target="#navbarNav" aria-controls="navbarNav" aria-
    expanded="false" aria-label="Toggle navigation">
      <span class="navbar-toggler-icon"></span>
    </button>
    <div class="collapse navbar-collapse" id="navbarNav">
      <ul class="navbar-nav">
        <li class="nav-item">
          <a class="nav-link active" aria-current="page" href="#">Home</a>
        </li>
        <li class="nav-item">
          <a class="nav-link" href="#">Invoices</a>
        </li>
        <li class="nav-item">
          <a class="nav-link" href="#">Clients</a>
        </li>
        <li class="nav-item">
          <a class="nav-link" href="#">Reports</a>
        </li>
      </ul>
      <ul class="navbar-nav ms-auto">
        <li class="nav-item">
          <button class="btn btn-outline-primary" id="theme-toggle">
            <i class="bi bi-moon-stars"></i>
          </button>
```

```
      </li>
    </ul>
  </div>
</div>
</nav>
```

This navbar includes:

- A brand/logo
- Navigation links
- A responsive toggle for mobile views
- A theme toggle button (which we'll implement shortly)

The navbar-expand-lg class ensures the navbar will collapse into a mobile-friendly hamburger menu on smaller screens, while expanding to show all links on larger screens.

6.8 Deep Dive: The Card Component

Before implementing cards in our application, let's explore this versatile component in more detail. Cards have become a fundamental UI pattern in modern web design, and Bootstrap's implementation offers exceptional flexibility.

6.8.1 The Anatomy of a Card

A Bootstrap card is a flexible container with several optional components:

1. **Card Container** (.card): The main wrapper that provides the card's structure and styling
2. **Card Header** (.card-header): An optional section at the top, often used for titles or actions
3. **Card Body** (.card-body): The primary content area of the card
4. **Card Footer** (.card-footer): An optional section at the bottom, often used for actions or metadata

5. **Card Image** (.card-img-top or .card-img-bottom): Images can be placed at the top or bottom

6. **Card Title** (.card-title) and **subtitle** (.card-subtitle): Formatted headings within the card

7. **Card Text** (.card-text): Formatted paragraph text within the card

8. **Card Links** (.card-link): Styled links within the card

The beauty of cards lies in their modularity – you can include only the elements you need for your specific use case.

6.8.2 Card Variants and Styling

Bootstrap offers several ways to customize cards:

6.8.2.1 Contextual Variants

Cards can use contextual background colors with the .bg-* and .text-* utility classes:

```
<div class="card bg-primary text-white">
  <div class="card-body">
    <h5 class="card-title">Primary Card</h5>
    <p class="card-text">A card with primary background.</p>
  </div>
</div>
```

Available contextual classes include primary, secondary, success, danger, warning, info, light, and dark.

6.8.2.2 Border Variants

For a more subtle approach, you can use border variants with .border-* classes:

```
<div class="card border-success">
  <div class="card-header bg-transparent border-success">Success Header</div>
  <div class="card-body text-success">
    <h5 class="card-title">Success Card</h5>
```

```
    <p class="card-text">A card with success borders.</p>
  </div>
  <div class="card-footer bg-transparent border-success">Success Footer</div>
</div>
```

6.8.2.3 Card Layout Options

Cards can be arranged in various layouts:

- **Card Groups** (.card-group): Attached cards with equal height
- **Card Decks** (deprecated in Bootstrap 5, use grid system instead): Separated cards with equal height
- **Card Columns** (deprecated in Bootstrap 5, use grid system with Masonry instead): Masonry-like card layout

6.8.3 Cards as Content Containers

Cards excel at containing and organizing different types of content:

- **Text Content**: Articles, posts, or descriptions
- **Media Content**: Images, videos, or audio players
- **Interactive Elements**: Forms, buttons, or toggles
- **Lists**: Item collections or feature lists
- **Pricing Tables**: Service or product pricing information

6.8.4 Card Design Principles

When designing with cards, consider these principles:

1. **Consistency**: Maintain consistent padding, typography, and imagery across cards
2. **Hierarchy**: Establish clear visual hierarchy within each card
3. **Actionability**: Make it clear which elements are interactive

4. **Density**: Balance information density to avoid overwhelming users
5. **Responsiveness**: Ensure cards adapt gracefully to different screen sizes

6.8.5 Using Cards for Content Organization

Next, let's use Bootstrap cards to better organize our invoice form and invoice list. Cards provide a clean, boxed container with optional headers and footers:

```
<div class="row mt-4">
  <div class="col-md-6">
    <div class="card">
      <div class="card-header">
        <h5 class="card-title mb-0">Create New Invoice</h5>
      </div>
      <div class="card-body">
        <!-- Invoice form goes here -->
        <form id="invoice-form">
          <!-- Form fields -->
        </form>
      </div>
      <div class="card-footer">
        <button type="submit" class="btn btn-primary" form="invoice-form">Create Invoice</button>
      </div>
    </div>
  </div>
  <div class="col-md-6">
    <div class="card">
      <div class="card-header">
        <h5 class="card-title mb-0">Invoice List</h5>
      </div>
      <div class="card-body">
        <div id="invoice-list">
```

```
        <!-- Invoice list will be rendered here -->
      </div>
    </div>
   </div>
  </div>
</div>
```

Cards help visually separate different functional areas of our application, making the interface more organized and easier to understand. The card header provides a clear title, the body contains the main content, and the footer is perfect for action buttons.

6.8.6 Implementing a Theme Toggle

Finally, let's implement a theme toggle to switch between light and dark modes. Bootstrap 5.3 includes built-in color mode support, which we can leverage:

```
<!-- Add this to the head section -->
<meta name="color-scheme" content="light dark">
<meta name="theme-color" content="#7952b3">
```

And here's the JavaScript to toggle between modes:

```
document.addEventListener('DOMContentLoaded', () => {
  const themeToggle = document.getElementById('theme-toggle');
  const icon = themeToggle.querySelector('i');

  // Check for saved theme preference or use device preference
  const savedTheme = localStorage.getItem('theme');
  const prefersDark = window.matchMedia('(prefers-color-scheme: dark)').matches;

  if (savedTheme === 'dark' || (!savedTheme && prefersDark)) {
    document.documentElement.setAttribute('data-bs-theme', 'dark');
    icon.classList.replace('bi-moon-stars', 'bi-sun');
  }
```

```
// Toggle theme on button click
themeToggle.addEventListener('click', () => {
  const currentTheme = document.documentElement.getAttribute('data-
  bs-theme');
  const newTheme = currentTheme === 'dark' ? 'light' : 'dark';

  document.documentElement.setAttribute('data-bs-theme', newTheme);
  localStorage.setItem('theme', newTheme);

  // Toggle icon
  if (newTheme === 'dark') {
    icon.classList.replace('bi-moon-stars', 'bi-sun');
  } else {
    icon.classList.replace('bi-sun', 'bi-moon-stars');
  }
});
});
```

This code:

1. Checks for a saved theme preference in localStorage

2. Falls back to the user's device preference if no saved preference exists

3. Sets the appropriate theme by adding a data-bs-theme attribute to the document

4. Toggles between themes when the button is clicked

5. Updates the button icon to reflect the current theme

With these enhancements, our invoice application now has a professional navigation system, well-organized content areas, and support for both light and dark themes.

6.9 The Finished Example

Here's the complete, finished example with the navbar, cards, and theme toggle functionality implemented:

```html
<!DOCTYPE html>
<html lang="en" data-bs-theme="light">
<head>
  <meta charset="UTF-8">
  <meta name="viewport" content="width=device-width, initial-scale=1.0">
  <meta name="color-scheme" content="light dark">
  <meta name="theme-color" content="#7952b3">
  <title>Invoice Maker</title>
  <link href="https://cdn.jsdelivr.net/npm/bootstrap@5.3.0/dist/css/bootstrap.min.css" rel="stylesheet">
  <link rel="stylesheet" href="https://cdn.jsdelivr.net/npm/bootstrap-icons@1.11.0/font/bootstrap-icons.css">
  <style>
    .card {
      transition: background-color 0.3s ease;
    }
    [data-bs-theme="dark"] .navbar-light {
      background-color: #212529 !important;
    }
    [data-bs-theme="dark"] .navbar-light .navbar-brand,
    [data-bs-theme="dark"] .navbar-light .nav-link {
      color: rgba(255, 255, 255, 0.85);
    }
    [data-bs-theme="dark"] .navbar-light .nav-link.active {
      color: #fff;
    }
  </style>
</head>
<body>

<nav class="navbar navbar-expand-lg navbar-light bg-light">
  <div class="container-fluid">
    <a class="navbar-brand" href="#">Invoice Maker</a>
    <button class="navbar-toggler" type="button" data-bs-toggle="collapse" data-bs-target="#navbarNav" aria-controls="navbarNav" aria-expanded="false" aria-label="Toggle navigation">
```

```html
          <span class="navbar-toggler-icon"></span>
      </button>
      <div class="collapse navbar-collapse" id="navbarNav">
        <ul class="navbar-nav">
          <li class="nav-item">
            <a class="nav-link active" aria-current="page" href="#">Home</a>
          </li>
          <li class="nav-item">
            <a class="nav-link" href="#">Invoices</a>
          </li>
          <li class="nav-item">
            <a class="nav-link" href="#">Clients</a>
          </li>
          <li class="nav-item">
            <a class="nav-link" href="#">Reports</a>
          </li>
        </ul>
        <ul class="navbar-nav ms-auto">
          <li class="nav-item">
            <button class="btn btn-outline-primary" id="theme-toggle">
              <i class="bi bi-moon-stars"></i>
            </button>
          </li>
        </ul>
      </div>
    </div>
</nav>

  <div class="container py-5">
    <div class="row justify-content-center">
      <div class="col-lg-10">
        <div class="card shadow-sm">
          <div class="card-body p-4">
            <h1 class="text-center mb-4">Invoice Maker</h1>

            <section class="mb-4">
```

```html
    <h2 class="h4 mb-3 border-bottom pb-2">Client Information</h2>
    <div class="row g-3">
      <div class="col-md-6">
        <label for="clientName" class="form-label">Client Name</label>
        <input type="text" class="form-control" id="clientName">
      </div>
      <div class="col-md-6">
        <label for="clientEmail" class="form-label">Client Email</label>
        <input type="email" class="form-control" id="clientEmail">
      </div>
      <div class="col-md-12">
        <label for="clientAddress" class="form-label">Client Address</label>
        <textarea class="form-control" id="clientAddress" rows="2"></textarea>
      </div>
    </div>
</section>

<section class="mb-4">
    <h2 class="h4 mb-3 border-bottom pb-2">Invoice Details</h2>
    <div class="row g-3">
      <div class="col-md-4">
        <label for="invoiceNumber" class="form-label">Invoice #</label>
        <input type="text" class="form-control" id="invoiceNumber">
      </div>
      <div class="col-md-4">
        <label for="invoiceDate" class="form-label">Date</label>
        <input type="date" class="form-control" id="invoiceDate">
      </div>
      <div class="col-md-4">
        <label for="dueDate" class="form-label">Due Date</label>
        <input type="date" class="form-control" id="dueDate">
      </div>
    </div>
</section>
```

```html
<section class="mb-4">
  <h2 class="h4 mb-3 border-bottom pb-2">Invoice Items</h2>
  <div class="card mb-3">
    <div class="card-body p-0">
      <div class="table-responsive">
        <table class="table table-striped table-bordered mb-0">
          <thead class="table-light">
            <tr>
              <th>Description</th>
              <th>Quantity</th>
              <th>Price</th>
              <th>Tax</th>
              <th>Total</th>
              <th>Actions</th>
            </tr>
          </thead>
          <tbody>
            <tr>
              <td>Web Design Services</td>
              <td>1</td>
              <td>$500.00</td>
              <td>10%</td>
              <td>$550.00</td>
              <td>
                <button type="button" class="btn btn-sm btn-danger">
                  <i class="bi bi-trash"></i> Remove
                </button>
              </td>
            </tr>
            <tr>
              <td>Logo Design</td>
              <td>1</td>
              <td>$200.00</td>
              <td>10%</td>
              <td>$220.00</td>
```

```html
                <td>
                  <button type="button" class="btn btn-sm btn-danger">
                    <i class="bi bi-trash"></i> Remove
                  </button>
                </td>
              </tr>
            </tbody>
          </table>
        </div>
      </div>
      <div class="card-footer">
        <button type="button" class="btn btn-sm btn-primary">
          <i class="bi bi-plus-circle"></i> Add Item
        </button>
      </div>
    </div>
</section>
<section class="mb-4">
  <div class="row justify-content-end">
    <div class="col-md-5">
      <div class="card">
        <div class="card-header">
          <h5 class="card-title mb-0">Summary</h5>
        </div>
        <div class="card-body">
          <div class="d-flex justify-content-between mb-2">
            <span>Subtotal:</span>
            <span>$700.00</span>
          </div>
          <div class="d-flex justify-content-between mb-2">
            <span>Tax:</span>
            <span>$70.00</span>
          </div>
          <div class="d-flex justify-content-between border-top pt-2 fw-bold">
```

```html
            <span>Total:</span>
            <span>$770.00</span>
          </div>
        </div>
      </div>
    </div>
  </div>
</section>

<div class="d-flex justify-content-between mt-4">
  <button type="button" class="btn btn-outline-secondary">
    <i class="bi bi-arrow-counterclockwise"></i> Reset
  </button>
  <button type="button" class="btn btn-success">
    <i class="bi bi-file-earmark-pdf"></i> Generate Invoice
  </button>
</div>
          </div>
        </div>
      </div>
    </div>
  </div>

  <!-- Bootstrap JS Bundle with Popper -->
  <script src="https://cdn.jsdelivr.net/npm/bootstrap@5.3.0/dist/js/
  bootstrap.bundle.min.js"></script>

  <!-- Theme Toggle Script -->
  <script>
    document.addEventListener('DOMContentLoaded', () => {
      const themeToggle = document.getElementById('theme-toggle');
      const icon = themeToggle.querySelector('i');

      // Check for saved theme preference or use device preference
      const savedTheme = localStorage.getItem('theme');
      const prefersDark = window.matchMedia('(prefers-color-scheme:
      dark)').matches;
```

```
      if (savedTheme === 'dark' || (!savedTheme && prefersDark)) {
        document.documentElement.setAttribute('data-bs-theme', 'dark');
        icon.classList.replace('bi-moon-stars', 'bi-sun');
      }

      // Toggle theme on button click
      themeToggle.addEventListener('click', () => {
        const currentTheme = document.documentElement.getAttribute('data-
        bs-theme');
        const newTheme = currentTheme === 'dark' ? 'light' : 'dark';

        document.documentElement.setAttribute('data-bs-theme', newTheme);
        localStorage.setItem('theme', newTheme);

        // Toggle icon
        if (newTheme === 'dark') {
          icon.classList.replace('bi-moon-stars', 'bi-sun');
        } else {
          icon.classList.replace('bi-sun', 'bi-moon-stars');
        }
      });
    });
  </script>
</body>
</html>
```

6.10 The Art of Component Composition

One of Bootstrap's greatest strengths is how its components can be combined to create more complex, feature-rich interfaces. This practice, known as component composition, allows you to build sophisticated UI patterns while maintaining the structure and consistency that Bootstrap provides.

6.10.1 Principles of Effective Component Composition

When combining Bootstrap components, keep these principles in mind:

1. **Maintain Hierarchy**: Establish clear visual and functional relationships between components. For example, a navbar might contain dropdowns, which in turn might contain badges.

2. **Respect Component Boundaries**: Each component should fulfill its intended purpose. Don't force a component to do something it wasn't designed for when another component would be more appropriate.

3. **Consider Interaction Patterns**: Think about how combined components will behave when users interact with them. Will clicking one component affect another? How will focus states work?

4. **Preserve Accessibility**: Ensure that your component combinations maintain proper accessibility. This might require additional ARIA attributes or keyboard navigation handling.

5. **Optimize for Responsiveness**: Component combinations should adapt gracefully to different screen sizes, just like individual components.

6.10.2 Common Component Combinations

Here are some effective component combinations that you'll often see in Bootstrap applications:

6.10.2.1 Navbar + Dropdown

Adding dropdowns to navbar items creates multi-level navigation:

```
<nav class="navbar navbar-expand-lg navbar-light bg-light">
  <div class="container-fluid">
    <a class="navbar-brand" href="#">Brand</a>
    <button class="navbar-toggler" type="button" data-bs-toggle="collapse"
    data-bs-target="#navbarNav">
```

```html
      <span class="navbar-toggler-icon"></span>
    </button>
    <div class="collapse navbar-collapse" id="navbarNav">
      <ul class="navbar-nav">
        <li class="nav-item dropdown">
          <a class="nav-link dropdown-toggle" href="#" id="navbarDropdown"
          role="button" data-bs-toggle="dropdown">
            Dropdown
          </a>
          <ul class="dropdown-menu" aria-labelledby="navbarDropdown">
            <li><a class="dropdown-item" href="#">Action</a></li>
            <li><a class="dropdown-item" href="#">Another action</a></li>
          </ul>
        </li>
      </ul>
    </div>
  </div>
</nav>
```

6.10.2.2 Card + List Group

Combining cards with list groups creates structured content lists:

```html
<div class="card">
  <div class="card-header">Featured</div>
  <ul class="list-group list-group-flush">
    <li class="list-group-item">Item 1</li>
    <li class="list-group-item">Item 2</li>
    <li class="list-group-item">Item 3</li>
  </ul>
  <div class="card-footer">Card footer</div>
</div>
```

6.10.2.3 Button + Badge

Adding badges to buttons provides contextual information about button actions:

```
<button type="button" class="btn btn-primary">
  Notifications <span class="badge bg-secondary">4</span>
</button>
```

6.10.2.4 Input Group + Button + Dropdown

This powerful combination creates advanced form controls with integrated actions:

```
<div class="input-group mb-3">
  <input type="text" class="form-control" placeholder="Search...">
  <button class="btn btn-outline-secondary dropdown-toggle" type="button"
  data-bs-toggle="dropdown">
    Filter
  </button>
  <ul class="dropdown-menu dropdown-menu-end">
    <li><a class="dropdown-item" href="#">Products</a></li>
    <li><a class="dropdown-item" href="#">Categories</a></li>
    <li><a class="dropdown-item" href="#">Tags</a></li>
  </ul>
  <button class="btn btn-primary" type="button">Search</button>
</div>
```

6.10.3 Nested Components in Our Invoice App

In our invoice application, we've already used component composition in several ways:

1. **Navbar with Button**: We added a theme toggle button to our navbar
2. **Card with Table**: We wrapped our invoice items table in a card for better organization
3. **Card with Form Elements**: We used cards to contain and structure our form inputs

These combinations create a more cohesive, organized interface than what we might have ended up with if we had used each component in isolation.

6.10.4 Advanced Component Composition Techniques

As you become more comfortable with Bootstrap components, consider these advanced techniques:

1. **Component States as Triggers**: Use the state of one component to trigger changes in another. For example, a form validation state could trigger an alert component.

2. **Dynamic Component Generation**: Use JavaScript to dynamically generate and combine components based on user actions or data.

3. **Custom Component Extensions**: Extend Bootstrap components with custom behaviors while maintaining their core functionality.

4. **Micro-Interactions**: Add subtle animations or transitions between component states to enhance the user experience.

Mastering component composition allows you to create interfaces that are both sophisticated and maintainable, leveraging Bootstrap's robust foundation while adding your own creative touches.

6.11 Conclusion

In this chapter, we've explored the world of Bootstrap components, from their historical evolution to practical implementation in our invoice application. We've seen how components provide a structured, consistent approach to building interfaces, and how they can be categorized based on complexity and behavior.

The components we've implemented – navbar, cards, and theme toggle – are just the beginning. Bootstrap offers dozens of components to address virtually any UI need you might encounter. While we've covered the basics here, the next chapter will delve into more JavaScript-heavy components like modals, tooltips, and popovers, which add even more interactivity and functionality to your applications.

Remember that effective use of components isn't just about knowing what they do, but understanding how they work together to create cohesive, intuitive interfaces. As you continue to build with Bootstrap, you'll develop an instinct for which components best serve particular needs and how to combine them effectively.

By thoughtfully applying these components, you're not just making your applications look better – you're making them more usable, accessible, and maintainable.

CHAPTER 7

JavaScript-Powered Components in Bootstrap 5.3

7.1 Introduction

In the previous chapter, we explored Bootstrap's component system and implemented several key components in our Invoice Maker application. While these components provided structure and visual appeal, they were largely static. Now it's time to bring our application to life with interactive features.

Bootstrap 5.3 includes a powerful set of JavaScript-powered components that enable rich user interactions without requiring you to write extensive custom code. In this chapter, we'll implement these interactive components and learn how to customize their behavior using JavaScript.

In this chapter, you'll learn:

1. **How to Implement Tab Navigation** – Create a tabbed interface that allows users to switch between table and card views of invoice items

2. **Working with Bootstrap Modals** – Build a form modal for adding new invoice items that appears when users click a button

3. **Dynamic Content Manipulation** – Update the DOM to add and remove invoice items in response to user actions

4. **Event Handling in JavaScript** – Understand how to listen for and respond to user interactions like clicks and form submissions

5. **Using Bootstrap's Spinner Component** – Implement loading indicators to provide visual feedback during operations

6. **Managing Application State** – Keep track of invoice items and ensure different views remain synchronized

7. **Responsive Design Considerations** – Ensure our interactive components work well across different screen sizes

We'll build on the foundation established in Chapter 1, where we briefly touched on JavaScript basics. This chapter will expand those concepts significantly, focusing on practical applications within our Invoice Maker app.

By the end of this chapter, you'll have transformed the static invoice application into an interactive tool where users can add items through a modal form, remove items with a click, switch between different views, and experience thoughtful UI touches like loading indicators.

Let's begin by enhancing our invoice application with tabbed navigation.

7.2 Implementing Tab Navigation

One of the most common UI patterns you'll encounter is the tabbed interface. Tabs allow users to switch between different views or sections of content without navigating to a new page. In our Invoice Maker application, we'll use tabs to offer two different ways to view invoice items: a traditional table view and a more visual card view.

Bootstrap makes implementing tabs straightforward, but there's still plenty to learn about how they work under the hood. Let's dive in.

7.2.1 Understanding Bootstrap's Tab Component

Before we start coding, it's worth understanding how Bootstrap's tab component works. At its core, the tab system consists of two main parts:

1. A set of tab triggers (usually links or buttons) that users click to switch tabs

2. The tab content panes that are shown or hidden based on which tab is active

Bootstrap handles the switching behavior through JavaScript, which listens for click events on the tab triggers and manages which content pane is visible.

The beauty of Bootstrap's implementation is that it's both accessible and flexible. The tabs are keyboard navigable, properly communicate their state to screen readers, and can be styled to match your design needs.

7.2.2 Adding Tabs to Our Invoice Items Section

Let's modify our Invoice Maker application to include tabs for switching between table and card views of our invoice items. We'll need to make changes to the HTML structure first, then we'll add the JavaScript functionality.

Note that in the examples that follow, we're using a combination of kebab-case and camelCase naming conventions just to show that it's possible. However, please note that the usual practice in development teams is to choose one approach and stick with it. This is what's referred to as a "naming convention", and it encompasses a lot more than what I've just mentioned. For now, it's enough to be aware of it, and to start getting an idea of potential naming conventions and discrepancies when producing your own code or reading other people's code. As a little side exercise, you can even try to spot the differences and try updating the code so that it follows whatever naming convention you pick.

Here's how our invoice items section currently looks:

```html
<section class="mb-4">
  <h2 class="h4 mb-3 border-bottom pb-2">Invoice Items</h2>
  <div class="card mb-3">
    <div class="card-body p-0">
      <div class="table-responsive">
        <table class="table table-striped table-bordered mb-0">
          <!-- Table content here -->
        </table>
      </div>
    </div>
    <div class="card-footer">
      <button type="button" class="btn btn-sm btn-primary">
        <i class="bi bi-plus-circle"></i> Add Item
      </button>
```

CHAPTER 7   JAVASCRIPT-POWERED COMPONENTS IN BOOTSTRAP 5.3

```
    </div>
  </div>
</section>
```

We need to modify this structure to include our tab navigation. Let's update it:

```
<section class="mb-4">
  <h2 class="h4 mb-3 border-bottom pb-2">Invoice Items</h2>

  <!-- Tab navigation -->
  <ul class="nav nav-tabs mb-3" id="itemViewTabs" role="tablist">
    <li class="nav-item" role="presentation">
      <button class="nav-link active" id="table-tab" data-bs-toggle="tab"
        data-bs-target="#table-view" type="button" role="tab" aria-
        controls="table-view" aria-selected="true">Table View</button>
    </li>
    <li class="nav-item" role="presentation">
      <button class="nav-link" id="card-tab" data-bs-toggle="tab" data-
        bs-target="#card-view" type="button" role="tab" aria-controls="card-
        view" aria-selected="false">Card View</button>
    </li>
  </ul>

  <!-- Tab content -->
  <div class="tab-content" id="itemViewTabsContent">
    <!-- Table View Tab -->
    <div class="tab-pane fade show active" id="table-view" role="tabpanel"
    aria-labelledby="table-tab">
      <div class="card mb-3">
        <div class="card-body p-0">
          <div class="table-responsive">
            <table class="table table-striped table-bordered mb-0">
              <thead class="table-light">
                <tr>
                  <th>Description</th>
                  <th>Quantity</th>
                  <th>Price</th>
```

```html
          <th>Tax</th>
          <th>Total</th>
          <th>Actions</th>
        </tr>
      </thead>
      <tbody id="invoice-items-table">
        <tr>
          <td>Web Design Services</td>
          <td>1</td>
          <td>$500.00</td>
          <td>10%</td>
          <td>$550.00</td>
          <td>
            <button type="button" class="btn btn-sm btn-danger
            remove-item">
              <i class="bi bi-trash"></i> Remove
            </button>
          </td>
        </tr>
        <tr>
          <td>Logo Design</td>
          <td>1</td>
          <td>$200.00</td>
          <td>10%</td>
          <td>$220.00</td>
          <td>
            <button type="button" class="btn btn-sm btn-danger
            remove-item">
              <i class="bi bi-trash"></i> Remove
            </button>
          </td>
        </tr>
      </tbody>
    </table>
  </div>
</div>
```

CHAPTER 7   JAVASCRIPT-POWERED COMPONENTS IN BOOTSTRAP 5.3

```html
      <div class="card-footer">
        <button type="button" class="btn btn-sm btn-primary" id="add-
        item-btn">
          <i class="bi bi-plus-circle"></i> Add Item
        </button>
      </div>
    </div>
</div>

<!-- Card View Tab -->
<div class="tab-pane fade" id="card-view" role="tabpanel" aria-
labelledby="card-tab">
  <div class="row row-cols-1 row-cols-md-2 row-cols-lg-4 g-4 mb-3"
  id="invoice-items-cards">
    <!-- Card for Web Design Services -->
    <div class="col">
      <div class="card h-100">
        <div class="card-header bg-transparent">
          <h5 class="card-title mb-0">Web Design Services</h5>
        </div>
        <div class="card-body">
          <ul class="list-group list-group-flush">
            <li class="list-group-item d-flex justify-content-between">
              <span>Quantity:</span>
              <span>1</span>
            </li>
            <li class="list-group-item d-flex justify-content-between">
              <span>Price:</span>
              <span>$500.00</span>
            </li>
            <li class="list-group-item d-flex justify-content-between">
              <span>Tax:</span>
              <span>10%</span>
            </li>
            <li class="list-group-item d-flex justify-content-between
            fw-bold">
```

```html
          <span>Total:</span>
          <span>$550.00</span>
        </li>
      </ul>
    </div>
    <div class="card-footer bg-transparent">
      <button type="button" class="btn btn-sm btn-danger remove-
      item w-100">
        <i class="bi bi-trash"></i> Remove
      </button>
    </div>
  </div>
</div>

<!-- Card for Logo Design -->
<div class="col">
  <div class="card h-100">
    <div class="card-header bg-transparent">
      <h5 class="card-title mb-0">Logo Design</h5>
    </div>
    <div class="card-body">
      <ul class="list-group list-group-flush">
        <li class="list-group-item d-flex justify-content-between">
          <span>Quantity:</span>
          <span>1</span>
        </li>
        <li class="list-group-item d-flex justify-content-between">
          <span>Price:</span>
          <span>$200.00</span>
        </li>
        <li class="list-group-item d-flex justify-content-between">
          <span>Tax:</span>
          <span>10%</span>
        </li>
        <li class="list-group-item d-flex justify-content-between
        fw-bold">
```

```html
              <span>Total:</span>
              <span>$220.00</span>
            </li>
          </ul>
        </div>
        <div class="card-footer bg-transparent">
          <button type="button" class="btn btn-sm btn-danger remove-
          item w-100">
            <i class="bi bi-trash"></i> Remove
          </button>
        </div>
      </div>
    </div>
  </div>

  <div class="text-center">
    <button type="button" class="btn btn-primary" id="add-item-btn-
    card-view">
      <i class="bi bi-plus-circle"></i> Add Item
    </button>
  </div>
    </div>
  </div>
</section>
```

That's quite a bit of code, so let's break down what we've done:

1. We've added a tab navigation system using Bootstrap's nav-tabs class

2. We've created two tab panes: one for the table view and one for the card view

3. We've moved our existing table into the first tab pane

4. We've created a new card-based layout for the second tab pane

5. We've added unique IDs to elements we'll need to reference with JavaScript

The tab navigation consists of two buttons with the nav-link class. The first button has the active class, which means it will be selected by default. Each button has several data attributes that connect it to its corresponding content pane.

The tab content is wrapped in a tab-content container, with each individual pane having the tab-pane class. The first pane also has the show active classes to make it visible by default.

7.2.3 How the Tab System Works

Let's take a closer look at the attributes in our tab system to understand how they work:

- data-bs-toggle="tab": Tells Bootstrap that this element should trigger the tab functionality
- data-bs-target="#table-view": Specifies which tab pane to show when this tab is clicked
- role="tab" and role="tabpanel": Accessibility attributes that help screen readers understand the relationship between tabs and their content
- aria-controls="table-view": Connects the tab to the content it controls
- aria-selected="true": Indicates whether the tab is currently selected

Bootstrap's JavaScript automatically handles the tab switching when a user clicks on a tab. It toggles the active class on the tabs and shows active classes on the tab panes.

7.2.4 The Card View Layout

For our card view, we've used Bootstrap's grid system with the row-cols-* classes. This creates a responsive layout where:

- On mobile, cards stack in a single column (row-cols-1)
- On medium screens, two cards appear per row (row-cols-md-2)
- On large screens, four cards appear per row (row-cols-lg-4)

Each card displays the same information as the table but in a more visual format. We've used list groups inside the cards to organize the details neatly.

7.2.5 Making the Tabs Interactive

With the HTML structure in place, the tabs will already work thanks to Bootstrap's JavaScript. However, we need to ensure that our "Add Item" functionality works in both views, and that removing an item in one view also removes it from the other.

Let's add some JavaScript to handle this synchronization:

```javascript
document.addEventListener('DOMContentLoaded', function() {
  // Get references to key elements
  const tableBody = document.getElementById('invoice-items-table');
  const cardsContainer = document.getElementById('invoice-items-cards');
  const addItemBtn = document.getElementById('add-item-btn');
  const addItemBtnCardView = document.getElementById('add-item-btn-card-view');

  // Function to remove an item
  function removeItem(event) {
    if (event.target.classList.contains('remove-item') ||
        event.target.closest('.remove-item')) {
      // Get the row or card to remove
      const itemElement = event.target.closest('tr') || event.target.closest('.col');

      // Get the item description to identify the corresponding element in the other view
      let itemDescription;
      if (itemElement.tagName === 'TR') {
        itemDescription = itemElement.cells[0].textContent;
      } else {
        itemDescription = itemElement.querySelector('.card-title').textContent;
      }

      // Remove from table view
      const tableRows = tableBody.querySelectorAll('tr');
```

CHAPTER 7 JAVASCRIPT-POWERED COMPONENTS IN BOOTSTRAP 5.3

```
      for (let row of tableRows) {
        if (row.cells[0].textContent === itemDescription) {
          row.remove();
        }
      }

      // Remove from card view
      const cards = cardsContainer.querySelectorAll('.col');
      for (let card of cards) {
        if (card.querySelector('.card-title').textContent ===
        itemDescription) {
          card.remove();
        }
      }

      // Update totals (we'll implement this later)
      updateTotals();
    }
  }
  // Add event listeners for remove buttons
  document.addEventListener('click', removeItem);

  // Placeholder function for updating totals
  function updateTotals() {
    // We'll implement this in a later section
    console.log('Updating totals...');
  }
});
```

This JavaScript code does several important things:

1. It waits for the DOM to be fully loaded before executing
2. It gets references to important elements in our HTML
3. It defines a function to handle removing items
4. It adds a click event listener to the document that delegates to the removeItem function

The removeItem function is particularly interesting. It uses event delegation to handle clicks on any remove button, whether in the table view or the card view. When a remove button is clicked, it:

1. Finds the parent row or card
2. Gets the item description to identify the corresponding element in the other view
3. Removes the item from both the table view and the card view
4. Updates the totals (which we'll implement later)

Event delegation is a powerful technique where we attach a single event listener to a parent element instead of attaching listeners to each individual button. This is more efficient and also works for elements that might be added to the page later.

7.2.6 Testing Our Tab Navigation

With these changes in place, we can now test our tab navigation. When you load the page, you should see the table view by default. Clicking on the "Card View" tab should switch to the card-based layout. The "Add Item" button should be visible in both views, and removing an item in one view should also remove it from the other.

In the next section, we'll implement the modal form for adding new invoice items.

7.3 Implementing a Modal Form

Modals are dialog boxes or popup windows that appear on top of the current page. They're perfect for forms that don't require a full page reload, like our "Add Item" form. Bootstrap provides a comprehensive modal component that we can easily customize for our needs.

7.3.1 Understanding Bootstrap Modals

Bootstrap modals consist of three main parts:

1. The modal container, which provides the overall structure and backdrop

2. The modal dialog, which controls the width and positioning

3. The modal content, which is divided into header, body, and footer sections

Modals can be triggered by buttons, links, or JavaScript. They can be static (requiring user interaction to close) or dismissible (can be closed by clicking outside or pressing the Escape key).

7.3.2 Creating the Add Item Modal

Let's create a modal form for adding new invoice items. We'll add this to our HTML, right before the closing </body> tag:

```html
<!-- Add Item Modal -->
<div class="modal fade" id="addItemModal" tabindex="-1" aria-labelledby="addItemModalLabel" aria-hidden="true">
  <div class="modal-dialog">
    <div class="modal-content">
      <div class="modal-header">
        <h5 class="modal-title" id="addItemModalLabel">Add Invoice Item</h5>
        <button type="button" class="btn-close" data-bs-dismiss="modal" aria-label="Close"></button>
      </div>
      <div class="modal-body">
        <form id="addItemForm">
          <div class="mb-3">
            <label for="itemDescription" class="form-label">Description</label>
            <input type="text" class="form-control" id="itemDescription" required>
          </div>
          <div class="row mb-3">
            <div class="col">
              <label for="itemQuantity" class="form-label">Quantity</label>
```

```
              <input type="number" class="form-control" id="itemQuantity"
              min="1" value="1" required>
            </div>
            <div class="col">
              <label for="itemPrice" class="form-label">Price ($)</label>
              <input type="number" class="form-control" id="itemPrice"
              min="0" step="0.01" required>
            </div>
          </div>
          <div class="mb-3">
            <label for="itemTax" class="form-label">Tax (%)</label>
            <input type="number" class="form-control" id="itemTax" min="0"
            max="100" value="10">
          </div>
        </form>
      </div>
      <div class="modal-footer">
        <button type="button" class="btn btn-secondary" data-bs-
        dismiss="modal">Cancel</button>
        <button type="button" class="btn btn-primary" id="saveItemBtn">Add
        Item</button>
      </div>
    </div>
  </div>
</div>
```

This modal contains a form with fields for the item description, quantity, price, and tax percentage. The form has validation attributes like required, min, and max to ensure users enter valid data.

7.3.3 Connecting the Modal to Our Buttons

Now we need to connect our "Add Item" buttons to the modal. We'll update the buttons in both the table view and card view to trigger the modal:

```html
<!-- In the table view -->
<button type="button" class="btn btn-sm btn-primary" id="add-item-btn"
data-bs-toggle="modal" data-bs-target="#addItemModal">
  <i class="bi bi-plus-circle"></i> Add Item
</button>

<!-- In the card view -->
<button type="button" class="btn btn-primary" id="add-item-btn-card-view"
data-bs-toggle="modal" data-bs-target="#addItemModal">
  <i class="bi bi-plus-circle"></i> Add Item
</button>
```

The data-bs-toggle="modal" and data-bs-target="#addItemModal" attributes tell Bootstrap to show the modal with the ID "addItemModal" when the button is clicked.

7.3.4 Handling Form Submission

Now let's add JavaScript to handle the form submission. We'll extend our existing JavaScript code:

```javascript
document.addEventListener('DOMContentLoaded', function() {
  // Get references to key elements (existing code)
  const tableBody = document.getElementById('invoice-items-table');
  const cardsContainer = document.getElementById('invoice-items-cards');
  const addItemBtn = document.getElementById('add-item-btn');
  const addItemBtnCardView = document.getElementById('add-item-btn-
  card-view');

  // New references for the modal form
  const addItemForm = document.getElementById('addItemForm');
  const saveItemBtn = document.getElementById('saveItemBtn');
  const addItemModal = document.getElementById('addItemModal');
  const modal = new bootstrap.Modal(addItemModal);

  // Function to remove an item (existing code)
  function removeItem(event) {
    // ... (existing code)
  }
```

CHAPTER 7   JAVASCRIPT-POWERED COMPONENTS IN BOOTSTRAP 5.3

```javascript
// Add event listeners for remove buttons (existing code)
document.addEventListener('click', removeItem);

// Function to add a new item
function addItem() {
  // Get form values
  const description = document.getElementById('itemDescription').value;
  const quantity = parseInt(document.getElementById('itemQuantity').value);
  const price = parseFloat(document.getElementById('itemPrice').value);
  const tax = parseFloat(document.getElementById('itemTax').value);

  // Calculate total
  const taxAmount = price * quantity * (tax / 100);
  const total = price * quantity + taxAmount;

  // Format currency values
  const formattedPrice = `$${price.toFixed(2)}`;
  const formattedTotal = `$${total.toFixed(2)}`;

  // Add to table view
  const tableRow = document.createElement('tr');
  tableRow.innerHTML = `
    <td>${description}</td>
    <td>${quantity}</td>
    <td>${formattedPrice}</td>
    <td>${tax}%</td>
    <td>${formattedTotal}</td>
    <td>
      <button type="button" class="btn btn-sm btn-danger remove-item">
        <i class="bi bi-trash"></i> Remove
      </button>
    </td>
  `;
  tableBody.appendChild(tableRow);

  // Add to card view
  const cardCol = document.createElement('div');
```

```
cardCol.className = 'col';
cardCol.innerHTML = `
  <div class="card h-100">
    <div class="card-header bg-transparent">
      <h5 class="card-title mb-0">${description}</h5>
    </div>
    <div class="card-body">
      <ul class="list-group list-group-flush">
        <li class="list-group-item d-flex justify-content-between">
          <span>Quantity:</span>
          <span>${quantity}</span>
        </li>
        <li class="list-group-item d-flex justify-content-between">
          <span>Price:</span>
          <span>${formattedPrice}</span>
        </li>
        <li class="list-group-item d-flex justify-content-between">
          <span>Tax:</span>
          <span>${tax}%</span>
        </li>
        <li class="list-group-item d-flex justify-content-between
        fw-bold">
          <span>Total:</span>
          <span>${formattedTotal}</span>
        </li>
      </ul>
    </div>
    <div class="card-footer bg-transparent">
      <button type="button" class="btn btn-sm btn-danger remove-
      item w-100">
        <i class="bi bi-trash"></i> Remove
      </button>
    </div>
  </div>
`;
cardsContainer.appendChild(cardCol);
```

```
    // Reset form and close modal
    addItemForm.reset();
    modal.hide();

    // Update totals
    updateTotals();
  }

  // Add event listener for the save button
  saveItemBtn.addEventListener('click', function() {
    // Check form validity
    if (addItemForm.checkValidity()) {
      addItem();
    } else {
      // Trigger browser's native form validation UI
      addItemForm.reportValidity();
    }
  });

  // Allow form submission with Enter key
  addItemForm.addEventListener('keyDown', function(event) {
    if (event.key === 'Enter') {
      event.preventDefault();
      saveItemBtn.click();
    }
  });

  // Placeholder function for updating totals (existing code)
  function updateTotals() {
    // We'll implement this in a later section
    console.log('Updating totals...');
  }
});
```

Let's break down what this code does:

1. We get references to the new modal elements

2. We create a Bootstrap Modal instance from our modal element

3. We define an addItem function that:

    a. Gets the form values

    b. Calculates the total price including tax

    c. Creates new elements for both the table and card views

    d. Resets the form and closes the modal

    e. Updates the totals

4. We add event listeners for:

    a. The save button click

    b. Enter key presses in the form

The addItem function is where most of the work happens. It creates new HTML elements for both the table view and the card view, ensuring that our data stays synchronized between the two views.

7.3.5 Form Validation

Notice how we're using the browser's built-in form validation:

1. We've added attributes like required, min, and max to our form inputs

2. We check if the form is valid with addItemForm.checkValidity()

3. If it's not valid, we trigger the browser's validation UI with addItemForm.reportValidity()

This gives us robust validation with minimal code. The browser will prevent submission and show error messages if the user tries to submit invalid data.

7.3.6 Understanding Dynamic DOM Manipulation

One of the most powerful aspects of JavaScript is its ability to manipulate the Document Object Model (DOM) dynamically. In our code, we're creating new elements and adding them to the page without a reload.

Here's a closer look at how we're creating a new table row:

```
const tableRow = document.createElement('tr');
tableRow.innerHTML = `
  <td>${description}</td>
  <td>${quantity}</td>
  <!-- ... more cells ... -->
`;
tableBody.appendChild(tableRow);
```

This code:

1. Creates a new <tr> element with document.createElement('tr')
2. Sets its inner HTML using a template literal (the backtick syntax)
3. Adds it to the table body with appendChild()

The template literal allows us to easily insert our variables into the HTML string using ${variableName} syntax. This is a modern JavaScript feature that makes dynamic HTML generation much cleaner than concatenating strings.

7.3.7 Testing the Modal Form

With these changes in place, let's test our modal form:

1. Click the "Add Item" button in either view
2. Fill out the form with item details
3. Click "Add Item" or press Enter

You should see the new item appear in both the table view and the card view. The form should reset, and the modal should close automatically.

In the next section, we'll implement the loading indicator for the reset button.

7.4 Implementing a Loading Indicator

Loading indicators provide visual feedback to users when an operation is in progress. They're especially important for operations that take more than a few hundred milliseconds, as they reassure users that something is happening and the application hasn't frozen.

Bootstrap 5.3 includes built-in spinner components that we can use as loading indicators. In this section, we'll add a loading indicator to our reset button, simulating a delay that might occur when resetting a form in a real application.

7.4.1 Understanding Bootstrap Spinners

Bootstrap offers two types of spinners:

1. **Border Spinners**: A circular loading indicator with a spinning border
2. **Growing Spinners**: A circular loading indicator that grows and fades

Both types come in different sizes and colors to match your application's design. They can be used standalone or inside buttons to indicate that the button's action is in progress.

7.4.2 Adding the Reset Button

First, let's add a proper reset button to our form. We'll place it next to the "Generate Invoice" button at the bottom of our page:

```
<div class="d-flex justify-content-between mt-4">
  <button type="button" class="btn btn-outline-secondary" id="reset-form-btn">
    <i class="bi bi-arrow-counterclockwise"></i> Reset
  </button>
  <button type="button" class="btn btn-success">
    <i class="bi bi-file-earmark-pdf"></i> Generate Invoice
  </button>
</div>
```

This button has an ID of reset-form-btn that we'll use to reference it in our JavaScript code.

7.4.3 Implementing the Loading State

Now let's modify our JavaScript to handle the reset button click and show a loading indicator. We'll add this to our existing JavaScript code:

```
document.addEventListener('DOMContentLoaded', function() {
  // Existing code...

  // Get reference to the reset button
  const resetFormBtn = document.getElementById('reset-form-btn');

  // Function to reset the form with a loading indicator
  function resetFormWithLoading() {
    // Disable the button and show loading state
    resetFormBtn.disabled = true;

    // Store the original button content
    const originalContent = resetFormBtn.innerHTML;

    // Replace with spinner
    resetFormBtn.innerHTML = `
      <span class="spinner-border spinner-border-sm" role="status" aria-hidden="true"></span>
      <span class="ms-1">Resetting...</span>
    `;

    // Simulate a delay (in a real app, this might be an API call)
    setTimeout(function() {
      // Clear all invoice items
      tableBody.innerHTML = '';
      cardsContainer.innerHTML = '';

      // Reset any form fields if needed
      // For example, if we had a client info form:
      // document.getElementById('clientName').value = '';

      // Update totals
      updateTotals();
```

```
      // Restore the button
      resetFormBtn.innerHTML = originalContent;
      resetFormBtn.disabled = false;
   }, 2000); // 2 second delay
 }
 // Add event listener for the reset button
 resetFormBtn.addEventListener('click', resetFormWithLoading);

 // Existing code...
});
```

This code does several important things:

1. It gets a reference to the reset button using its ID

2. It defines a function resetFormWithLoading that:

    a. Disables the button to prevent multiple clicks

    b. Stores the original button content

    c. Replaces the button content with a spinner and "Resetting..." text

    d. Uses setTimeout to simulate a 2-second delay

    e. Clears all invoice items from both views

    f. Updates the totals

    g. Restores the button to its original state

3. It adds a click event listener to the reset button

7.4.4 Understanding setTimeout

The setTimeout function is a core JavaScript feature that allows you to delay the execution of code. It takes two arguments:

1. A function to execute

2. A delay in milliseconds

In our example, we're using setTimeout to simulate a delay that might occur in a real application when resetting a form. This could represent time spent making an API call, processing data, or performing other operations.

```
setTimeout(function() {
  // Code to execute after the delay
}, 2000); // 2 second delay
```

The code inside the function will execute after 2000 milliseconds (2 seconds) have passed. During this time, our loading indicator will be visible, giving the user feedback that something is happening.

7.4.5 The Spinner Component

Let's take a closer look at the spinner component we're using:

```
<span class="spinner-border spinner-border-sm" role="status" aria-hidden="true"></span>
```

This creates a small border spinner with the following classes:

- spinner-border: Creates the basic spinner animation
- spinner-border-sm: Makes the spinner smaller to fit nicely in a button

We've also added accessibility attributes:

- role="status": Tells screen readers that this is a status indicator
- aria-hidden="true": Hides the spinner from screen readers since we provide text ("Resetting...") that already communicates the status

7.4.6 Testing the Loading Indicator

With these changes in place, let's test our loading indicator:

1. Add a few invoice items using the modal form
2. Click the "Reset" button

3. Observe the button change to show a spinner and "Resetting…" text
4. After 2 seconds, all invoice items should be removed, and the button should return to its original state

This provides a much better user experience than an instant reset, especially in real applications where there might be actual processing happening behind the scenes.

7.4.7 Variations of the Spinner Component

Bootstrap offers several variations of the spinner component that you can use in different contexts:

7.4.7.1 Different Sizes

```
<!-- Regular size (default) -->
<div class="spinner-border" role="status">
  <span class="visually-hidden">Loading...</span>
</div>

<!-- Small size -->
<div class="spinner-border spinner-border-sm" role="status">
  <span class="visually-hidden">Loading...</span>
</div>
```

7.4.7.2 Different Colors

```
<div class="spinner-border text-primary" role="status"></div>
<div class="spinner-border text-secondary" role="status"></div>
<div class="spinner-border text-success" role="status"></div>
<div class="spinner-border text-danger" role="status"></div>
<div class="spinner-border text-warning" role="status"></div>
<div class="spinner-border text-info" role="status"></div>
<div class="spinner-border text-light" role="status"></div>
<div class="spinner-border text-dark" role="status"></div>
```

7.4.7.3 Growing Spinner

```
<div class="spinner-grow" role="status">
  <span class="visually-hidden">Loading...</span>
</div>
```

These variations give you flexibility in how you present loading states throughout your application.

7.4.8 Best Practices for Loading Indicators

When using loading indicators, keep these best practices in mind:

1. **Use Them for Operations That Take Time**: Only show loading indicators for operations that take more than a few hundred milliseconds. Instant operations don't need them.

2. **Provide Context**: Accompany spinners with text that explains what's happening (like "Resetting..." or "Saving...").

3. **Disable Interactive Elements**: Prevent users from triggering the same action multiple times by disabling buttons or forms during loading.

4. **Consider Placement**: Place the indicator near the action that triggered it, so users understand what's loading.

5. **Be Consistent**: Use the same style of loading indicators throughout your application for a cohesive experience.

By following these practices, you can create a more polished and professional user experience in your applications.

In the next section, we'll update our code to calculate and display invoice totals.

7.5 Calculating and Displaying Invoice Totals

An essential feature of any invoice application is the ability to calculate and display totals. In this section, we'll implement functionality to calculate subtotals, tax amounts, and the grand total for all invoice items.

7.5.1 Setting Up the Totals Section

First, let's add a section to our HTML to display the totals. We'll place this below the invoice items section:

```
<div class="card mt-4">
  <div class="card-header bg-light">
    <h5 class="mb-0">Invoice Summary</h5>
  </div>
  <div class="card-body">
    <div class="row">
      <div class="col-md-6 offset-md-6">
        <table class="table table-sm">
          <tbody>
            <tr>
              <th>Subtotal:</th>
              <td class="text-end" id="subtotal">$0.00</td>
            </tr>
            <tr>
              <th>Tax:</th>
              <td class="text-end" id="tax-amount">$0.00</td>
            </tr>
            <tr class="table-active fw-bold">
              <th>Total:</th>
              <td class="text-end" id="grand-total">$0.00</td>
            </tr>
          </tbody>
        </table>
      </div>
    </div>
  </div>
</div>
```

This creates a card with a table showing the subtotal, tax amount, and grand total. Each value has an ID that we'll use to update it from our JavaScript code.

7.5.2 Implementing the updateTotals Function

Now let's implement the updateTotals function that we've been calling in our code. We'll replace the placeholder function with a real implementation:

```javascript
document.addEventListener('DOMContentLoaded', function() {
  // Existing code...

  // Function to update invoice totals
  function updateTotals() {
    // Get all table rows (excluding the header row)
    const tableRows = tableBody.querySelectorAll('tr');

    let subtotal = 0;
    let taxAmount = 0;

    // Calculate totals from table rows
    tableRows.forEach(row => {
      const cells = row.querySelectorAll('td');
      if (cells.length >= 5) { // Make sure we have enough cells
        // Get quantity from the second cell
        const quantity = parseInt(cells[1].textContent);

        // Get price from the third cell (remove $ and convert to number)
        const price = parseFloat(cells[2].textContent.replace('$', ''));

        // Get tax percentage from the fourth cell (remove % and convert to number)
        const taxPercent = parseFloat(cells[3].textContent.replace('%', ''));

        // Calculate item subtotal and tax
        const itemSubtotal = quantity * price;
        const itemTax = itemSubtotal * (taxPercent / 100);

        // Add to running totals
        subtotal += itemSubtotal;
        taxAmount += itemTax;
      }
    });
```

```javascript
    // Calculate grand total
    const grandTotal = subtotal + taxAmount;

    // Update the DOM elements
    document.getElementById('subtotal').textContent = `$${subtotal.
    toFixed(2)}`;
    document.getElementById('tax-amount').textContent = `$${taxAmount.
    toFixed(2)}`;
    document.getElementById('grand-total').textContent = `$${grandTotal.
    toFixed(2)}`;

    // If we have no items, reset to $0.00
    if (tableRows.length === 0) {
      document.getElementById('subtotal').textContent = '$0.00';
      document.getElementById('tax-amount').textContent = '$0.00';
      document.getElementById('grand-total').textContent = '$0.00';
    }
  }

  // Existing code...
});
```

This function does several important things:

1. It gets all the table rows from the invoice items table

2. It initializes variables to track the subtotal and tax amount

3. It iterates through each row, extracting the quantity, price, and tax percentage

4. It calculates the subtotal and tax for each item and adds them to the running totals

5. It calculates the grand total by adding the subtotal and tax amount

6. It updates the DOM elements with the formatted totals

7. It handles the case where there are no items by resetting the totals to $0.00

7.5.3 Understanding the DOM Traversal

In this function, we're using DOM traversal to extract data from the table rows. Let's look at how this works:

```
const cells = row.querySelectorAll('td');
if (cells.length >= 5) { // Make sure we have enough cells
  // Get quantity from the second cell
  const quantity = parseInt(cells[1].textContent);

  // Get price from the third cell (remove $ and convert to number)
  const price = parseFloat(cells[2].textContent.replace('$', ''));

  // Get tax percentage from the fourth cell (remove % and convert
  to number)
  const taxPercent = parseFloat(cells[3].textContent.replace('%', ''));

  // ...
}
```

This code:

1. Gets all the <td> elements in the current row
2. Checks that we have at least five cells (to avoid errors)
3. Extracts the quantity from the second cell (index 1)
4. Extracts the price from the third cell (index 2), removing the dollar sign
5. Extracts the tax percentage from the fourth cell (index 3), removing the percent sign

We're using parseInt and parseFloat to convert the text content to numbers, and replace to remove currency and percentage symbols.

7.5.4 Calling updateTotals

We need to make sure updateTotals is called whenever the invoice items change. We're already calling it in several places:

1. After adding a new item

2. After resetting the form

But we also need to call it when removing an item. Let's update the removeItem function:

```
// Function to remove an item
function removeItem(event) {
  // Check if the clicked element is a remove button
  if (event.target.closest('.remove-item')) {
    const button = event.target.closest('.remove-item');

    // Find the parent row or card
    const row = button.closest('tr');
    const card = button.closest('.col');

    // Remove the elements
    if (row) row.remove();
    if (card) card.remove();

    // Update totals
    updateTotals();
  }
}
```

We've added a call to updateTotals() after removing the elements, ensuring that the totals are always up to date.

7.5.5 Testing the Totals Calculation

With these changes in place, let's test our totals calculation:

1. Add a few invoice items using the modal form

2. Verify that the subtotal, tax amount, and grand total are calculated correctly

3. Remove an item and verify that the totals update

4. Reset the form and verify that the totals reset to $0.00

The totals should update in real-time as you add, remove, or reset items.

7.5.6 Understanding Data Flow

It's worth noting the data flow in our application:

1. User input (adding/removing items) ➤ DOM changes ➤ Total calculation

In a more complex application, you might use a different approach:

1. User input ➤ Data model changes ➤ DOM updates ➤ Total calculation

This second approach, known as the Model-View-Controller (MVC) pattern or similar architectures, separates data from presentation. It's more maintainable for larger applications but requires more code.

For our invoice maker, the direct DOM manipulation approach is simpler and works well for the scope of this project.

7.5.7 Enhancing the User Experience

To enhance the user experience, we could add some visual feedback when the totals update. Let's add a subtle animation to the totals when they change:

```
// Function to update invoice totals with animation
function updateTotals() {
  // Existing calculation code...

  // Update the DOM elements with animation
  const elements = [
    document.getElementById('subtotal'),
    document.getElementById('tax-amount'),
    document.getElementById('grand-total')
  ];

  // Update text content
  elements[0].textContent = `$${subtotal.toFixed(2)}`;
  elements[1].textContent = `$${taxAmount.toFixed(2)}`;
  elements[2].textContent = `$${grandTotal.toFixed(2)}`;
```

```
  // Add highlight class for animation
  elements.forEach(el => {
    el.classList.add('highlight-change');
    setTimeout(() => {
      el.classList.remove('highlight-change');
    }, 500);
  });

  // If we have no items, reset to $0.00
  if (tableRows.length === 0) {
    elements[0].textContent = '$0.00';
    elements[1].textContent = '$0.00';
    elements[2].textContent = '$0.00';
  }
}
```

We'll need to add a CSS class for the animation. Add this to your CSS:

```
.highlight-change {
  animation: highlight 0.5s ease-in-out;
}

@keyframes highlight {
  0% { background-color: rgba(255, 255, 0, 0.5); }
  100% { background-color: transparent; }
}
```

This creates a subtle yellow flash animation when the totals update, drawing the user's attention to the change.

7.6 Conclusion

We've now implemented a complete invoice maker application with the following JavaScript-powered features:

1. Tab navigation between table and card views
2. A modal form for adding new items

3. Dynamic removal of items
4. A loading indicator for the reset button
5. Real-time calculation and display of totals

These features demonstrate how Bootstrap's JavaScript components can be combined with custom JavaScript code to create interactive web applications. The declarative nature of Bootstrap's components makes it easy to add complex UI elements like tabs and modals, while JavaScript gives us the power to handle user interactions and update the UI dynamically.

In the next chapter, we'll explore how to deploy our invoice maker app to a live site on Netlify using GitHub.

CHAPTER 8

Sharing Your Invoice Maker App with the World

8.1 Introduction

Congratulations! In the previous chapter, we built a fully functional Invoice Maker app with Bootstrap and JavaScript. You've created something valuable that could help people manage their invoices more efficiently.

But what good is an amazing app if it only lives on your computer? In this chapter, we'll take your Invoice Maker app from your local machine to the internet, where anyone can access it from anywhere in the world.

The good news is that after all the complex JavaScript work we did in the previous chapter, deploying your app online is relatively straightforward. We'll break it down into simple steps that anyone can follow, even if you've never published a website before.

In this chapter, you'll learn:

- How to use Git as your project's safety net – think of it as a super-powered undo button that protects all your hard work
- How GitHub helps you store your code securely in the cloud and collaborate with others
- How Netlify can automatically publish your website from your GitHub repository with just a few clicks
- Why this approach to deployment gives you both simplicity and powerful features for free

8.2 Understanding Git: Your Code's Safety Net

Before we deploy our Invoice Maker app, let's talk about Git. If you've never used Git before, you can think of it as a time machine for your code.

8.2.1 What Is Git?

Git is a version control system that tracks changes to your files over time. Here's what makes it essential for developers:

- **History Tracking**: Git remembers every change you make to your files, allowing you to go back to any previous version if something breaks.

- **Parallel Development**: It allows you to create "branches" to experiment with new features without affecting your working code.

- **Collaboration**: Multiple people can work on the same project without overwriting each other's changes.

For our purposes in this chapter, we'll focus on the most basic Git functionality: saving snapshots of your project that you can return to if needed.

8.2.2 Git Basics: The Three-Step Process

Using Git involves a simple three-step process that we'll use to prepare our Invoice Maker app for deployment:

1. **Initialize**: Tell Git to start tracking your project (this must be done once per project)

2. **Stage**: Select which files you want to include in your next snapshot

3. **Commit**: Save a permanent snapshot of those files with a message describing what changed

Think of it like taking a photo:

1. You set up your camera (initialize)

2. You decide what to include in the frame (stage)

3. You take the picture and write a caption (commit)

8.2.3 A Note on Best Practices

It's worth mentioning that what we'll cover in this chapter is a simplified approach to Git. Professional developers use more advanced Git workflows with branches, pull requests, and other features. However, the basics we'll learn here will give you a solid foundation, and more importantly, they'll help protect your code as you continue to develop your skills.

The worst thing that can happen when learning to code is spending hours building something amazing, only to accidentally break it with no way to get back to the working version. Git prevents this disaster scenario, which is why we'll use it throughout the rest of this book.

8.3 GitHub: Your Code's Home in the Cloud

Now that we understand what Git is, let's talk about GitHub.

8.3.1 What Is GitHub?

GitHub is a web-based platform that uses Git in the background but adds a visual interface and many additional features:

- **Remote Storage**: Your code is safely stored in the cloud, protected from computer crashes or losses
- **Visual Interface**: See your project's history, changes, and structure through a web browser
- **Collaboration Tools**: Features that make it easier to work with others on the same codebase
- **Integration**: Connects with deployment platforms like Netlify for easy publishing

For our Invoice Maker app, GitHub will serve as both a backup of our code and the connection point to our deployment platform.

8.4 Netlify: From Code to Live Website

The final piece of our deployment puzzle is Netlify.

8.4.1 What Is Netlify?

Netlify is a web hosting platform specifically designed for modern web projects. It takes your code from GitHub and turns it into a live website automatically. Here's why it's perfect for our Bootstrap app:

- **Simple Deployment**: Connect to your GitHub repository and your site goes live with just a few clicks
- **Automatic Updates**: When you update your code on GitHub, Netlify automatically rebuilds and deploys your site
- **Free SSL Certificates**: Your site gets HTTPS security automatically
- **Global CDN**: Your site loads quickly for visitors anywhere in the world
- **Advanced Features**: As your needs grow, Netlify offers form handling, serverless functions, and more

The combination of Git, GitHub, and Netlify creates a streamlined workflow that's both beginner-friendly and powerful enough for professional development.

In the following sections, we'll walk through the step-by-step process of setting up Git for our project, creating a GitHub repository, and deploying our Invoice Maker app on Netlify.

8.5 Setting Up Git for Your Invoice Maker App (Optional)

Before we upload our app to GitHub and deploy it, it's a good idea to set up Git locally. This step is optional but recommended as it gives you a safety net for your code right on your computer.

8.5.1 What Is Git Again?

Remember, Git is like a time machine for your code. It lets you save snapshots of your project at different points in time, so you can always go back if something breaks. Think of it as creating save points in a video game.

8.5.2 The Simplest Git Setup

Here's the most straightforward way to set up Git for your Invoice Maker project:

1. **Install Git**: If you don't already have Git installed, download it from git-scm.com and run the installer with default settings.

2. **Open Your Project Folder**: Right-click inside your Invoice Maker project folder and select "Git Bash Here" (on Windows) or open Terminal and navigate to your project folder (on Mac/Linux).

3. **Initialize Git**: Type this simple command and press Enter:

   ```
   git init
   ```

   This tells Git to start watching your project folder.

4. **Save Your First Snapshot**: Type these two commands:

   ```
   git add .
   git commit -m "Initial version of Invoice Maker app"
   ```

The first command (git add .) stages all the files for commit, and the second command (git commit –m) creates a snapshot with your message.

That's it! You now have a local Git repository that's tracking your project. If you make changes and want to save another snapshot, just repeat the git add . and git commit -m "Your message here" commands.

8.5.3 Why This Matters

Even this simple Git setup gives you powerful protection:

- If you accidentally delete something important, you can recover it
- If you make changes that break your app, you can go back to a working version

- You have a history of all the major changes you've made to your project

For now, we don't need to worry about more advanced Git features. This basic setup is enough to give you a safety net as you continue developing your skills.

8.6 Creating a GitHub Repository

Now that we have our project tracked with Git locally, let's create a GitHub repository to store it in the cloud.

A repository, aka a "repo" is simply your code as a stand-alone project that is stored on GitHub.

The concept of a repository in the git world is so common that developers use the word "repository" interchangeably with the words "project" or "folder."

Now that we have the minimum-needed theoretical background, let's start with our app's deployment.

8.6.1 Step 1: Create a GitHub Account

If you don't already have a GitHub account, you'll need to create one:

1. Go to github.com
2. Click "Sign up"
3. Follow the instructions to create your account

8.6.2 Step 2: Create a New Repository

Once you're logged in to GitHub:

1. Click the "+" icon in the top-right corner and select "New repository"
2. Name your repository (e.g., "invoice-maker")
3. Add a description if you want (e.g., "A Bootstrap 5.3 Invoice Maker application")

4. Keep the repository Public (unless you have a specific reason to make it Private)

5. Do NOT initialize the repository with a README, .gitignore, or license since we already have our files

6. Click "Create repository"

8.6.3 Step 3: Upload Your Files to GitHub

Pro Tip Although uploading via GitHub's web interface works, a better practice is to connect your local Git repository to GitHub using git remote add origin <repo-url> command, then push your commits using git push. This allows smoother syncing between local and remote versions – however, it does require setting up Git authentication for a given developer right inside the command line (console) of that user's operating system, which introduces various complications. That's why I've chosen to offer you an easier alternative, which, in real-life development, is seldom used. But it's a very simple one, and it's easy to do, so I've opted for doing it this way. The goal of the chapter is to guide you to deploy your site, not get bogged down in setting up Git authentication on your local machine.

Instead of using complex command-line operations that require setting up authentication, let's use GitHub's simple web interface to upload our files:

1. After creating your repository, you'll see a page with several options. Look for the "uploading an existing file" link and click it.

2. You'll be taken to a page where you can drag and drop files from your computer directly into GitHub.

3. Drag all your Invoice Maker files – likely, just one (or a few at most) – and folders from your file explorer into the GitHub upload area. You can select multiple files at once to upload them together.

4. After dragging your files, scroll down to the "Commit changes" section at the bottom of the page.

5. Enter a commit message like "Initial upload: Complete Invoice Maker app" in the first text box.

6. Leave the "Add an optional extended description…" field empty or add more details if you wish.

7. Make sure the "Commit directly to the main branch" option is selected.

8. Click the green "Commit changes" button to upload your files.

8.6.4 Step 4: Verify Your Repository

Go back to your browser and refresh the GitHub page. You should now see all your Invoice Maker files in your GitHub repository!

Congratulations! Your code is now safely stored in the cloud, and you're ready to deploy it with Netlify.

8.7 Deploying Your App with Netlify

Now that your code is on GitHub, deploying it with Netlify is surprisingly easy.

8.7.1 Step 1: Create a Netlify Account

1. Go to netlify.com
2. Click "Sign up"
3. Choose to sign up with GitHub (this makes the connection easier)
4. Follow the authorization steps

8.7.2 Step 2: Create a New Site from Git

Once you're logged in to Netlify:

1. Click the "New site from Git" button
2. Choose "GitHub" as your Git provider

CHAPTER 8   SHARING YOUR INVOICE MAKER APP WITH THE WORLD

3. Authorize Netlify to access your GitHub repositories if prompted

4. Select your "invoice-maker" repository from the list

8.7.3 Step 3: Configure Your Build Settings

For a simple HTML/CSS/JavaScript project like our Invoice Maker, you don't need any special build settings:

1. Leave the "Branch to deploy" as "main"

2. Leave the "Build command" field empty

3. Set the "Publish directory" to the directory containing your HTML file (usually just "." for the root directory)

4. Click "Deploy site"

8.7.4 Step 4: Wait for Deployment

Netlify will now deploy your site. This usually takes less than a minute for a simple site like our Invoice Maker.

Once the deployment is complete, Netlify will assign your site a random subdomain like random-words-123456.netlify.app.

8.7.5 Step 5: Customize Your Site Name (Optional)

If you want a more memorable URL:

1. Go to "Site settings"

2. Click "Change site name"

3. Enter a new name (e.g., "my-invoice-maker")

4. Your site will now be available at my-invoice-maker.netlify.app

8.7.6 Step 6: Visit Your Live Site

Click on the URL Netlify has provided, and you should see your Invoice Maker app live on the internet!

Congratulations! You've successfully deployed your Bootstrap 5.3 Invoice Maker app to the internet, where anyone can access it.

8.8 Making Updates to Your Live Site

One of the best features of this workflow is how easy it is to update your site after it's deployed. Here's the process using GitHub's web interface:

1. Make changes to your files on your computer
2. Go to your GitHub repository in your web browser
3. Navigate to the file you want to update
4. Click the pencil icon (Edit this file) in the upper right corner of the file view
5. Make your changes in the editor
6. Scroll down to the "Commit changes" section
7. Enter a brief description of your changes (e.g., "Update invoice styling")
8. Click "Commit changes"
9. Netlify automatically detects the changes and redeploys your site

For uploading new files:

1. Navigate to the folder where you want to add the file
2. Click "Add file" ➤ "Upload files" at the top of the file list
3. Drag and drop your new files
4. Commit the changes as described above

That's it! Within a minute or two, your changes will be live on your Netlify site.

8.9 Conclusion

In this chapter, we've taken our Invoice Maker app from a local project to a live website on the internet. Along the way, we've learned:

- How to use Git to track changes and protect our code
- How to store our code on GitHub for safekeeping and collaboration
- How to deploy our site to Netlify for free, professional web hosting
- How to update our site when we make changes

This workflow might seem like a lot of steps the first time through, but it becomes second nature with practice. More importantly, you're now using the same tools and processes that professional web developers use every day.

In the remaining chapters of this book, we'll switch gears and look at how the Bootstrap framework fits in with the wider front-end web development ecosystem, starting with npm - the Node package manager.

PART III

Your Third Layout: Bootstrap 5.3 and React

CHAPTER 9

Modern Front-End Tooling

9.1 Introduction

So, you've made it this far! You've built a functional invoice application with Bootstrap, learned about responsive design, and even deployed your creation to the web. But if you've been browsing developer forums or job listings lately, you might be feeling a bit overwhelmed by the sheer number of tools, frameworks, and buzzwords being thrown around.

> "What's this Webpack thing? Do I need to learn Node.js? What's npm? Why can't I just keep using script tags like we've been doing?"

I get it. Looking at modern front-end development can feel like staring at a mountain of knowledge that seems impossible to climb. But here's a secret: it's all about perspective. Instead of seeing it as a boring mountain of technical jargon to memorize, try viewing it as an exciting mystery with many moving parts where you get to uncover how everything fits together. It's like being a detective in a tech thriller rather than a student cramming for an exam.

This chapter isn't about hands-on coding (we'll get back to that in the next chapter), but it's crucial for understanding the ecosystem you're about to enter. Think of it as the map you need before embarking on a journey. Without it, you might wander aimlessly, not knowing which tools matter and which ones you can safely ignore for now.

We'll explore how we got to where we are today in front-end development, focusing on what's important for you as a beginner or mid-level developer. By the end, you'll have enough context to make sense of modern JavaScript development and be prepared for our upcoming dive into React.

Let's start unraveling this mystery together!

9.2 The Evolution of JavaScript: From ES5 to Modern Times

Remember when phones had physical keyboards and websites were mostly static pages? That was roughly the era of ES5 (ECMAScript 5), the version of JavaScript that dominated the web from 2009 until around 2015. It was reliable but limited compared to what we have today.

JavaScript's transformation really kicked into high gear with ES6 (also called ES2015) – a massive update that changed how we write JavaScript forever. If you've seen code with arrow functions (=>) or variables declared with let and const instead of var, you're looking at post-ES5 JavaScript.

Here's a quick before-and-after to show you the difference:

ES5 (Old Way):

```
var getName = function(person) {
  return person.firstName + ' ' + person.lastName;
};
```

ES6+ (Modern Way):

```
const getName = (person) => {
  return `${person.firstName} ${person.lastName}`;
};
```

ES6 introduced a ton of improvements that made JavaScript more powerful and pleasant to work with:

- Arrow functions (as shown above)
- Template literals using backticks (`Hello, ${name}!`)
- Classes (though they're really just syntactic sugar over the prototype system)
- Promises for better async handling
- Destructuring assignments (const { firstName, lastName } = person;)
- Default parameters

- Spread and rest operators (...)
- Modules (we'll talk more about these in a moment)

The above, in and of itself, might feel a bit too much if you have never used it or seen it. But, it's important to know it's out there and it exists – that's all there is to it. If you haven't used it before, do not worry – you'll learn it in time. Right now, don't even try to memorize it.

Since ES6, JavaScript has continued to evolve with yearly updates (ES2016, ES2017, etc.), each adding new features. But ES6 was the watershed moment that modernized the language.

But why does any of this matter to you? Because modern frameworks like React assume you're familiar with these features. The good news is that you don't need to memorize everything – you'll pick up what you need as you go along.

9.3 The Module Revolution: Why JavaScript Needed a Better Way to Organize Code

As web applications grew more complex, developers faced a problem: how do you organize thousands of lines of JavaScript in a way that's maintainable?

In most programming languages, this problem was solved long ago with modules – a way to split code into separate files and explicitly import what you need. But JavaScript was designed in the 1990s for simple webpage interactions, not complex applications. It didn't have a native module system.

Early solutions were messy. Developers would either:

1. Put everything in one massive file (nightmare to maintain)
2. Split into multiple files but risk variable name collisions
3. Use patterns like the Immediately Invoked Function Expression (IIFE) to create private scopes
4. Adopt third-party module systems like AMD or CommonJS

None of these solutions was ideal. JavaScript needed a better way.

9.4 Enter Node.js: JavaScript Beyond the Browser

In 2009, a developer named Ryan Dahl had a revolutionary idea: what if we could take the JavaScript engine from a browser (specifically Chrome's V8 engine) and let it run outside the browser as a standalone program?

This idea became Node.js, and it changed everything.

To understand why Node.js was revolutionary, let's quickly look at how browsers work. When you visit a website, your browser:

1. Requests HTML, CSS, and JavaScript files from a server
2. Parses the HTML to build the DOM (Document Object Model)
3. Applies CSS styles to the DOM elements
4. Executes JavaScript to add interactivity

The JavaScript engine is the part that executes the code. Chrome uses V8, Firefox uses SpiderMonkey, Safari uses JavaScriptCore, etc.

Node.js essentially extracted the V8 engine from Chrome and wrapped it with additional APIs for file system access, networking, and other server-side tasks. Suddenly, JavaScript could be used for much more than just making websites interactive – it could run servers, build tools, and even desktop applications.

But Node.js didn't just bring JavaScript to the server side; it also introduced a consistent module system based on CommonJS, which lets you organize code like this:

```
// In math.js
function add(a, b) {
  return a + b;
}

module.exports = { add };

// In another file
const math = require('./math.js');
console.log(math.add(2, 3)); // Outputs: 5
```

This might not look revolutionary now, but it was a game-changer for JavaScript development. Finally, there was a standard way to split code into modules!

9.5 The Client-Server Model and REST: How Websites Traditionally Work

Before we go further, let's take a quick detour to understand how websites traditionally work, because this context helps explain why modern tools evolved the way they did.

In the traditional web model,

1. Your browser (the client) requests a page from a server.
2. The server sends back HTML, CSS, and JavaScript.
3. When you interact with the page (like submitting a form), the browser makes a new request to the server.
4. The server processes the request and sends back a completely new page.
5. Your browser replaces the current page with the new one.

This is why old-school websites have that "flash" when you navigate between pages – you're getting a completely new page each time.

When you submit a form in HTML, it uses HTTP methods (also called REST verbs) like

- GET: Request data (like loading a page)
- POST: Submit data (like sending a form)
- PUT: Update existing data
- DELETE: Remove data

The default behavior of a form in HTML is to send a POST request to the server and load a new page with the response:

```
<form action="/submit-data" method="post">
  <!-- form fields here -->
  <button type="submit">Submit</button>
</form>
```

This model worked fine for document-centric websites but felt clunky for interactive applications. Each interaction required a full page reload, making for a jarring user experience.

9.6 The Rise of React and the Virtual DOM

As web applications became more complex, developers grew frustrated with directly manipulating the DOM. It was error-prone, hard to maintain, and slow for complex updates.

Facebook faced this problem on a massive scale. Their solution, released in 2013, was React – a JavaScript library that introduced a revolutionary concept: the Virtual DOM.

Instead of directly manipulating the DOM (which is slow), React creates a lightweight copy of it in memory (the Virtual DOM). When your data changes:

1. React updates this virtual copy
2. Compares it to the previous version (a process called "reconciliation")
3. Calculates the minimal set of changes needed to update the real DOM
4. Applies only those specific changes

This approach made complex UI updates much more efficient and gave developers a more declarative way to build interfaces. Instead of saying "add this element, then update this text, then change this color," you simply describe what the UI should look like based on the current data, and React figures out how to update the DOM efficiently.

React also popularized component-based architecture, where UIs are built from reusable, self-contained components. This made it easier to build and maintain complex interfaces.

But to use React effectively, developers needed a better way to manage dependencies and build their applications. This is where npm and the Node.js ecosystem became crucial.

9.7 npm: The Package Manager That Changed Everything

When Node.js gained popularity, it needed a way for developers to share and reuse code. This led to the creation of npm (Node Package Manager), which has become one of the largest software registries in the world.

npm is both a command-line tool and an online repository of JavaScript packages. It lets you easily install, manage, and share code packages.

The beauty of npm is that it gives you access to thousands of ready-made solutions. Need to add date manipulation to your project? Instead of writing complex date logic yourself, you can just run:

`npm install moment`

And suddenly you have access to Moment.js, a library that makes working with dates much easier. It's like standing on the shoulders of giants – leveraging the work of other programmers so you don't have to reinvent the wheel.

Every npm project typically has a package.json file, which acts as a manifest for your project. It lists:

- Your project's name, version, and description
- Dependencies (packages your project needs to run)
- Development dependencies (packages needed during development but not in production)
- Scripts for common tasks like starting the development server or building for production

Here's a simple example:

```
{
  "name": "my-awesome-project",
  "version": "1.0.0",
  "dependencies": {
    "react": "^17.0.2",
    "react-dom": "^17.0.2"
  },
  "devDependencies": {
    "webpack": "^5.52.0"
  },
  "scripts": {
    "start": "webpack serve --mode development",
    "build": "webpack --mode production"
  }
}
```

With this file, anyone can clone your project and run npm install to automatically download all the necessary dependencies. No need to manually include script tags or download files!

9.8 Installing Node.js and npm

Before you can use npm, you need to install Node.js, which includes npm by default. Here's how to do it on different operating systems:

9.8.1 Windows:

1. Visit the official Node.js website at https://nodejs.org/
2. Download the LTS (Long Term Support) version for Windows
3. Run the installer and follow the prompts
4. To verify installation, open Command Prompt and type:node –version
npm --version

9.8.2 macOS:

1. Visit https://nodejs.org/
2. Download the macOS LTS installer
3. Run the installer
4. Alternatively, if you use Homebrew, you can run:brew install node
5. Verify with:node –version
npm --version

9.8.3 Ubuntu/Debian Linux:

1. Open Terminal
2. Update your package index:sudo apt update

3. Install Node.js and npm:sudo apt install nodejs npm

4. Verify with:node –version
   npm --version

Once installed, you can start using npm commands to install packages and manage your projects.

9.9 Modern Project Starters: From Create React App to Vite

Setting up a modern JavaScript project involves configuring many tools: transpilers, bundlers, linters, etc. This can be overwhelming for beginners.

To solve this problem, the community created project starters that set everything up for you with sensible defaults:

Create React App was the first major solution:

```
npx create-react-app my-new-project
```

This command creates a new React project with a pre-configured build system. It hides all the complexity behind a single dependency called react-scripts.

More recently, **Vite** has emerged as a faster alternative:

```
npm create vite@latest my-new-project -- --template react
```

Vite (French for "quick") uses newer technologies like ES modules and esbuild to provide an extremely fast development experience.

Both tools let you focus on writing code instead of configuring build systems. For beginners, this is a huge win!

Before we continue, let's make a small detour so that I can explain these npm create and npx create commands to you.

9.9.1 The npm create and npx create Commands

Both commands are modern shortcuts for setting up new projects, with some slight difference.

When you use the npm create <package> command, it runs the npm init <package> command under the hood. It downloads and executes a package named create-<package>. For example: npm create react-app my-app will run create-react-app.

When you use the npx create-<package>, this will directly execute the create-<package> without installing it globally. It will download, run, and discard the package. It will have the same result as the previous command (npm create) command, but it will get the latest version, and it won't be added to npm's cache.

As a rule of thumb, you can use npm create <pacakge> when you scaffold projects frequently, and npx create-<package> when you want to be explicit and ensure you get the latest version.

9.10 CDNs vs. npm: Different Ways to Include Dependencies

Up until now in this book, we've been including Bootstrap using a Content Delivery Network (CDN) link:

```
<link href="https://cdn.jsdelivr.net/npm/bootstrap@5.3.0/dist/css/bootstrap.min.css" rel="stylesheet">
```

```
<script src="https://cdn.jsdelivr.net/npm/bootstrap@5.3.0/dist/js/bootstrap.bundle.min.js"></script>
```

A CDN is a network of servers distributed globally that deliver web content to users based on their geographic location. Using a CDN has several advantages:

- **Simplicity**: Just add a link tag, and you're done
- **Caching**: If a user has visited another site that uses the same CDN link, the file might already be cached in their browser
- **No Build Step**: Your HTML file works immediately without any compilation

You might have noticed the .min.css and .min.js in those URLs. These refer to "minified" versions of the files, where all unnecessary characters (whitespace, comments, long variable names) have been removed to make the file smaller. This makes the page load faster but makes the code harder for humans to read.

While CDNs are convenient, the npm approach offers several advantages for larger projects:

- **Version Control**: Your dependencies are locked to specific versions.
- **Offline Development**: You can work without an internet connection.
- **Tree Shaking**: Modern build tools can remove unused code to reduce file size.
- **Customization**: Some libraries allow you to import only the parts you need.

With npm, instead of CDN links, you'd do:

```
npm install bootstrap
```

Then in your JavaScript:

```
import 'bootstrap/dist/css/bootstrap.min.css';
import 'bootstrap';
```

This approach requires a build step to bundle everything together, which is where tools like Webpack or Vite come in.

9.11 Understanding Node Modules and Bundlers

When you run npm install, packages are downloaded to a folder called node_modules in your project. This folder can get huge – often hundreds of megabytes or even gigabytes for complex projects!

Fortunately, you don't need to include this folder when sharing your code. Since all the dependencies are listed in your package.json, others can regenerate the node_modules folder by running npm install.

But browsers can't directly use files from node_modules. This is where bundlers come in. A bundler:

1. Starts with your entry point file (usually something like src/index.js)
2. Follows all the imports to find every file your app needs

3. Transforms them as needed (e.g., transpiling newer JavaScript to older versions for compatibility)
4. Combines everything into one or more "bundle" files that browsers can understand

Popular bundlers include:

- **Webpack**: The most widely used bundler, extremely flexible but complex to configure
- **Parcel**: Aims to be zero-configuration while still being powerful
- **Rollup**: Specializes in creating efficient bundles for libraries
- **esbuild**: Extremely fast bundler written in Go
- **Vite**: Uses esbuild for production builds and native ES modules during development

Most project starters like Create React App or Vite set up the bundler for you, so you don't need to configure it manually.

9.12 Bringing It All Together: The Modern Front-End Workflow

Now that we've covered the individual pieces, let's see how they fit together in a typical modern front-end workflow:

1. **Initialize a new project:**

    ```
    npm init -y
    # or use a starter like:
    npm create vite@latest my-app -- --template react
    ```

2. **Install dependencies:**

    ```
    npm install react react-dom
    npm install --save-dev vite @vitejs/plugin-react
    ```

3. **Write your code** using modern JavaScript features and imports:

   ```
   // src/App.jsx
   import { useState } from 'react';

   function App() {
     const [count, setCount] = useState(0);
     return (
       <div>
         <p>You clicked {count} times</p>
         <button onClick={() => setCount(count + 1)}>
           Click me
         </button>
       </div>
     );
   }

   export default App;
   ```

4. **Run a development server** with hot reloading:

   ```
   npm run dev
   ```

5. **Build for production** when you're ready to deploy:

   ```
   npm run build
   ```

This workflow is quite different from what we've been doing so far with plain HTML, CSS, and JavaScript files, but it offers significant advantages for larger projects.

9.13 What This Means for Bootstrap

Remember when we visited the Bootstrap website and saw installation instructions that mentioned npm?

```
npm install bootstrap@5.3.0
```

Now you understand what this means! Instead of using CDN links, you can install Bootstrap as a package and import it into your project.

This approach gives you more control. For example, you can import only the parts of Bootstrap you need to reduce your bundle size:

```
// Import only the Bootstrap components you need
import 'bootstrap/js/dist/modal';
import 'bootstrap/js/dist/tooltip';
```

While we've been using the CDN approach for simplicity, the npm approach becomes more beneficial as your projects grow in complexity.

9.14 Conclusion: Staying on the Edge of Competence

We've covered a lot in this chapter – the evolution of JavaScript, Node.js, npm, bundlers, React, and how they all fit together in the modern front-end ecosystem. It might feel overwhelming, and that's completely normal.

The front-end landscape is vast, and no one knows everything about it. Even experienced developers are constantly learning new tools and techniques.

The key is to approach learning like weight training: lift weights that are proportional to your strength. Stay on the "edge of competence" – push yourself to learn new things, but don't try to learn everything at once. It's better to understand one concept deeply than to have a shallow understanding of ten.

Remember that imposter syndrome – the feeling that you don't know enough or don't belong – is incredibly common in web development because the field is so broad. But here's the truth: we're all just humans figuring things out as we go. The experts you admire were beginners once too.

In the next chapter, we'll start applying what we've learned by diving into React concepts. We'll build on the foundation of Bootstrap we've established, but take it to the next level with component-based architecture. Don't worry if you don't understand everything right away – learning is a journey, not a destination.

The most important thing is to keep coding, keep experimenting, and keep your curiosity alive. That's how you grow as a developer.

CHAPTER 10

React Concepts You Need to Know to Code Your Layout

10.1 Introduction

Welcome to the exciting world of React! In the previous chapter, we explored the modern front-end ecosystem and learned about tools like Node.js and npm. Now, it's time to dive into React itself – a powerful JavaScript library that has revolutionized how developers build user interfaces.

Don't worry if you're feeling a bit intimidated. We're going to take this step by step, focusing only on the core concepts you need to get started. By the end of this chapter, you'll be able to build a static restaurant website with multiple components – all without diving into the more complex aspects of React.

Here's what we'll cover

1. Setting up a simple React project
2. Understanding JSX – React's special syntax
3. Creating and composing components
4. Passing data to components using props
5. Building a complete restaurant website with Bootstrap styling

The beauty of React lies in its component-based approach. Instead of building one massive page, you'll create small, reusable pieces that fit together like building blocks. This makes your code more organized, easier to maintain, and simpler to understand.

So, let's get started on our journey to build "Pizza Paradise" – a fictional restaurant website that will showcase the power of React components!

10.2 Setting Up Your First React Project

Before we dive into coding, let's set up a simple React project. There are several ways to do this, but we'll use the most straightforward approach for beginners.

10.2.1 Option 1: Using an Online Code Editor

If you want to avoid installing anything on your computer, you can use an online code editor like CodeSandbox or StackBlitz. These platforms allow you to write React code directly in your browser.

1. Visit CodeSandbox
2. Click on "Create Sandbox"
3. Select the "React" template

And you're ready to go! The editor will create a basic React project for you with all the necessary files.

10.2.2 Option 2: Using Vite Locally

If you prefer to work on your local machine (which I recommend for a better development experience), you can use Vite – a modern, faster build tool that sets up a React project with a single command.

First, make sure you have Node.js and npm installed (as we discussed in the previous chapter). Then, open your terminal or command prompt and run:

```
npm create vite@latest pizza-paradise -- --template react
cd pizza-paradise
npm install
npm run dev
```

This will create a new folder called "pizza-paradise" with all the necessary files, navigate into that folder, install dependencies, and start a development server. Your browser should automatically open with your new React application running at http://localhost:5173.

10.2.3 Understanding the Project Structure

Whether you're using an online editor or a local setup with Vite, your React project will have a similar structure. Let's take a quick look at the most important files in a Vite React project:

```
pizza-paradise/
├── node_modules/      # All the dependencies installed by npm
├── public/            # Static files like images and other assets
│   └── ...
├── src/               # Your source code
│   ├── App.jsx        # The main component
│   ├── main.jsx       # The entry point of your application
│   └── ...
├── index.html         # The main HTML file (in root, not in public)
├── package.json       # Project configuration and dependencies
├── vite.config.js     # Vite configuration file
└── ...
```

There are a few key features of React projects built with Vite:

1. Vite uses .jsx extension by default (though .js works too)
2. The main HTML file is in the root directory
3. The entry point is typically named main.jsx instead of index.js
4. Vite includes a configuration file (vite.config.js)

For now, we'll focus mainly on the files in the src directory, as that's where we'll be writing our React code.

10.2.4 Adding Bootstrap to Our Project

Since we'll be using Bootstrap for styling our restaurant website, let's add it to our project. The simplest way is to use a CDN link.

With Vite, the main HTML file is located in the root directory. Open the index.html file and add the following line inside the <head> section:

```
<link href="https://cdn.jsdelivr.net/npm/bootstrap@5.3.0/dist/css/bootstrap.min.css" rel="stylesheet">
```

And add this line just before the closing </body> tag:

```
<script src="https://cdn.jsdelivr.net/npm/bootstrap@5.3.0/dist/js/bootstrap.bundle.min.js"></script>
```

Now we have Bootstrap available throughout our application!

Alternatively, you could install Bootstrap as a dependency using npm:

```
npm install bootstrap
```

And then import it in your main.jsx file:

```
import 'bootstrap/dist/css/bootstrap.min.css'
import 'bootstrap/dist/js/bootstrap.bundle.min.js'
```

For this tutorial, we'll stick with the CDN approach for simplicity.

10.3 Understanding JSX: React's Special Syntax

Before we start building components, we need to understand JSX-a syntax extension for JavaScript that looks similar to HTML but comes with some special rules and capabilities.

10.3.1 What Is JSX?

JSX stands for JavaScript XML. It allows you to write HTML-like code directly in your JavaScript files. Here's a simple example:

```
const element = <h1>Hello, Pizza Lovers!</h1>;
```

This might look like HTML, but it's actually JSX that will be transformed into regular JavaScript by a tool called Babel before it runs in the browser.

The equivalent JavaScript without JSX would be much more verbose:

```
const element = React.createElement('h1', null, 'Hello, Pizza Lovers!');
```

As you can see, JSX makes your code more readable and intuitive, especially when creating complex UI elements.

The end result of using JSX is that you can write HTML-looking code right inside a JavaScript file (or, more precisely, a JSX file).

10.3.2 JSX Rules and Quirks

While JSX looks like HTML, there are some important differences to be aware of:

1. **Use className instead of class**

    Since class is a reserved keyword in JavaScript, you need to use className for CSS classes:

    ```
    // Wrong
    <div class="container">...</div>

    // Correct
    <div className="container">...</div>
    ```

2. **Self-closing tags must have a slash**

    In HTML, you can write <img src="pizza.jpg">, but in JSX, you must include a closing slash: <img src="pizza.jpg" />.

3. **JavaScript expressions in curly braces**

    You can embed JavaScript expressions within JSX using curly braces:

    ```
    const name = "Margherita";
    const element = <h1>The best pizza is {name}!</h1>;
    ```

    Think of it like this: The HTML-like syntax inside a JSX file is **static**. But having curly braces allows you to "inject" dynamic sections into this otherwise static HTML-like structure. In other words, like in the exampl above, you use the curly braces in your JSX HTML-like code to add in dynamic values – such as variables – and have the resuting website show these dynamic values. Why is that important – because these dynamic values can change based on how the user interacts with the app (by, say, clicking a button) – thus making the entire user experience have a real interactive, dynamic feel.

4. **Inline styles use objects**

   CSS properties are written in camelCase and values are provided as strings:

   ```
   const style = {
     backgroundColor: "red",
     fontSize: "20px"
   };

   const element = <div style={style}>Spicy Pizza!</div>;

   // Or inline
   const element = <div style={{ backgroundColor: "red", fontSize: "20px" }}>Spicy Pizza!</div>;
   ```

   Note above that we have nested curly braces. The first pair of curly braces is there to allow for the dynamic syntax: style={}, and the second (inner) pair of curly braces is the JS object itself – the dynamic value that will be processed by JS as needed.

5. **Comments are written inside curly braces**

   ```
   const element = (
     <div>
       {/* This is a comment in JSX */}
       <h1>Pizza Paradise</h1>
     </div>
   );
   ```

6. **Adjacent JSX elements must be wrapped in a container**

```
// Wrong
const element = (
  <h1>Pizza Paradise</h1>
  <p>The best pizza in town!</p>
);

// Correct
const element = (
  <div>
    <h1>Pizza Paradise</h1>
    <p>The best pizza in town!</p>
  </div>
);

// Also correct (using React fragment)
const element = (
  <>
    <h1>Pizza Paradise</h1>
    <p>The best pizza in town!</p>
  </>
);
```

Note that a React fragment is simply an "empty element" which will not be shown (rendered) in the resulting web page, but is used in React to help developers adhere to the rule of wrapping adjacent elements in a single wrapping element. A fragment is essentially like a <div> that wraps the sibiling elements.

Understanding these JSX quirks will help you avoid common pitfalls when writing React components.

10.3.3 JSX and HTML Attributes

Most HTML attributes work the same way in JSX, but some have different names to avoid conflicts with JavaScript keywords:

- class becomes className
- for becomes htmlFor

- tabindex becomes tabIndex
- onclick becomes onClick (and all event handlers follow this camelCase pattern)

For example, to create a Bootstrap button with an onClick event:

```
<button className="btn btn-primary" onClick={() => console.log('Clicked!')}>
  Order Now
</button>
```

Now that we understand the basics of JSX, let's move on to creating our first React component!

10.4 Creating Your First React Component

In React, a component is a reusable piece of UI. Think of it as a custom HTML element that you define. Components can be as simple as a button or as complex as an entire page. The idea of a React component is not that much different from a pure Bootstrap component. It's just that a React component has more capabilities and is adapted to the React way of doing things.

10.4.1 Basic Component Structure

Let's create a simple component for our restaurant website. Open your src/App.jsx file and replace its contents with the following code:

```
import React from 'react';

function App() {
  return (
    <div className="container mt-5">
      <h1>Pizza Paradise</h1>
      <p>Welcome to the best pizza restaurant in town!</p>
    </div>
  );
}

export default App;
```

Let's break down what's happening here:

1. We import the React library (this is required for JSX to work)
2. We define a function called App
3. The function returns JSX that describes what should be rendered
4. We export the component so it can be used elsewhere

When you save this file, you should see the changes reflected in your browser. Congratulations! You've just created your first React component.

10.4.2 Creating a Header Component

Now, let's create a separate component for our restaurant's header. This demonstrates the concept of component composition-building larger components from smaller ones.

Create a new file called Header.jsx in the src directory and add the following code:

```
import React from 'react';

function Header() {
  return (
    <nav className="navbar navbar-expand-lg navbar-dark bg-dark">
      <div className="container">
        <a className="navbar-brand" href="#">Pizza Paradise</a>
        <button className="navbar-toggler" type="button" data-bs-
        toggle="collapse" data-bs-target="#navbarNav">
          <span className="navbar-toggler-icon"></span>
        </button>
        <div className="collapse navbar-collapse" id="navbarNav">
          <ul className="navbar-nav ms-auto">
            <li className="nav-item">
              <a className="nav-link active" href="#">Home</a>
            </li>
            <li className="nav-item">
              <a className="nav-link" href="#">Menu</a>
            </li>
            <li className="nav-item">
```

```
              <a className="nav-link" href="#">About</a>
            </li>
            <li className="nav-item">
              <a className="nav-link" href="#">Contact</a>
            </li>
          </ul>
        </div>
      </div>
    </nav>
  );
}

export default Header;
```

This component creates a Bootstrap navbar with links to different sections of our restaurant website.

10.4.3 Using the Header Component

Now, let's use our new Header component in the main App component. Update your App.jsx file:

```
import React from 'react';
import Header from './Header';

function App() {
  return (
    <div>
      <Header />
      <div className="container mt-5">
        <h1>Pizza Paradise</h1>
        <p>Welcome to the best pizza restaurant in town!</p>
      </div>
    </div>
  );
}

export default App;
```

Notice how we:

1. Import the Header component
2. Use it in our JSX just like an HTML tag: <Header />

This is the power of component composition-we can build complex UIs by combining simpler components.

10.4.4 Creating a Hero Section Component

Next, let's create a component for our hero section (or jumbotron) to showcase a special offer. Create a new file called Hero.jsx in the src directory:

```
import React from 'react';

function Hero() {
  return (
    <div className="bg-primary text-white py-5">
      <div className="container">
        <div className="row">
          <div className="col-md-6">
            <h1 className="display-4">Special Offer!</h1>
            <p className="lead">Buy 3 pizzas, get 1 free. Limited time
            only!</p>
            <button className="btn btn-light btn-lg">Order Now</button>
          </div>
          <div className="col-md-6 d-flex justify-content-center">
            <img
              src="https://images.unsplash.com/photo-1513104890138-7c74965
              9a591?ixlib=rb-4.0.3&auto=format&fit=crop&w=500&q=80"
              alt="Delicious pizza"
              className="img-fluid rounded"
              style={{ maxHeight: '300px' }}
            />
          </div>
        </div>
      </div>
    </div>
```

```
      </div>
    );
}

export default Hero;
```

This component creates a colorful section with a promotional message and an image of a delicious pizza. We're using an image from Unsplash, but you could replace it with your own image.

10.4.5 Adding the Hero Component to Our App

Now, let's update our App.js to include the new Hero component:

```
import React from 'react';
import Header from './Header';
import Hero from './Hero';

function App() {
  return (
    <div>
      <Header />
      <Hero />
      <div className="container mt-5">
        <h1>Welcome to Pizza Paradise</h1>
        <p>Serving the best pizzas since 1990.</p>
      </div>
    </div>
  );
}

export default App;
```

Save the file and check your browser. You should now see a complete header and hero section for our restaurant website!

This is the beauty of React's component-based architecture-we're building our UI piece by piece, with each component responsible for a specific part of the interface. This makes our code more organized and easier to maintain.

10.5 Understanding Props: Passing Data to Components

So far, our components have been static-they always render the same content. But in real applications, components need to be dynamic and adapt to different data. This is where **props** come in.

10.5.1 What Are Props?

Props (short for "properties") are a way to pass data from a parent component to a child component. Think of them as custom HTML attributes that you can define and use in your components.

Before we dive into props, let's quickly refresh our understanding of JavaScript objects, as props are essentially JavaScript objects.

10.5.2 A Quick Refresher on JavaScript Objects

In JavaScript, an object is a collection of key-value pairs. Here's a simple example:

```
const pizza = {
  name: "Margherita",
  price: 12.99,
  toppings: ["Tomato Sauce", "Mozzarella", "Basil"]
};

// Accessing object properties
console.log(pizza.name); // "Margherita"
console.log(pizza.price); // 12.99
console.log(pizza.toppings[0]); // "Tomato Sauce"
```

Objects allow you to group related data together, making it easier to manage and pass around in your code.

10.5.3 How Props Work in React

In React, props work like this:

1. The parent component passes data to the child component using attributes in JSX

2. The child component receives this data as a single object called props

3. The child component can access the data using props. attributeName

Let's see this in action by creating a reusable PizzaCard component for our menu.

10.5.4 Creating a Reusable PizzaCard Component

Create a new file called PizzaCard.jsx in the src directory:

```jsx
import React from 'react';

function PizzaCard(props) {
  return (
    <div className="card mb-4">
      <img src={props.imageUrl} className="card-img-top" alt={props.name} />
      <div className="card-body">
        <h5 className="card-title">{props.name}</h5>
        <p className="card-text">{props.description}</p>
        <div className="d-flex justify-content-between align-items-center">
          <span className="h5 mb-0">${props.price.toFixed(2)}</span>
          <button className="btn btn-primary">Add to Cart</button>
        </div>
      </div>
    </div>
  );
}

export default PizzaCard;
```

In this component:

- We define a function called PizzaCard that takes a props parameter
- We use various props (imageUrl, name, description, price) to customize the content of the card
- We access these props using the dot notation: props.propertyName

10.5.5 Creating a Menu Section Component

Now, let's create a menu section that will contain multiple pizza cards. Create a new file called Menu.jsx in the src directory:

```
import React from 'react';
import PizzaCard from './PizzaCard';

function Menu() {
  return (
    <div className="container my-5">
      <h2 className="text-center mb-4">Our Pizza Menu</h2>
      <div className="row">
        <div className="col-md-4">
          <PizzaCard
            name="Margherita"
            description="Classic pizza with tomato sauce, mozzarella, and fresh basil."
            price={12.99}
            imageUrl="https://images.unsplash.com/photo-1574071318508-1cdb ab80d002?ixlib=rb-4.0.3&auto=format&fit=crop&w=500&q=80"
          />
        </div>
        <div className="col-md-4">
          <PizzaCard
            name="Pepperoni"
            description="America's favorite! Tomato sauce, mozzarella, and pepperoni."
            price={14.99}
```

```jsx
          imageUrl="https://images.unsplash.com/photo-1628840042765-356c
          da07504e?ixlib=rb-4.0.3&auto=format&fit=crop&w=500&q=80"
        />
      </div>
      <div className="col-md-4">
        <PizzaCard
          name="Vegetarian"
          description="Loaded with bell peppers, mushrooms, onions,
          olives, and mozzarella."
          price={13.99}
          imageUrl="https://images.unsplash.com/photo-1604917877934-07d
          8d248d396?ixlib=rb-4.0.3&auto=format&fit=crop&w=500&q=80"
        />
      </div>
    </div>
    <div className="row mt-4">
      <div className="col-md-4">
        <PizzaCard
          name="Hawaiian"
          description="A tropical blend of ham, pineapple, and
          mozzarella cheese."
          price={15.99}
          imageUrl="https://images.unsplash.com/photo-1565299624946-b28f
          40a0ae38?ixlib=rb-4.0.3&auto=format&fit=crop&w=500&q=80"
        />
      </div>
      <div className="col-md-4">
        <PizzaCard
          name="Meat Lovers"
          description="For carnivores! Pepperoni, sausage, bacon, and
          ground beef."
          price={16.99}
          imageUrl="https://images.unsplash.com/photo-1571407970349-bc81
          e7e96d47?ixlib=rb-4.0.3&auto=format&fit=crop&w=500&q=80"
        />
```

```
      </div>
      <div className="col-md-4">
        <PizzaCard
          name="BBQ Chicken"
          description="Grilled chicken, BBQ sauce, red onions, and cilantro."
          price={15.99}
          imageUrl="https://images.unsplash.com/photo-1593246049226-ded77bf90326?ixlib=rb-4.0.3&auto=format&fit=crop&w=500&q=80"
        />
      </div>
    </div>
    <div className="row mt-4 justify-content-center">
      <div className="col-md-4">
        <PizzaCard
          name="Supreme"
          description="The works! Pepperoni, sausage, bell peppers, onions, and olives."
          price={17.99}
          imageUrl="https://images.unsplash.com/photo-1595708684082-a173bb3a06c5?ixlib=rb-4.0.3&auto=format&fit=crop&w=500&q=80"
        />
      </div>
    </div>
  </div>
  );
}

export default Menu;
```

In this component:

- We import and use the PizzaCard component multiple times
- For each pizza, we pass different props to customize its appearance and content
- We organize the cards in a responsive grid using Bootstrap's row and column classes

Notice that we're not using a .map() function to loop over an array of pizzas. Instead, we're explicitly adding each PizzaCard component with its specific props. This approach is more straightforward for beginners and makes it clear exactly what's being rendered.

10.5.6 Adding the Menu to Our App

Now, let's update our App.js to include the new Menu component:

```
import React from 'react';
import Header from './Header';
import Hero from './Hero';
import Menu from './Menu';

function App() {
  return (
    <div>
      <Header />
      <Hero />
      <Menu />
      <div className="container mt-5 mb-5">
        <h2 className="text-center">Welcome to Pizza Paradise</h2>
        <p className="text-center">Serving the best pizzas since 1990.</p>
      </div>
    </div>
  );
}

export default App;
```

Save the file and check your browser. You should now see a complete menu section with different pizza cards!

10.5.7 Understanding Props in More Detail

Let's take a closer look at how props work by examining our PizzaCard component:

```
<PizzaCard
  name="Margherita"
```

```
        description="Classic pizza with tomato sauce, mozzarella, and
        fresh basil."
        price={12.99}
        imageUrl="https://images.unsplash.com/photo-1574071318508-1cdbab80d002?ix
lib=rb-4.0.3&auto=format&fit=crop&w=500&q=80"
/>
```

Here, we're passing four props to the PizzaCard component:

1. name: A string prop (notice the quotes)

2. description: Another string prop

3. price: A number prop (notice the curly braces, not quotes)

4. imageUrl: A string prop for the image URL

Inside the PizzaCard component, all these props are accessible through the props object:

```
function PizzaCard(props) {
  // props = {
  //   name: "Margherita",
  //   description: "Classic pizza with tomato sauce, mozzarella, and fresh
        basil.",
  //   price: 12.99,
  //   imageUrl: "https://images.unsplash.com/photo-1574071318508-1cdbab8
        0d002?ixlib=rb-4.0.3&auto=format&fit=crop&w=500&q=80"
  // }

  return (
    // JSX that uses props.name, props.description, etc.
  );
}
```

10.5.8 Props vs. Hardcoded Values

You might be wondering: why use props instead of just hardcoding values in the component? The answer is reusability and flexibility.

Without props, we would need to create a separate component for each pizza, like MargheritaPizzaCard, PepperoniPizzaCard, etc. That would be repetitive and hard to maintain.

With props, we can create a single PizzaCard component that can be customized for any pizza. This makes our code more DRY (Don't Repeat Yourself) and easier to update.

10.5.9 Props Are Read-Only

One important rule about props: they are read-only. A component should never modify its own props. Think of props as arguments to a function-the function can use the arguments, but it shouldn't change them.

If you need to modify data, you would typically use state (which we're not covering in this chapter) or create a new value based on the props.

10.6 Building a Testimonials Section

Now that we understand props, let's create a testimonials section for our restaurant website. This will give us more practice with components and props.

10.6.1 Creating a Testimonial Component

First, let's create a reusable component for individual testimonials. Create a new file called Testimonial.jsx in the src directory:

```
import React from 'react';

function Testimonial(props) {
  return (
    <div className="col-md-4 mb-4">
      <div className="card h-100">
        <div className="card-body">
          <div className="d-flex justify-content-center mb-3">
            <img
              src={props.avatar}
              alt={props.name}
              className="rounded-circle"
```

```
          style={{ width: '80px', height: '80px', objectFit: 'cover' }}
        />
      </div>
      <h5 className="card-title text-center">{props.name}</h5>
      <div className="text-center mb-3">
        {[...Array(5)].map((_, i) => (
          <span key={i} className={i < props.rating ? "text-warning" :
          "text-muted"}>
             ★
          </span>
        ))}
      </div>
      <p className="card-text text-center">"{props.comment}"</p>
    </div>
   </div>
  </div>
 );
}

export default Testimonial;
```

In this component:

- We create a card to display the testimonial
- We use props to customize the avatar, name, rating, and comment
- We use a simple technique to display star ratings based on the rating prop

---

Note We're using a simple array mapping technique to render the stars. Don't worry too much about this part-it's just a convenient way to render multiple similar elements. The key point is that we're using props to determine how many stars should be highlighted.

10.6.2 Creating a Testimonials Section Component

Now, let's create a component that will contain multiple testimonials. Create a new file called Testimonials.jsx in the src directory:

```jsx
import React from 'react';
import Testimonial from './Testimonial';

function Testimonials() {
  return (
    <div className="container my-5">
      <h2 className="text-center mb-4">What Our Customers Say</h2>
      <div className="row">
        <Testimonial
          name="John Smith"
          rating={5}
          comment="Best pizza I've ever had! The crust is perfect and the toppings are always fresh."
          avatar="https://randomuser.me/api/portraits/men/32.jpg"
        />
        <Testimonial
          name="Sarah Johnson"
          rating={4}
          comment="Love their Meat Lovers pizza. Great service and quick delivery too!"
          avatar="https://randomuser.me/api/portraits/women/44.jpg"
        />
        <Testimonial
          name="Michael Brown"
          rating={5}
          comment="The BBQ Chicken pizza is to die for! I order at least once a week."
          avatar="https://randomuser.me/api/portraits/men/22.jpg"
        />
      </div>
    </div>
```

```
  );
}
export default Testimonials;
```

In this component:

- We import and use the Testimonial component three times
- For each testimonial, we pass different props to customize its appearance and content
- We're using the Random User Generator API to get placeholder avatar images

10.6.3 Adding the Testimonials to Our App

Now, let's update our App.js to include the new Testimonials component:

```
import React from 'react';
import Header from './Header';
import Hero from './Hero';
import Menu from './Menu';
import Testimonials from './Testimonials';

function App() {
  return (
    <div>
      <Header />
      <Hero />
      <Menu />
      <Testimonials />
      <div className="container mt-5 mb-5">
        <h2 className="text-center">Welcome to Pizza Paradise</h2>
        <p className="text-center">Serving the best pizzas since 1990.</p>
      </div>
    </div>
  );
}
```

```
export default App;
```

Save the file and check your browser. You should now see a testimonials section with customer reviews!

10.7 Creating a Footer Component

To complete our restaurant website, let's add a footer section. Create a new file called Footer.jsx in the src directory:

```
import React from 'react';

function Footer() {
  return (
    <footer className="bg-dark text-white py-4">
      <div className="container">
        <div className="row">
          <div className="col-md-4 mb-3 mb-md-0">
            <h5>Pizza Paradise</h5>
            <p className="text-muted">Serving the best pizzas since
            1990.</p>
          </div>
          <div className="col-md-4 mb-3 mb-md-0">
            <h5>Opening Hours</h5>
            <ul className="list-unstyled text-muted">
              <li>Monday - Friday: 11am - 10pm</li>
              <li>Saturday - Sunday: 11am - 11pm</li>
            </ul>
          </div>
          <div className="col-md-4">
            <h5>Contact Us</h5>
            <ul className="list-unstyled text-muted">
              <li>123 Pizza Street, New York, NY</li>
              <li>Phone: (555) 123-4567</li>
              <li>Email: info@pizzaparadise.com</li>
```

```
          </ul>
        </div>
      </div>
      <hr className="my-4" />
      <div className="row">
        <div className="col-md-6 text-center text-md-start">
          <p className="mb-0 text-muted">&copy; 2023 Pizza Paradise. All
          rights reserved.</p>
        </div>
        <div className="col-md-6 text-center text-md-end">
          <ul className="list-inline mb-0">
            <li className="list-inline-item"><a href="#" className="text-
            muted">Terms of Use</a></li>
            <li className="list-inline-item"><a href="#" className="text-
            muted">Privacy Policy</a></li>
          </ul>
        </div>
      </div>
    </div>
  </footer>
 );
}

export default Footer;
```

This component creates a footer with information about the restaurant, opening hours, contact details, and copyright information.

10.7.1 Adding the Footer to Our App

Now, let's update our App.js to include the new Footer component:

```
import React from 'react';
import Header from './Header';
import Hero from './Hero';
import Menu from './Menu';
import Testimonials from './Testimonials';
```

```
import Footer from './Footer';

function App() {
  return (
    <div>
      <Header />
      <Hero />
      <Menu />
      <Testimonials />
      <Footer />
    </div>
  );
}

export default App;
```

Save the file and check your browser. You should now see a complete restaurant website with a header, hero section, menu, testimonials, and footer!

10.8 Importing Assets in React

So far, we've been using external URLs for our images, but in a real project, you might want to include images and other assets directly in your project. Let's see how to do that.

10.8.1 Adding Images to Your Project

1. Create a new folder called assets in the src directory (Vite conventionally uses 'assets' instead of 'images')
2. Download some pizza images and save them in this folder (or use your own images)
3. Import and use these images in your components

For example, to use a local image in the Hero component:

```
import React from 'react';
import pizzaImage from './assets/pizza.jpg'; // Import the image
```

```jsx
function Hero() {
  return (
    <div className="bg-primary text-white py-5">
      <div className="container">
        <div className="row">
          <div className="col-md-6">
            <h1 className="display-4">Special Offer!</h1>
            <p className="lead">Buy 3 pizzas, get 1 free. Limited time
            only!</p>
            <button className="btn btn-light btn-lg">Order Now</button>
          </div>
          <div className="col-md-6 d-flex justify-content-center">
            <img
              src={pizzaImage} // Use the imported image
              alt="Delicious pizza"
              className="img-fluid rounded"
              style={{ maxHeight: '300px' }}
            />
          </div>
        </div>
      </div>
    </div>
  );
}

export default Hero;
```

10.8.2 Adding CSS Files

You can also import CSS files directly into your components. For example, if you want to add some custom styles:

1. Create a file called PizzaCard.css in the src directory

2. Add some CSS rules to this file:

```css
.card {
  transition: transform 0.3s;
}

.card:hover {
  transform: translateY(-5px);
  box-shadow: 0 10px 20px rgba(0, 0, 0, 0.1);
}

.card-img-top {
  height: 200px;
  object-fit: cover;
}
```

3. Import this CSS file in your PizzaCard component:

```jsx
import React from 'react';
import './PizzaCard.css'; // Import the CSS file

function PizzaCard(props) {
  // Component code...
}

export default PizzaCard;
```

Now, the CSS rules will be applied to your PizzaCard component, adding hover effects and consistent image sizing.

10.9 Conclusion: Bringing It All Together

Congratulations! You've built a complete restaurant website using React components. Let's recap what we've learned:

1. **React Basics**: We've learned how to set up a React project and understand its structure.

2. **JSX**: We've explored JSX, React's special syntax that looks like HTML but comes with some differences (like className instead of class).

3. **Components**: We've created multiple components, each responsible for a specific part of the UI:

    a. Header: The navigation bar

    b. Hero: The promotional section

    c. PizzaCard: A reusable card for displaying pizza information

    d. Menu: A collection of pizza cards

    e. Testimonial: A card for customer reviews

    f. Testimonials: A collection of testimonials

    g. Footer: The website footer

4. **Props**: We've learned how to pass data to components using props, making our components flexible and reusable.

5. **Importing Assets**: We've seen how to import and use images and CSS files in our components.

This is just the beginning of your React journey. React offers many more powerful features like state management, lifecycle methods, hooks, and more. But with the foundation you've built in this chapter, you're well-equipped to start exploring these advanced concepts.

10.9.1 What's Next: Adding Interactivity

Congratulations on building your first React application! You've learned the core concepts of components, JSX, and props, which form the foundation of React development. In this chapter, we've focused on creating a static website to help you understand these fundamental concepts without overwhelming you with too many new ideas at once.

CHAPTER 10   REACT CONCEPTS YOU NEED TO KNOW TO CODE YOUR LAYOUT

In the next chapter, we'll take your Pizza Paradise application to the next level by adding interactivity. We'll continue using Bootstrap from a CDN for styling, but we'll make your Bootstrap and React web app much more capable by:

- Handling user-triggered events like clicks and form submissions
- Update the UI dynamically based on user interactions

The beauty of React is that it handles all the complex DOM updates for you behind the scenes. This means you can focus on your application logic rather than worrying about manually selecting and updating DOM elements.

Keep practicing what you've learned in this chapter, and you'll be well-prepared for the interactive features we'll explore next!

CHAPTER 11

Adding Interactivity to Your React Restaurant Website

11.1 Introduction

In the previous chapter, we built a static restaurant website using React components, JSX, and props. While the site looks good, it doesn't actually *do* anything yet. A user can't interact with it in any meaningful way – they can't order food, customize their pizzas, or add items to a cart.

In this chapter, we'll transform our static website into an interactive application by introducing a fundamental React concept: **state**. Before we dive in, it's worth noting that while these React-specific mechanics aren't directly related to Bootstrap, understanding them is crucial. React has become the de-facto standard for modern web development, and to fully utilize Bootstrap in a React environment (which we'll do in Chapter 12 with react-bootstrap), we need to master these core React concepts first.

11.2 Understanding State in React

You might be surprised to learn that we've already been working with a form of state in our application. Remember props? Props are essentially a type of state – they're data that influences how a component renders. The difference is that props are passed *to* a component from its parent, making them a form of **external state**.

Let's clarify this with a definition:

State in React refers to data that can change over time and affects what a component renders.

There are two main types of state in React:

1. **External State (Props)**: Data passed to a component from outside (its parent)

2. **Internal State**: Data that belongs to and is managed by the component itself

We've already worked extensively with props. Now let's explore internal state.

11.2.1 Props vs. Internal State

Here's a quick comparison to help you understand the difference:

Table 11-1. Props vs. Internal State Comparison

Props	Internal State
Passed from parent to child	Created and managed within the component
Read-only (immutable)	Mutable (can be updated)
Changes when parent re-renders	Changes when explicitly updated
Accessed via function parameters	Accessed via React's useState hook

Let's look at an example from our Pizza Paradise website. In the previous chapter, we created a PizzaCard component that received props like name, description, and price:

```
function PizzaCard(props) {
  return (
    <div className="card mb-4">
      <img src={props.imageUrl} className="card-img-top" alt={props.name} />
      <div className="card-body">
        <h5 className="card-title">{props.name}</h5>
        <p className="card-text">{props.description}</p>
        <p className="card-text fw-bold">${props.price}</p>
```

```
      <button className="btn btn-primary">Add to Cart</button>
    </div>
  </div>
);
}
```

This component is entirely driven by props – external state. But what if we want to make the "Add to Cart" button actually do something? That's where internal state comes in.

11.3 Introducing React Hooks and useState

To manage internal state in a functional component, React provides a feature called **Hooks**. Hooks are special functions that let you "hook into" React features. The most basic hook for state management is useState.

Before we implement useState in our Pizza Paradise application, let's take a step back and understand a JavaScript concept that's crucial for working with hooks: **destructuring**.

11.3.1 Understanding Destructuring in JavaScript

Destructuring is a JavaScript feature that allows you to extract values from arrays or properties from objects and assign them to variables in a more concise way. It's a powerful feature that's used extensively in modern React code.

Let's start with some basic examples:

11.3.1.1 Object Destructuring

Object destructuring extracts properties from objects:

```
// Without destructuring
const person = { firstName: 'John', lastName: 'Doe', age: 30 };
const firstName = person.firstName;
const lastName = person.lastName;
```

```
// With destructuring
const { firstName, lastName } = person;
console.log(firstName); // 'John'
console.log(lastName);  // 'Doe'
```

You can also assign to different variable names:

```
const { firstName: fName, lastName: lName } = person;
console.log(fName); // 'John'
console.log(lName); // 'Doe'
```

And provide default values:

```
const { firstName, middleName = 'M.' } = person;
console.log(middleName); // 'M.' (default value since it doesn't exist in person)
```

11.3.1.2 Array Destructuring

Array destructuring works similarly but uses position rather than property names:

```
// Without destructuring
const colors = ['red', 'green', 'blue'];
const firstColor = colors[0];
const secondColor = colors[1];

// With destructuring
const [firstColor, secondColor] = colors;
console.log(firstColor);  // 'red'
console.log(secondColor); // 'green'
```

You can skip elements you're not interested in:

```
const [firstColor, , thirdColor] = colors;
console.log(firstColor);  // 'red'
console.log(thirdColor);  // 'blue'
```

And provide default values:

```
const [firstColor, secondColor, thirdColor, fourthColor = 'yellow']
= colors;
console.log(fourthColor); // 'yellow' (default value since it doesn't exist
in colors)
```

11.3.2 Object vs. Array Destructuring: Why React Uses Array Destructuring for useState

Now that we understand both types of destructuring, let's discuss why React's useState hook uses array destructuring instead of object destructuring.

The key difference is **naming flexibility**:

- With object destructuring, the variable names must match the property names (unless you explicitly rename them).

- With array destructuring, you can name the variables whatever you want because they're based on position, not property names.

This flexibility is crucial for useState because:

1. You often need to create multiple state variables in a component

2. The names should be descriptive of what the state represents

3. The setter function should clearly indicate what state it updates

Imagine if useState used object destructuring:

```
// Hypothetical object-based useState
const { state, setState } = React.useState(0);
```

If you needed multiple state variables, you'd have naming conflicts:

```
// This wouldn't work!
const { state, setState } = React.useState(0);
const { state, setState } = React.useState(''); // Error: Duplicate
declaration
```

You'd need to rename each one:

```
const { state: count, setState: setCount } = React.useState(0);
const { state: name, setState: setName } = React.useState('');
```

With array destructuring, React can provide a cleaner API:

```
const [count, setCount] = React.useState(0);
const [name, setName] = React.useState('');
```

This is more concise and allows you to name your state variables and setters in a way that makes sense for your application.

11.3.3 How useState Works

Now that we understand destructuring, let's look at how useState actually works:

```
const [state, setState] = React.useState(initialValue);
```

Here's what's happening:

1. useState is a function that takes an initial value as its argument
2. It returns an array with exactly two elements:
    a. The current state value (initially set to the initial value)
    b. A function to update that state value
3. We use array destructuring to assign these two elements to variables

When you call the update function (the second element), React:

1. Updates the state value
2. Re-renders the component with the new value

Let's see a simple example:

```
import React, { useState } from 'react';

function Counter() {
  // useState returns an array with two elements
  // We use array destructuring to assign them to variables
```

```
  const [count, setCount] = useState(0);

  return (
    <div>
      <p>You clicked {count} times</p>
      <button onClick={() => setCount(count + 1)}>
        Click me
      </button>
    </div>
  );
}
```

In this example:

1. We initialize a state variable count with a value of 0
2. We get a function setCount that we can use to update the count
3. When the button is clicked, we call setCount with the new value (count + 1)
4. React re-renders the component with the updated count

11.3.4 Using Multiple State Variables

You can use useState multiple times in a single component for different pieces of state:

```
function UserProfile() {
  const [name, setName] = useState('');
  const [age, setAge] = useState(0);
  const [isLoggedIn, setIsLoggedIn] = useState(false);

  // Component logic...
}
```

Each state variable is completely independent and can be updated separately.

11.3.5 Using Objects with useState

Sometimes it makes sense to group related state variables into an object:

```
function PizzaCustomizer() {
  const [pizza, setPizza] = useState({
    size: 'medium',
    crust: 'thin',
    toppings: ['cheese']
  });

  // To update just one property, we need to spread the existing state
  const changeSize = (newSize) => {
    setPizza({ ...pizza, size: newSize });
  };

  // Component rendering...
}
```

When updating an object state, remember that you need to include all the existing properties you want to keep, as the state setter completely replaces the previous state.

11.4 Event Handling in React

Now that we understand state, let's look at the other side of the coin: events. State by itself isn't very useful without a way to change it, and that's where events come in.

In React, event handling is similar to handling events in vanilla JavaScript, but with some key differences:

1. React events are named using camelCase (e.g., onClick instead of onclick)
2. In JSX, you pass a function as the event handler, not a string
3. You can't return false to prevent default behavior; you must call preventDefault explicitly

Here's a comparison:

Vanilla JavaScript:

```
<button onclick="handleClick()">Click Me</button>

<script>
function handleClick() {
  console.log('Button clicked!');
}
</script>
```

React:

```
function Button() {
  const handleClick = () => {
    console.log('Button clicked!');
  };

  return (
    <button onClick={handleClick}>Click Me</button>
  );
}
```

11.4.1 Common Events in React

React supports all the standard DOM events. Here are some of the most common ones:

- onClick: Triggered when an element is clicked
- onChange: Triggered when the value of an input element changes
- onSubmit: Triggered when a form is submitted
- onMouseEnter / onMouseLeave: Triggered when the mouse enters/leaves an element
- onFocus / onBlur: Triggered when an element gains/loses focus

11.4.2 Handling Form Inputs

Form handling is a common use case for combining state and events. Let's see how we can create a controlled input:

```
function NameForm() {
  const [name, setName] = useState('');

  const handleChange = (event) => {
    setName(event.target.value);
  };

  const handleSubmit = (event) => {
    event.preventDefault(); // Prevent the form from submitting normally
    alert(`Hello, ${name}!`);
  };

  return (
    <form onSubmit={handleSubmit}>
      <label>
        Name:
        <input type="text" value={name} onChange={handleChange} />
      </label>
      <button type="submit">Submit</button>
    </form>
  );
}
```

In this example:

1. We create a state variable name to store the input value
2. The handleChange function updates the state when the input changes
3. The input's value attribute is set to the state variable, creating a "controlled component"
4. The handleSubmit function prevents the default form submission and shows an alert

11.4.3 Adding Interactivity to Our Pizza Paradise Website

Now let's apply what we've learned to our restaurant website. Let's modify our PizzaCard component to allow users to add pizzas to a cart:

```
import React, { useState } from 'react';

function PizzaCard(props) {
  const [quantity, setQuantity] = useState(1);

  const increaseQuantity = () => {
    setQuantity(quantity + 1);
  };

  const decreaseQuantity = () => {
    if (quantity > 1) {
      setQuantity(quantity - 1);
    }
  };

  const addToCart = () => {
    alert(`Added ${quantity} ${props.name}(s) to cart!`);
    // In a real app, we would update a cart state here
  };

  return (
    <div className="card mb-4">
      <img src={props.imageUrl} className="card-img-top" alt={props.name} />
      <div className="card-body">
        <h5 className="card-title">{props.name}</h5>
        <p className="card-text">{props.description}</p>
        <p className="card-text fw-bold">${props.price}</p>

        <div className="d-flex align-items-center mb-3">
          <button
            className="btn btn-sm btn-outline-secondary"
            onClick={decreaseQuantity}
          >
```

CHAPTER 11 ADDING INTERACTIVITY TO YOUR REACT RESTAURANT WEBSITE

```
          -
        </button>
        <span className="mx-2">{quantity}</span>
        <button
          className="btn btn-sm btn-outline-secondary"
          onClick={increaseQuantity}
        >
          +
        </button>
      </div>

      <button
        className="btn btn-primary"
        onClick={addToCart}
      >
        Add to Cart
      </button>
    </div>
  </div>
  );
}

export default PizzaCard;
```

This updated PizzaCard component now:

1. Maintains its own internal state for the quantity
2. Provides buttons to increase and decrease the quantity
3. Has a functional "Add to Cart" button that shows an alert

However, there's a limitation: each PizzaCard manages its own isolated state. What if we want to keep track of all the pizzas in a shopping cart? This is where we need to understand how state flows through a component hierarchy.

11.5 Component Hierarchy and State Flow in React

In React applications, data flows in a unidirectional manner, typically from parent components down to child components. This concept is often referred to as "one-way data flow" and is a fundamental principle of React's design.

Let's visualize the component hierarchy in our Pizza Paradise application:

```
App
├── Header
├── Hero
├── Menu
│   ├── PizzaCard
│   ├── PizzaCard
│   └── PizzaCard
├── Testimonials
│   ├── Testimonial
│   ├── Testimonial
│   └── Testimonial
└── Footer
```

In this hierarchy, App is the root component, and it has several child components like Header, Hero, Menu, etc. The Menu component itself has multiple PizzaCard children, and Testimonials has multiple Testimonial children.

11.5.1 State Lifting

When multiple components need to share and modify the same state, we can "lift the state up" to their closest common ancestor. This allows the state to be shared among all the components that need it.

For example, if we want to implement a shopping cart for our Pizza Paradise website, we would:

1. Move the cart state up to the App component
2. Pass down the cart data and functions to modify it as props to the components that need them

CHAPTER 11　ADDING INTERACTIVITY TO YOUR REACT RESTAURANT WEBSITE

Let's see how this would work:

```jsx
import React, { useState } from 'react';
import Header from './Header';
import Hero from './Hero';
import Menu from './Menu';
import Testimonials from './Testimonials';
import Footer from './Footer';

function App() {
  // Cart state lifted up to the App component
  const [cart, setCart] = useState([]);

  // Function to add a pizza to the cart
  const addToCart = (pizza, quantity) => {
    // Check if this pizza is already in the cart
    const existingItemIndex = cart.findIndex(item => item.id === pizza.id);

    if (existingItemIndex >= 0) {
      // If it is, update the quantity
      const updatedCart = [...cart];
      updatedCart[existingItemIndex].quantity += quantity;
      setCart(updatedCart);
    } else {
      // If not, add it as a new item
      setCart([...cart, { ...pizza, quantity }]);
    }
  };

  // Function to remove a pizza from the cart
  const removeFromCart = (pizzaId) => {
    setCart(cart.filter(item => item.id !== pizzaId));
  };

  // Calculate total items in cart
  const cartItemCount = cart.reduce((total, item) => total + item.
  quantity, 0);
```

```
  return (
    <div className="App">
      <Header cartItemCount={cartItemCount} />
      <Hero />
      <Menu pizzas={pizzaData} addToCart={addToCart} />
      <Testimonials />
      <Footer />
    </div>
  );
}

export default App;
```

In this example, we've lifted the cart state up to the App component. We've also defined functions to add and remove items from the cart, and we're passing these down as props to the components that need them.

Now let's update our Menu component to pass the addToCart function down to each PizzaCard:

```
import React from 'react';
import PizzaCard from './PizzaCard';

function Menu({ pizzas, addToCart }) {
  return (
    <section className="container my-5" id="menu">
      <h2 className="text-center mb-4">Our Menu</h2>
      <div className="row">
        {pizzas.map(pizza => (
          <div className="col-md-4" key={pizza.id}>
            <PizzaCard
              {...pizza}
              addToCart={addToCart}
            />
          </div>
        ))}
```

```
      </div>
    </section>
  );
}

export default Menu;
```

And finally, let's update our PizzaCard component to use the passed-down addToCart function:

```
import React, { useState } from 'react';

function PizzaCard(props) {
  const [quantity, setQuantity] = useState(1);

  const increaseQuantity = () => {
    setQuantity(quantity + 1);
  };

  const decreaseQuantity = () => {
    if (quantity > 1) {
      setQuantity(quantity - 1);
    }
  };

  const handleAddToCart = () => {
    // Call the addToCart function that was passed down as a prop
    props.addToCart({
      id: props.id,
      name: props.name,
      price: props.price,
      imageUrl: props.imageUrl
    }, quantity);

    // Reset quantity after adding to cart
    setQuantity(1);
  };
```

```jsx
  return (
    <div className="card mb-4">
      <img src={props.imageUrl} className="card-img-top" alt={props.name} />
      <div className="card-body">
        <h5 className="card-title">{props.name}</h5>
        <p className="card-text">{props.description}</p>
        <p className="card-text fw-bold">${props.price}</p>

        <div className="d-flex align-items-center mb-3">
          <button
            className="btn btn-sm btn-outline-secondary"
            onClick={decreaseQuantity}
          >
            -
          </button>
          <span className="mx-2">{quantity}</span>
          <button
            className="btn btn-sm btn-outline-secondary"
            onClick={increaseQuantity}
          >
            +
          </button>
        </div>

        <button
          className="btn btn-primary"
          onClick={handleAddToCart}
        >
          Add to Cart
        </button>
      </div>
    </div>
  );
}

export default PizzaCard;
```

11.5.2 Understanding the Flow of Data

Let's break down what's happening in this example:

1. **State Initialization**: The cart state is initialized in the App component.

2. **Passing State Down**: The App component passes the addToCart function down to the Menu component as a prop.

3. **Prop Drilling**: The Menu component doesn't use the addToCart function directly but passes it further down to each PizzaCard component.

4. **Using Props to Update Parent State**: When a user clicks the "Add to Cart" button in a PizzaCard, it calls the handleAddToCart function, which in turn calls the addToCart function that was passed down from App. This updates the cart state in the App component.

5. **Re-rendering**: When the cart state changes in the App component, React re-renders the affected components. In this case, the Header component would update to show the new cart item count.

This pattern of "lifting state up" and passing down functions as props is a common way to share state between components in React. It maintains the principle of one-way data flow while allowing child components to communicate with their parents.

11.5.3 Child-to-Parent Communication

In React, child components can't directly modify their parent's state. Instead, they communicate with their parents through callback functions that are passed down as props.

In our example:

- The App component defines the addToCart function and passes it down to Menu and then to PizzaCard.

- When a user interacts with a PizzaCard, it calls this function to communicate back to the App component.

This pattern is sometimes called "lifting state up" because we're moving the state management up to a common ancestor component.

11.5.4 Grandparent-to-Grandchild Communication

Sometimes you need to pass data from a component to a grandchild (or even further down). In our example, we passed the addToCart function from App through Menu to PizzaCard.

As applications grow more complex, this "prop drilling" can become cumbersome. For more complex state management needs, React provides the Context API and there are also third-party libraries like Redux. However, for many applications, lifting state up is sufficient and keeps the code simpler.

11.6 Building a Shopping Cart Component

Now that we understand how state flows through our component hierarchy, let's create a simple shopping cart component for our Pizza Paradise website.

First, let's update our Header component to display the cart:

```
import React, { useState } from 'react';

function Header({ cartItemCount, cart, removeFromCart }) {
  const [cartOpen, setCartOpen] = useState(false);

  const toggleCart = () => {
    setCartOpen(!cartOpen);
  };

  // Calculate total price
  const totalPrice = cart.reduce((total, item) => {
    return total + (item.price * item.quantity);
  }, 0);

  return (
    <header className="navbar navbar-expand-lg navbar-dark bg-dark
    sticky-top">
      <div className="container">
        <a className="navbar-brand" href="#">Pizza Paradise</a>
```

CHAPTER 11   ADDING INTERACTIVITY TO YOUR REACT RESTAURANT WEBSITE

```
<button className="navbar-toggler" type="button" data-bs-
toggle="collapse" data-bs-target="#navbarNav">
  <span className="navbar-toggler-icon"></span>
</button>

<div className="collapse navbar-collapse" id="navbarNav">
  <ul className="navbar-nav me-auto">
    <li className="nav-item">
      <a className="nav-link" href="#">Home</a>
    </li>
    <li className="nav-item">
      <a className="nav-link" href="#menu">Menu</a>
    </li>
    <li className="nav-item">
      <a className="nav-link" href="#testimonials">Testimonials</a>
    </li>
    <li className="nav-item">
      <a className="nav-link" href="#contact">Contact</a>
    </li>
  </ul>

  <div className="position-relative">
    <button
      className="btn btn-outline-light position-relative"
      onClick={toggleCart}
    >
      <i className="bi bi-cart"></i> Cart
      {cartItemCount > 0 && (
        <span className="position-absolute top-0 start-100
        translate-middle badge rounded-pill bg-danger">
          {cartItemCount}
        </span>
      )}
    </button>
```

CHAPTER 11   ADDING INTERACTIVITY TO YOUR REACT RESTAURANT WEBSITE

```
{cartOpen && (
  <div className="position-absolute end-0 mt-2 p-3 bg-white
  shadow rounded" style={{ width: '300px', zIndex: 1000 }}>
    <h6 className="border-bottom pb-2 mb-3">Shopping Cart</h6>

    {cart.length === 0 ? (
      <p className="text-muted">Your cart is empty</p>
    ) : (
      <>
        {cart.map(item => (
          <div key={item.id} className="d-flex justify-content-
          between align-items-center mb-2">
            <div>
              <h6 className="mb-0">{item.name}</h6>
              <small className="text-muted">${item.price} x
              {item.quantity}</small>
            </div>
            <div>
              <span className="me-2">${(item.price * item.
              quantity).toFixed(2)}</span>
              <button
                className="btn btn-sm btn-outline-danger"
                onClick={() => removeFromCart(item.id)}
              >
                &times;
              </button>
            </div>
          </div>
        ))}

        <div className="border-top pt-2 mt-3">
          <div className="d-flex justify-content-between">
            <strong>Total:</strong>
            <strong>${totalPrice.toFixed(2)}</strong>
          </div>
```

CHAPTER 11   ADDING INTERACTIVITY TO YOUR REACT RESTAURANT WEBSITE

```
                    <button className="btn btn-success w-100
                    mt-2">Checkout</button>
                  </div>
              )}
            </div>
          )}
        </div>
      </div>
    </div>
  </header>
 );
}

export default Header;
```

Now, let's update our App component to pass the cart data and the removeFromCart function to the Header component:

```
import React, { useState } from 'react';
import Header from './Header';
import Hero from './Hero';
import Menu from './Menu';
import Testimonials from './Testimonials';
import Footer from './Footer';

// Sample pizza data
const pizzaData = [
  {
    id: 1,
    name: 'Margherita',
    description: 'Classic pizza with tomato sauce, mozzarella, and basil',
    price: 12.99,
    imageUrl: 'https://source.unsplash.com/random/300x200/?pizza,margherita
'
  },
```

```
  {
    id: 2,
    name: 'Pepperoni',
    description: 'Pizza with tomato sauce, mozzarella, and pepperoni',
    price: 14.99,
    imageUrl: 'https://source.unsplash.com/random/300x200/?pizza,pepperoni'
  },
  {
    id: 3,
    name: 'Vegetarian',
    description: 'Pizza with tomato sauce, mozzarella, and assorted
    vegetables',
    price: 13.99,
    imageUrl: 'https://source.unsplash.com/random/300x200/?pizza,vegetable'
  },
  // Add more pizzas as needed
];

function App() {
  // Cart state lifted up to the App component
  const [cart, setCart] = useState();

  // Function to add a pizza to the cart
  const addToCart = (pizza, quantity) => {
    // Check if this pizza is already in the cart
    const existingItemIndex = cart.findIndex(item => item.id === pizza.id);

    if (existingItemIndex >= 0) {
      // If it is, update the quantity
      const updatedCart = [...cart];
      updatedCart[existingItemIndex].quantity += quantity;
      setCart(updatedCart);
    } else {
      // If not, add it as a new item
      setCart([...cart, { ...pizza, quantity }]);
    }
  };
```

```
// Function to remove a pizza from the cart
const removeFromCart = (pizzaId) => {
  setCart(cart.filter(item => item.id !== pizzaId));
};

// Calculate total items in cart
const cartItemCount = cart.reduce((total, item) => total + item.
quantity, 0);

return (
  <div className="App">
    <Header
      cartItemCount={cartItemCount}
      cart={cart}
      removeFromCart={removeFromCart}
    />
    <Hero />
    <Menu pizzas={pizzaData} addToCart={addToCart} />
    <Testimonials />
    <Footer />
  </div>
);
}
export default App;
```

11.7 Passing Event Handlers as Props

As you've seen in our shopping cart implementation, passing event handlers as props is a powerful pattern in React. It allows child components to communicate with their parents and trigger state changes higher up in the component tree.

Let's explore this pattern in more detail with another example. Imagine we want to add a pizza customization feature to our website. Users should be able to select toppings for their pizza before adding it to the cart.

CHAPTER 11   ADDING INTERACTIVITY TO YOUR REACT RESTAURANT WEBSITE

First, let's create a PizzaCustomizer component:

```
import React, { useState } from 'react';

function PizzaCustomizer({ pizza, onAddToCart, onClose }) {
  const [selectedToppings, setSelectedToppings] = useState([]);
  const [size, setSize] = useState('medium');
  const [quantity, setQuantity] = useState(1);

  // Available toppings
  const availableToppings = [
    { id: 1, name: 'Extra Cheese', price: 1.5 },
    { id: 2, name: 'Pepperoni', price: 2.0 },
    { id: 3, name: 'Mushrooms', price: 1.5 },
    { id: 4, name: 'Onions', price: 1.0 },
    { id: 5, name: 'Bell Peppers', price: 1.0 },
    { id: 6, name: 'Olives', price: 1.5 },
    { id: 7, name: 'Bacon', price: 2.0 },
  ];

  // Size options and their price multipliers
  const sizeOptions = {
    small: { name: 'Small', multiplier: 0.8 },
    medium: { name: 'Medium', multiplier: 1.0 },
    large: { name: 'Large', multiplier: 1.2 },
    'extra-large': { name: 'Extra Large', multiplier: 1.5 }
  };

  // Toggle a topping selection
  const toggleTopping = (topping) => {
    if (selectedToppings.find(t => t.id === topping.id)) {
      setSelectedToppings(selectedToppings.filter(t => t.id !==
      topping.id));
    } else {
      setSelectedToppings([...selectedToppings, topping]);
    }
  };
```

275

CHAPTER 11   ADDING INTERACTIVITY TO YOUR REACT RESTAURANT WEBSITE

```jsx
// Calculate total price
const calculateTotalPrice = () => {
  const basePrice = pizza.price * sizeOptions[size].multiplier;
  const toppingsPrice = selectedToppings.reduce((total, topping) => total
  + topping.price, 0);
  return (basePrice + toppingsPrice) * quantity;
};

// Handle adding to cart
const handleAddToCart = () => {
  const customizedPizza = {
    ...pizza,
    size,
    toppings: selectedToppings,
    totalPrice: calculateTotalPrice() / quantity, // Price per pizza
  };

  onAddToCart(customizedPizza, quantity);
  onClose(); // Close the customizer after adding to cart
};

return (
  <div className="modal-content">
    <div className="modal-header">
      <h5 className="modal-title">Customize Your {pizza.name}</h5>
      <button type="button" className="btn-close"
      onClick={onClose}></button>
    </div>

    <div className="modal-body">
      <div className="mb-4">
        <h6>Select Size:</h6>
        <div className="btn-group w-100">
          {Object.entries(sizeOptions).map(([sizeKey, sizeData]) => (
            <button
              key={sizeKey}
              type="button"
```

```
          className={`btn ${size === sizeKey ? 'btn-primary' : 'btn-
          outline-primary'}`}
          onClick={() => setSize(sizeKey)}
        >
          {sizeData.name}
        </button>
      ))}
    </div>
</div>

<div className="mb-4">
  <h6>Select Toppings:</h6>
  <div className="row g-2">
    {availableToppings.map(topping => {
      const isSelected = selectedToppings.some(t => t.id ===
      topping.id);
      return (
        <div className="col-6" key={topping.id}>
          <div
            className={`card p-2 ${isSelected ? 'bg-light border-
            primary' : ''}`}
            onClick={() => toggleTopping(topping)}
            style={{ cursor: 'pointer' }}
          >
            <div className="d-flex justify-content-between align-
            items-center">
              <span>{topping.name}</span>
              <span>${topping.price.toFixed(2)}</span>
            </div>
            {isSelected && (
              <div className="text-end text-primary">
                <i className="bi bi-check-circle-fill"></i>
              </div>
            )}
```

```jsx
            </div>
          </div>
        );
      })}
    </div>
  </div>

  <div className="mb-4">
    <h6>Quantity:</h6>
    <div className="d-flex align-items-center">
      <button
        className="btn btn-outline-secondary"
        onClick={() => quantity > 1 && setQuantity(quantity - 1)}
      >
        -
      </button>
      <span className="mx-3">{quantity}</span>
      <button
        className="btn btn-outline-secondary"
        onClick={() => setQuantity(quantity + 1)}
      >
        +
      </button>
    </div>
  </div>

  <div className="alert alert-info">
    <div className="d-flex justify-content-between">
      <strong>Total Price:</strong>
      <strong>${calculateTotalPrice().toFixed(2)}</strong>
    </div>
  </div>
</div>

<div className="modal-footer">
  <button type="button" className="btn btn-secondary"
  onClick={onClose}>Cancel</button>
```

CHAPTER 11   ADDING INTERACTIVITY TO YOUR REACT RESTAURANT WEBSITE

```
      <button type="button" className="btn btn-primary"
      onClick={handleAddToCart}>
         Add to Cart
      </button>
    </div>
  </div>
 );
}

export default PizzaCustomizer;
```

Now, let's update our PizzaCard component to use this customizer:

```
import React, { useState } from 'react';
import PizzaCustomizer from './PizzaCustomizer';

function PizzaCard(props) {
  const [showCustomizer, setShowCustomizer] = useState(false);

  const openCustomizer = () => {
    setShowCustomizer(true);
  };

  const closeCustomizer = () => {
    setShowCustomizer(false);
  };

  return (
      <div className="card mb-4">
        <img src={props.imageUrl} className="card-img-top" alt={props.
        name} />
        <div className="card-body">
          <h5 className="card-title">{props.name}</h5>
          <p className="card-text">{props.description}</p>
          <p className="card-text fw-bold">${props.price.toFixed(2)}</p>
```

```
      <button
        className="btn btn-primary w-100"
        onClick={openCustomizer}
      >
        Customize & Order
      </button>
    </div>
  </div>

  {showCustomizer && (
    <div className="modal-backdrop show">
      <div className="modal d-block" tabIndex="-1">
        <div className="modal-dialog modal-lg">
          <PizzaCustomizer
            pizza={props}
            onAddToCart={props.addToCart}
            onClose={closeCustomizer}
          />
        </div>
      </div>
    </div>
  )}
 );
}

export default PizzaCard;
```

In this example, we're passing two event handlers as props to the PizzaCustomizer component:

1. onAddToCart: A function that allows the customizer to add the customized pizza to the cart

2. onClose: A function that allows the customizer to close itself

This pattern gives child components the ability to trigger actions in their parent components, creating a two-way communication flow while still maintaining React's unidirectional data flow principle.

11.8 Conclusion

In this chapter, we've transformed our static Pizza Paradise website into an interactive application by adding state management and event handling. We've learned about:

1. **Internal State**: Using the useState hook to manage component-specific state

2. **Destructuring**: Understanding how array and object destructuring work in JavaScript

3. **Event Handling**: Responding to user interactions in React components

4. **Component Hierarchy**: Managing state flow between parent and child components

5. **Lifting State Up**: Moving shared state to a common ancestor component

6. **Passing Event Handlers as Props**: Enabling child-to-parent communication

These concepts form the foundation of interactive React applications. By understanding how state flows through your component hierarchy, you can build complex, interactive UIs while keeping your code organized and maintainable.

In the next chapter, we'll explore how to use react-bootstrap, a library that provides Bootstrap components built specifically for React. This will allow us to leverage Bootstrap's styling while taking full advantage of React's component model and state management capabilities.

Remember that while the concepts we've covered in this chapter aren't directly related to Bootstrap, they're essential for working with any UI library or framework in React. By mastering these fundamentals, you'll be well-equipped to build sophisticated web applications using React and Bootstrap together.

CHAPTER 12

Improving Your Restaurant Website Using the React-Bootstrap npm Package

12.1 Introduction

In the previous chapter, we built an interactive restaurant website using React's core features like state management, event handling, and component composition. While we used Bootstrap for styling via CDN, we had to manually integrate it with React, which led to some limitations:

1. We had to use string-based class names for styling.
2. We couldn't easily access Bootstrap's JavaScript functionality.
3. We had to write more boilerplate code for interactive components like modals and dropdowns.

In this chapter, we'll address these limitations by introducing **React-Bootstrap** – a library that provides Bootstrap components built specifically for React. This will allow us to leverage Bootstrap's styling while taking full advantage of React's component model.

12.2 Understanding React-Bootstrap

12.2.1 What Is React-Bootstrap?

React-Bootstrap is a complete re-implementation of the Bootstrap components using React. It replaces the Bootstrap JavaScript with React components, providing a more React-friendly way to use Bootstrap's UI components.

12.2.2 How Does React-Bootstrap Work?

Instead of using class names and data attributes to create Bootstrap components, React-Bootstrap provides ready-made React components that encapsulate both the styling and behavior of Bootstrap elements.

For example, instead of writing:

```
<button className="btn btn-primary" data-bs-toggle="modal" data-bs-target="#exampleModal">
  Launch Modal
</button>

<div className="modal fade" id="exampleModal" tabIndex="-1" aria-labelledby="exampleModalLabel" aria-hidden="true">
  {/* Modal content */}
</div>
```

With React-Bootstrap, you can write:

```
import { Button, Modal } from 'react-bootstrap';
import { useState } from 'react';

function MyComponent() {
  const [show, setShow] = useState(false);

  return (
    <>
      <Button variant="primary" onClick={() => setShow(true)}>
        Launch Modal
      </Button>
```

```
    <Modal show={show} onHide={() => setShow(false)}>
      {/* Modal content */}
    </Modal>
  );
}
```

This approach has several advantages:

1. **Declarative API**: Components are controlled through props rather than imperative DOM manipulation

2. **Type Safety**: Props have defined types, making it easier to catch errors

3. **React Integration**: Components work seamlessly with React's state and lifecycle

4. **React-First Implementation**: Uses React's component model instead of Bootstrap's JavaScript implementation

12.2.3 React-Bootstrap vs. Bootstrap

Here's a comparison between React-Bootstrap and the core Bootstrap framework:

Table 12-1. React-Bootstrap and Core Bootstrap Framework Comparison

Feature	Bootstrap	React-Bootstrap
Implementation	CSS + JavaScript	React Components
Usage	Class names + data attributes	React components + props
Control Flow	Imperative (manual DOM manipulation)	Declarative (controlled by state)
Integration with React	Manual	Built for React
Bundle Size	Larger (includes full Bootstrap JS)	Smaller (only includes needed components)
Typings	None	TypeScript support

12.2.4 Completeness and Community

React-Bootstrap is a mature project that implements all the core Bootstrap components. It closely follows Bootstrap's versioning, with React-Bootstrap v2.x corresponding to Bootstrap 5.x.

The project is actively maintained by a community of developers and has over 20,000 stars on GitHub. It welcomes contributions from the community, and there are clear guidelines for contributing to their documentation.

To contribute to React-Bootstrap:

1. Fork the repository on GitHub
2. Create a feature branch
3. Write tests for your changes
4. Submit a pull request

The project maintains an issue tracker where you can find bugs to fix or features to implement if you're interested in contributing.

12.3 Setting Up React-Bootstrap in Our Project

Let's start by adding React-Bootstrap to our Pizza Paradise project. We'll need to install both React-Bootstrap and Bootstrap itself (for the CSS).

12.3.1 Step 1: Install the Dependencies

First, let's install the required packages:

```
npm install react-bootstrap bootstrap
```

12.3.2 Step 2: Import the Bootstrap CSS

We need to import the Bootstrap CSS. The best place to do this is in the main entry file of our application (main.jsx or index.jsx):

```
// In main.jsx or index.jsx
import React from 'react';
```

```
import ReactDOM from 'react-dom/client';
import App from './App';

// Import Bootstrap CSS
import 'bootstrap/dist/css/bootstrap.min.css';

ReactDOM.createRoot(document.getElementById('root')).render(
  <React.StrictMode>
    <App />
  </React.StrictMode>
);
```

Now we're ready to start using React-Bootstrap components in our application!

12.4 Refactoring Our Components with React-Bootstrap

Let's start refactoring our Pizza Paradise website to use React-Bootstrap components. We'll go through each component one by one, explaining the changes and benefits.

12.4.1 Refactoring the Header Component

Let's start with the Header component. Here's how we can refactor it using React-Bootstrap:

```
import React, { useState } from 'react';
import { Navbar, Container, Nav, Button, Badge, Offcanvas } from 'react-bootstrap';

function Header({ cartItemCount, cart, removeFromCart }) {
  const [showCart, setShowCart] = useState(false);

  const handleCartClose = () => setShowCart(false);
  const handleCartShow = () => setShowCart(true);

  // Calculate total price
  const totalPrice = cart.reduce((total, item) => {
    return total + (item.price * item.quantity);
  }, 0);
```

CHAPTER 12   IMPROVING YOUR RESTAURANT WEBSITE USING THE REACT-BOOTSTRAP NPM PACKAGE

```
return (
  <Navbar bg="dark" variant="dark" expand="lg" sticky="top">
    <Container>
      <Navbar.Brand href="#">Pizza Paradise</Navbar.Brand>

      <Navbar.Toggle aria-controls="basic-navbar-nav" />

      <Navbar.Collapse id="basic-navbar-nav">
        <Nav className="me-auto">
          <Nav.Link href="#">Home</Nav.Link>
          <Nav.Link href="#menu">Menu</Nav.Link>
          <Nav.Link href="#testimonials">Testimonials</Nav.Link>
          <Nav.Link href="#contact">Contact</Nav.Link>
        </Nav>

        <Button
          variant="outline-light"
          onClick={handleCartShow}
          className="position-relative"
        >
          <i className="bi bi-cart"></i> Cart
          {cartItemCount > 0 && (
            <Badge
              bg="danger"
              pill
              className="position-absolute top-0 start-100 translate-middle"
            >
              {cartItemCount}
            </Badge>
          )}
        </Button>
      </Navbar.Collapse>
    </Container>
```

CHAPTER 12 IMPROVING YOUR RESTAURANT WEBSITE USING THE REACT-BOOTSTRAP NPM PACKAGE

```
<Offcanvas show={showCart} onHide={handleCartClose} placement="end">
  <Offcanvas.Header closeButton>
    <Offcanvas.Title>Shopping Cart</Offcanvas.Title>
  </Offcanvas.Header>
  <Offcanvas.Body>
    {cart.length === 0 ? (
      <p className="text-muted">Your cart is empty</p>
    ) : (
      <>
        {cart.map(item => (
          <div key={item.id} className="d-flex justify-content-
          between align-items-center mb-2">
            <div>
              <h6 className="mb-0">{item.name}</h6>
              <small className="text-muted">${item.price} x {item.
              quantity}</small>
            </div>
            <div>
              <span className="me-2">${(item.price * item.quantity).
              toFixed(2)}</span>
              <Button
                variant="outline-danger"
                size="sm"
                onClick={() => removeFromCart(item.id)}
              >
                &times;
              </Button>
            </div>
          </div>
        ))}
        <div className="border-top pt-2 mt-3">
          <div className="d-flex justify-content-between">
            <strong>Total:</strong>
            <strong>${totalPrice.toFixed(2)}</strong>
          </div>
```

```
                    <Button variant="success" className="w-100
                    mt-2">Checkout</Button>
                </div>
            )}
            </Offcanvas.Body>
        </Offcanvas>
    </Navbar>
  );
}

export default Header;
```

12.4.2 Key Changes and Benefits

Let's analyze the changes we made to the Header component:

1. **Component-Based Structure**: We replaced HTML elements with React-Bootstrap components like Navbar, Nav, and Button.

2. **Props Instead of Classes**: Instead of using className="navbar-dark bg-dark", we use props like bg="dark" variant="dark".

3. **Improved Cart Display**: We replaced our custom dropdown with React-Bootstrap's Offcanvas component, which provides better mobile support and animations out of the box.

4. **Simplified Structure**: The component structure is cleaner and more semantic, with nested components like Navbar.Brand and Nav.Link making the hierarchy clear.

5. **Automatic Accessibility**: React-Bootstrap components include proper ARIA attributes and keyboard navigation support by default.

12.4.3 Refactoring the Hero Component

Now let's refactor the Hero component:

```
import React from 'react';
import { Container, Row, Col, Button } from 'react-bootstrap';

function Hero() {
  return (
    <div className="bg-dark text-white py-5">
      <Container>
        <Row className="align-items-center">
          <Col md={6}>
            <h1>Welcome to Pizza Paradise</h1>
            <p className="lead">
              Discover the best pizza in town. Made with fresh ingredients
              and baked to perfection.
            </p>
            <Button variant="primary" size="lg" href="#menu">
              View Our Menu
            </Button>
          </Col>
          <Col md={6}>
            <img
              src="https://source.unsplash.com/random/600x400/?pizza"
              alt="Delicious Pizza"
              className="img-fluid rounded"
            />
          </Col>
        </Row>
      </Container>
    </div>
  );
}

export default Hero;
```

12.4.4 Refactoring the PizzaCard Component

Let's refactor the PizzaCard component to use React-Bootstrap:

```
import React, { useState } from 'react';
import { Card, Button, Modal, InputGroup, Form } from 'react-bootstrap';
import PizzaCustomizer from './PizzaCustomizer';

function PizzaCard(props) {
  const [quantity, setQuantity] = useState(1);
  const [showCustomizer, setShowCustomizer] = useState(false);

  const handleCustomizerShow = () => setShowCustomizer(true);
  const handleCustomizerClose = () => setShowCustomizer(false);

  const increaseQuantity = () => {
    setQuantity(quantity + 1);
  };

  const decreaseQuantity = () => {
    if (quantity > 1) {
      setQuantity(quantity - 1);
    }
  };

  const handleAddToCart = () => {
    props.addToCart({
      id: props.id,
      name: props.name,
      price: props.price,
      imageUrl: props.imageUrl
    }, quantity);

    setQuantity(1);
  };

  return (
      <Card className="h-100">
        <Card.Img variant="top" src={props.imageUrl} alt={props.name} />
```

CHAPTER 12   IMPROVING YOUR RESTAURANT WEBSITE USING THE REACT-BOOTSTRAP NPM PACKAGE

```
<Card.Body>
  <Card.Title>{props.name}</Card.Title>
  <Card.Text>{props.description}</Card.Text>
  <Card.Text className="fw-bold">${props.price.toFixed(2)}
  </Card.Text>

  <InputGroup className="mb-3">
    <Button
      variant="outline-secondary"
      onClick={decreaseQuantity}
    >
      -
    </Button>
    <Form.Control
      value={quantity}
      readOnly
      className="text-center"
    />
    <Button
      variant="outline-secondary"
      onClick={increaseQuantity}
    >
      +
    </Button>
  </InputGroup>

  <div className="d-grid gap-2">
    <Button
      variant="primary"
      onClick={handleAddToCart}
    >
      Add to Cart
    </Button>
    <Button
      variant="outline-primary"
      onClick={handleCustomizerShow}
    >
```

CHAPTER 12   IMPROVING YOUR RESTAURANT WEBSITE USING THE REACT-BOOTSTRAP NPM PACKAGE

```
              Customize
            </Button>
          </div>
        </Card.Body>
      </Card>

      <Modal show={showCustomizer} onHide={handleCustomizerClose}
      size="lg">
        <PizzaCustomizer
          pizza={props}
          onAddToCart={props.addToCart}
          onClose={handleCustomizerClose}
        />
      </Modal>
    );
}

export default PizzaCard;
```

12.4.5 Refactoring the PizzaCustomizer Component

Now let's refactor the PizzaCustomizer component:

```
import React, { useState } from 'react';
import { Modal, Button, ButtonGroup, Row, Col, Card, Form, Alert } from
'react-bootstrap';

function PizzaCustomizer({ pizza, onAddToCart, onClose }) {
  const [selectedToppings, setSelectedToppings] = useState();
  const [size, setSize] = useState('medium');
  const [quantity, setQuantity] = useState(1);

  // Available toppings
  const availableToppings = [
    { id: 1, name: 'Extra Cheese', price: 1.5 },
    { id: 2, name: 'Pepperoni', price: 2.0 },
    { id: 3, name: 'Mushrooms', price: 1.5 },
```

294

```
    { id: 4, name: 'Onions', price: 1.0 },
    { id: 5, name: 'Bell Peppers', price: 1.0 },
    { id: 6, name: 'Olives', price: 1.5 },
    { id: 7, name: 'Bacon', price: 2.0 },
];
// Size options and their price multipliers
const sizeOptions = {
  small: { name: 'Small', multiplier: 0.8 },
  medium: { name: 'Medium', multiplier: 1.0 },
  large: { name: 'Large', multiplier: 1.2 },
  'extra-large': { name: 'Extra Large', multiplier: 1.5 }
};

// Toggle a topping selection
const toggleTopping = (topping) => {
  if (selectedToppings.find(t => t.id === topping.id)) {
    setSelectedToppings(selectedToppings.filter(t => t.id !==
    topping.id));
  } else {
    setSelectedToppings([...selectedToppings, topping]);
  }
};

// Calculate total price
const calculateTotalPrice = () => {
  const basePrice = pizza.price * sizeOptions[size].multiplier;
  const toppingsPrice = selectedToppings.reduce((total, topping) => total
  + topping.price, 0);
  return (basePrice + toppingsPrice) * quantity;
};

// Handle adding to cart
const handleAddToCart = () => {
  const customizedPizza = {
    ...pizza,
    size,
```

CHAPTER 12   IMPROVING YOUR RESTAURANT WEBSITE USING THE REACT-BOOTSTRAP NPM PACKAGE

```
    toppings: selectedToppings,
    totalPrice: calculateTotalPrice() / quantity, // Price per pizza
  };

  onAddToCart(customizedPizza, quantity);
  onClose(); // Close the customizer after adding to cart
};

return (

    <Modal.Header closeButton>
      <Modal.Title>Customize Your {pizza.name}</Modal.Title>
    </Modal.Header>

    <Modal.Body>
      <Form>
        <Form.Group className="mb-4">
          <Form.Label>Select Size:</Form.Label>
          <ButtonGroup className="w-100">
            {Object.entries(sizeOptions).map(([sizeKey, sizeData]) => (
              <Button
                key={sizeKey}
                variant={size === sizeKey ? 'primary' : 'outline-
                primary'}
                onClick={() => setSize(sizeKey)}
              >
                {sizeData.name}
              </Button>
            ))}
          </ButtonGroup>
        </Form.Group>

        <Form.Group className="mb-4">
          <Form.Label>Select Toppings:</Form.Label>
          <Row xs={1} md={2} className="g-2">
            {availableToppings.map(topping => {
              const isSelected = selectedToppings.some(t => t.id ===
              topping.id);
```

```jsx
    return (
      <Col key={topping.id}>
        <Card
          className={isSelected ? 'border-primary' : ''}
          onClick={() => toggleTopping(topping)}
          style={{ cursor: 'pointer' }}
        >
          <Card.Body className="p-2">
            <div className="d-flex justify-content-between
            align-items-center">
              <span>{topping.name}</span>
              <span>${topping.price.toFixed(2)}</span>
            </div>
            {isSelected && (
              <div className="text-end text-primary">
                <i className="bi bi-check-circle-fill"></i>
              </div>
            )}
          </Card.Body>
        </Card>
      </Col>
    );
  })}
  </Row>
</Form.Group>

<Form.Group className="mb-4">
  <Form.Label>Quantity:</Form.Label>
  <div className="d-flex align-items-center">
    <Button
      variant="outline-secondary"
      onClick={() => quantity > 1 && setQuantity(quantity - 1)}
    >
      -
    </Button>
```

```
              <span className="mx-3">{quantity}</span>
              <Button
                variant="outline-secondary"
                onClick={() => setQuantity(quantity + 1)}
              >
                +
              </Button>
            </div>
          </Form.Group>

          <Alert variant="info">
            <div className="d-flex justify-content-between">
              <strong>Total Price:</strong>
              <strong>${calculateTotalPrice().toFixed(2)}</strong>
            </div>
          </Alert>
        </Form>
      </Modal.Body>

      <Modal.Footer>
        <Button variant="secondary" onClick={onClose}>Cancel</Button>
        <Button variant="primary" onClick={handleAddToCart}>
          Add to Cart
        </Button>
      </Modal.Footer>
    );
}

export default PizzaCustomizer;
```

12.4.6 Refactoring the Menu Component

Let's refactor the Menu component:

```
import React from 'react';
import { Container, Row, Col } from 'react-bootstrap';
import PizzaCard from './PizzaCard';
```

```
function Menu({ pizzas, addToCart }) {
  return (
    <Container as="section" className="my-5" id="menu">
      <h2 className="text-center mb-4">Our Menu</h2>
      <Row>
        {pizzas.map(pizza => (
          <Col md={4} key={pizza.id} className="mb-4">
            <PizzaCard
              {...pizza}
              addToCart={addToCart}
            />
          </Col>
        ))}
      </Row>
    </Container>
  );
}

export default Menu;
```

12.4.7 Refactoring the App Component

Finally, let's update our App component to use React-Bootstrap:

```
import React, { useState } from 'react';
import { Container } from 'react-bootstrap';
import Header from './Header';
import Hero from './Hero';
import Menu from './Menu';
import Testimonials from './Testimonials';
import Footer from './Footer';

// Sample pizza data
const pizzaData = [
  {
    id: 1,
    name: 'Margherita',
```

```
    description: 'Classic pizza with tomato sauce, mozzarella, and basil',
    price: 12.99,
    imageUrl: 'https://source.unsplash.com/random/300x200/?pizza,margherita'
  },
  {
    id: 2,
    name: 'Pepperoni',
    description: 'Pizza with tomato sauce, mozzarella, and pepperoni',
    price: 14.99,
    imageUrl: 'https://source.unsplash.com/random/300x200/?pizza,pepperoni'
  },
  {
    id: 3,
    name: 'Vegetarian',
    description: 'Pizza with tomato sauce, mozzarella, and assorted
    vegetables',
    price: 13.99,
    imageUrl: 'https://source.unsplash.com/random/300x200/?pizza,vegetable'
  },
  // Add more pizzas as needed
];

function App() {
  // Cart state lifted up to the App component
  const [cart, setCart] = useState();

  // Function to add a pizza to the cart
  const addToCart = (pizza, quantity) => {
    // Check if this pizza is already in the cart
    const existingItemIndex = cart.findIndex(item => item.id === pizza.id);

    if (existingItemIndex >= 0) {
      // If it is, update the quantity
      const updatedCart = [...cart];
      updatedCart[existingItemIndex].quantity += quantity;
      setCart(updatedCart);
```

```
    } else {
      // If not, add it as a new item
      setCart([...cart, { ...pizza, quantity }]);
    }
  };

  // Function to remove a pizza from the cart
  const removeFromCart = (pizzaId) => {
    setCart(cart.filter(item => item.id !== pizzaId));
  };

  // Calculate total items in cart
  const cartItemCount = cart.reduce((total, item) => total + item.
  quantity, 0);

  return (
    <>
      <Header
        cartItemCount={cartItemCount}
        cart={cart}
        removeFromCart={removeFromCart}
      />
      <Hero />
      <Menu pizzas={pizzaData} addToCart={addToCart} />
      <Testimonials />
      <Footer />
    </>
  );
}

export default App;
```

12.5 Benefits of Using React-Bootstrap

Now that we've refactored our Pizza Paradise website to use React-Bootstrap, let's discuss the key benefits and improvements:

12.5.1 Declarative Component API

React-Bootstrap provides a declarative API that aligns with React's philosophy. Instead of manipulating the DOM imperatively (as with vanilla Bootstrap), we declare what we want through props and let React handle the updates.

For example, with vanilla Bootstrap, showing/hiding a modal requires:

```
// Vanilla Bootstrap
const modal = new bootstrap.Modal(document.getElementById('myModal'));
modal.show(); // Show the modal
modal.hide(); // Hide the modal
```

With React-Bootstrap, it's simply:

```
// React-Bootstrap
const [show, setShow] = useState(false);

// To show the modal
setShow(true);

// To hide the modal
setShow(false);

// In the JSX
<Modal show={show} onHide={() => setShow(false)}>
  {/* Modal content */}
</Modal>
```

This declarative approach is more consistent with React's state-driven UI model and easier to reason about.

12.5.2 Component Composition

React-Bootstrap leverages React's component composition model, allowing for cleaner and more maintainable code. For example, the Navbar component has child components like Navbar.Brand, Navbar.Toggle, and Navbar.Collapse that make the structure more explicit and self-documenting.

12.5.3 Improved Type Safety

React-Bootstrap comes with TypeScript definitions, providing better type checking and autocompletion in modern IDEs. This helps catch errors at compile time rather than runtime.

12.5.4 Accessibility Improvements

React-Bootstrap components are designed with accessibility in mind. They include proper ARIA attributes, keyboard navigation support, and focus management out of the box.

12.5.5 Reduced Bundle Size

By using React-Bootstrap, we can potentially reduce our bundle size as we only import the specific components we need, rather than including the entire Bootstrap JavaScript library. This targeted approach to imports helps optimize our application size.

12.5.6 Better Integration with React Patterns

React-Bootstrap components work seamlessly with React patterns like controlled components, context, and hooks. This makes it easier to integrate them into a React application's state management and component hierarchy.

12.6 Common Pitfalls and How to Avoid Them

While React-Bootstrap offers many benefits, there are some common pitfalls to be aware of.

12.6.1 Mixing Bootstrap Classes with React-Bootstrap Components

One common mistake is mixing direct Bootstrap class usage with React-Bootstrap components. While React-Bootstrap components accept className props for additional styling, it's best to use the component props when available.

Avoid:

```
<Button className="btn-primary">Click Me</Button>
```

Prefer:

```
<Button variant="primary">Click Me</Button>
```

12.6.2 Not Importing the Bootstrap CSS

React-Bootstrap provides the component structure but relies on Bootstrap's CSS for styling. Don't forget to import the Bootstrap CSS in your project.

```
// In your entry file (e.g., main.jsx or index.jsx)
import 'bootstrap/dist/css/bootstrap.min.css';
```

12.6.3 Using Imperative Code with React-Bootstrap Components

Avoid using imperative code to control React-Bootstrap components. Instead, use state and props to control their behavior.

Avoid:

```
// Don't do this
const modalElement = document.getElementById('myModal');
modalElement.style.display = 'block';
```

Prefer:

```
const [show, setShow] = useState(false);

// Later in your component
<Modal show={show} onHide={() => setShow(false)}>
  {/* Modal content */}
</Modal>
```

12.7 Conclusion

In this chapter, we've successfully refactored our Pizza Paradise website to use React-Bootstrap, making it more maintainable, accessible, and aligned with React's component model. We've seen how React-Bootstrap provides a more declarative API for Bootstrap components, eliminating the need for jQuery and making our code more React-idiomatic.

Key takeaways from this chapter include:

1. React-Bootstrap provides React components that encapsulate Bootstrap's styling and behavior
2. It offers a more declarative API that aligns with React's philosophy
3. It improves type safety, accessibility, and integration with React patterns
4. It provides a more React-idiomatic way to use Bootstrap components

By using React-Bootstrap, we've made our Pizza Paradise website more maintainable and easier to extend. The component-based approach aligns perfectly with React's philosophy and makes our code more readable and self-documenting.

12.8 Things That We Didn't Discuss

The web development world is in constant flux, especially the front-end web development part. In addition, the JS ecosystem is huge and ever-evolving, and sometimes it can be hard to surf the technology wave. For that reason, I focused on HTML, CSS, JS, Bootstrap, and React, with particular focus on the react-bootstrap npm package.

That being said, here are some honorable mentions of technologies we glazed over or completely skipped:

12.8.1 State Management Solutions

- **Redux:** A predictable state container for JavaScript apps that helps manage application state with a unidirectional data flow pattern

- **MobX:** A simple, scalable state management solution with reactive capabilities

- **Zustand:** A small, fast, and scalable state-management solution using simplified flux principles

- **Recoil:** An experimental state management library for React that provides several capabilities that are difficult to achieve with React alone

- **Jotai:** An atomic approach to global React state management with a minimal API

12.8.2 Type Systems and Tooling

- **TypeScript:** A strongly typed programming language that builds on JavaScript, giving you better tooling at any scale

- **PropTypes:** Runtime type checking for React props and similar objects

- **Flow:** A static type checker for JavaScript

12.8.3 Build Tools and Module Bundlers

- **Webpack:** A static module bundler for modern JavaScript applications

- **Vite:** A build tool that aims to provide a faster and leaner development experience for modern web projects

- **Rollup:** A module bundler for JavaScript which compiles small pieces of code into something larger and more complex

- **Parcel:** A zero configuration web application bundler
- **Esbuild:** An extremely fast JavaScript bundler and minifier

12.8.4 CSS Solutions

- **CSS-in-JS:** Libraries like styled-components and emotion that allow you to write CSS directly in your JavaScript
- **CSS Modules:** A CSS file in which all class names and animation names are scoped locally by default
- **Tailwind CSS:** A utility-first CSS framework packed with classes that can be composed to build any design
- **SASS/SCSS:** CSS preprocessors that add features like variables, nesting, and mixins to CSS

12.8.5 UI Component Libraries

- **Material-UI:** A popular React UI framework implementing Google's Material Design
- **Chakra UI:** A simple, modular and accessible component library for React applications
- **Ant Design:** An enterprise-class UI design language and React UI library
- **Semantic UI:** A development framework that helps create beautiful, responsive layouts using human-friendly HTML

12.8.6 Modern React Patterns

- **React Hooks:** Functions that let you "hook into" React state and lifecycle features from function components
- **React Context API:** A way to pass data through the component tree without having to pass props down manually at every level

- **React Suspense:** A feature that lets your components "wait" for something before they render
- **Server Components:** A new React feature that allows components to be rendered on the server

12.8.7 State-Driven UI Approaches

- **Finite State Machines:** Libraries like XState that model UI as explicit states and transitions
- **Declarative UI Patterns:** Approaches that focus on describing what the UI should look like rather than how to update it

Many of these technologies could complement or provide alternative approaches to modern web development, especially in terms of state management and declarative UI patterns.

12.9 Conclusion

This brings us to the end of this book. I hope it was as fun for you learning all about the Bootstrap framework and the modern ecosystem of front-end development as it was for my writing about it.

If you'd like to learn more, there are a number of titles in the Apress library to explore more advanced React concepts and how to apply them to your day to day work – be it your personal or professional projects.

Some of those titles are

- *Web Forms with React: Build Robust and Scalable Forms with React Hook Form* (Apress Pocket Guides), First Edition, by Usman Abdur Rehman
- *Crafting Clean Code with JavaScript and React: A Practical Guide to Sustainable Front-End Development*, First Edition, by Héla Ben Khalfallah
- *Advanced Front-End Development: Building Scalable and High-Performance Web Applications with React*, First Edition, by Nitesh Upadhyaya

Index

A

Abstraction layer, 68–70
addToCart function, 265, 266, 268, 269
Ant design, 307
App component, 230, 263, 265, 268, 272, 299–301
App.js, 230, 232, 238, 243, 245
Array destructuring, 254
    cleaner API, 256
    naming flexibility, 255
    vs. object destructuring, 255, 256

B

Block Element Modifier (BEM) methodology, 117, 118
Bootstrap, 224, 250
    component combinations, *see* Component combinations
    component composition, *see* Component composition
    component library, 77, 78
    components, 122, 133 (*see also* Components)
    CSS display properties, 57, 58
    documentation, 54
    drawbacks, 53, 54
    grid-based web layout system, 58
    960 grid system, 59, 60
    grid system, 53, 68, 74, 78
    innovations, 61
    web design, 61
    website, 219
Bootstrap 5.x, 286
Breakpoints, 46, 47, 50
Browser
    DOCTYPE, 29
    h1 tag, 14
    html pages, 14
    metadata, 29
    web pages, 39–41
Buttons, 113, 133, 155

C

Card component
    components, 140, 141
    content containers, 142
    content organization, 143, 144
    design principles, 142
    implementation, 145–152
    layouts, 142
    variants, 141
CDN, *see* Content Delivery Network (CDN)
Chakra UI, 307
Column system and breakpoints
    browser results, 73
    chrome extensions, 74, 75
    full spectrum of contextual colors, 70, 71
    portfolio page, 71–73
        contextual colors, 75
        header and footer, 75

INDEX

Column system and breakpoints (*cont.*)
    main layout, 75
    project cards, 75
  shape-shifts, 76, 77
Command-line operations, 199
Component-based
    approach, 221, 305
Component-based design, 132, 133
Component combinations
  buttons+badges, 155
  card +list groups, 154
  input group + button +
    dropdown, 155
  navbar + dropdowns, 153, 154
Component composition
  definition, 152
  principles, 153
  techniques, 156
Component hierarchy
  build shopping cart
    component, 269–272
  child components, 263
  grandparent-to-grandchild
    communication, 269
  pass state down, 268
  in Pizza Paradise application, 263
  prop drilling, 268
  props to update Parent State, 268
  re-rendering, 268
  state initialization, 268
  state lifting, 263–267
Components, 156, 157
  base components, 133
  card component (*see* Card
    component)
  compound/dynamic, 134
  form, 135
  layout, 135
  navbar component (*see* Navbar
    component)
  utility, 135
Containers, 46, 51, 52
  fixed-width container, 46, 48, 53
  fluid container, 46, 48, 53
  nesting rules, 53
  responsive container, 46, 49
  types, 46, 48
Content Delivery Network (CDN),
    216, 220
  advantages, 216
  npm approach, 217
Contextual colors, 50, 51, 70–71,
    75, 77, 78
CSS
  box model, 44–46
  class selectors, 35–37
  content display, 21
  CSS-in-JS, 307
  declaration, 31
  display: inline, 22
  files, 247
  grid layout, 63–68
  id selectors, 35–37
  modules, 307
  paris, 22
  rules, 248
  specificity, 34, 35
  styles, 24

D

Declarative UI patterns, 308
Design patterns, 131
Destructuring
  array destructuring, 254
  object destructuring, 253

useState, 256
Devtools, 29, 30, 37, 38, 40
Document Object Model (DOM), 159, 169, 177, 178, 187, 188, 190, 210, 212, 250
DOM, *see* Document Object Model (DOM)

E

Esbuild, 218, 307
Event handling, React
    comparison, 258
    create controlled input, 260
    PizzaCard component, 261, 262
    standard DOM events, 259
    vanilla JavaScript, 258

F

Facebook, 212
File editing, notepad, 9
    close program, 10
    CTRL key, 11
    index.html file, 9, 10
    interface, 9
    text font, 11
    text, zoom in, 11
    zoom level, 10
File extensions, 3, 4
    HTML, 8
    itinerary.txt
        desktop visible, 4
        index.html, 6–8
        index.txt, 5, 6
        New command, 5
        steps, 4
        Text Document, 5
        troubleshooting, 7

Finite state machines, 308
Flexbox, 62, 63, 65, 67, 68
Flow, 306
Footer component, 244–246
Footer.jsx, 244
Forms
    BEM methodology, 117, 118
    controls, 120, 121
    definition, 111
    elements *vs.* components, 122
    horizontal forms, 119
    HTML (*see* HTML forms)
    inline forms, 119, 120
    layout options
        default layout stacks, 118
        horizontal forms, 119
        inline forms, 119, 120
    principles, 117
    validation, 121
Forms styling
    challenges, 116
    cross-browser compatibility, 116
    focus states/accessibility, 116
    inconsistent browser defaults, 115
    pseudo-elements, 115
    responsive forms, 116
    Shadow DOM elements, 115
Front-end development, 207, 308
Front-end ecosystem, 220, 221
Front-end landscape, 220
Front-end workflow, 218–219

G

Git, 194, 197
    developers, 194
    GitHub and Netlify, 196
    process, 194

INDEX

Git (*cont.*)
  repository, 198
  setup, 197
  version control system, 194
  workflows, 195
GitHub, 195, 196, 198, 200
  account, 198
  features, 195
  web interface, 202

H

handleAddToCart function, 268
Header component, 229–231, 268, 269, 272, 287–290
Header.jsx, 229
Hero component, 232, 246, 291
Hero.jsx, 231
Hero section components, 231–232
Hooks, 253
  destructuring, 253
  useState hook, 281
HTML
  add borders, 23
  attributes, 19
    align="right, 19, 21
    style attribute, 20, 21
  block-level and inline elements, 24
  button element, 37, 38
  clearIt(), 38
  cosmetic updates, 25
  display value, 26
  DOCTYPE, 27, 28
  elements, 17
  elements styles, 24
  formatting, 22
  h1 element, 22–24
  h1 styles to external stylesheet, 32
  heading tags, 18
  index.html file, 25, 26, 37
  index.html page, 23
  inline elements and block elements, 43
  metadata, 27, 28
  p elements, 23, 24
  p styles to external stylesheet, 33
  span elements, 23, 37
  span styles to external stylesheet, 33, 34
  style attribute, 25
  style sheets, 26
    testing, 30, 31
  tags, 22
HTML forms
  form controls, 112
    attributes, 114
    buttons, 113
    elements, 113
  <form> element, 111, 112
    labels, 114
    selection controls, 113
    text input, 112
HTTP methods, 211

I

Images
  classes, 95, 99, 100
  portfolio
    figure, 99
    figure caption, 99
    profile image, 96
    project images, 97
    shape options, 98
index.html file
  annotate text, 11
  notepad results, 13
  open file in browser, 13

tags, 11, 12
    add text, 12
    closing heading 1 tag, 12
    opening heading 1 tag, 12
Invoice application
    development, 136
    navbar component, 139, 140
    nested components, 155, 156
Invoice Maker app, 193, 194, 203
Invoice Maker project, 197
    client information section, 124
    completion, 128
    HTML structure, 123, 124
    invoice details, 124, 125
    item entry form, 125, 126
    items table, 126, 127
    overview, 123
    totals section, 127, 128
Invoice totals
    data flow, 190
    DOM traversal, 188
    totals calculation, 189
    total section, 185
    updateTotals function, 186–189
    user experience, 190, 191

J, K

JavaScript (JS), 38
    development, 210
    engine, 210
JavaScript-powered components, 159–192
JavaScript-powered features, 191, 192
JavaScript's transformation, 208
    ES6, 208
    Node.js, 210
    web applications, 209

Jotai, 306
JS, *see* JavaScript (JS)
JSX-a syntax, 224
    CSS classes, 225
    HTML attributes, 227
    JavaScript XML, 224
    quirks, 227

L

Labels, 114
Loading indicators, 178
    best practices, 184
    loading state, 180, 181
    reset button, 179
    setTimeout function, 181, 182
    spinner component, 182, 183
    testing, 182

M

map() function, 238
Material-UI, 307
Menu component, 238, 263, 265, 268, 298–299
Menu.jsx, 235
Mobile-first approach, 61, 136
MobX, 306
Modals
    add item modal, 171, 172
    connect to buttons, 172
    definition, 170
    DOM, 177, 178
    form submission, 173–177
    form validation, 177
    parts, 170
    static/dismissible, 171
    testing, 178

INDEX

Model-View-Controller (MVC), 190
Modern JavaScript project, 215
Moment.js, 213
MVC, *see* Model-View-Controller (MVC)

N

Navbar component
    accessibility considerations, 138
    classes, 138
    color schemes, 138
    components, 137
    implementation, 145–152
    invoice application, 139, 140
    navbar-expand-{breakpoint} classes, 136
    placement options, 137, 138
    responsive behavior, 137
Nested components, 155, 156
Nested flexbox, 65, 66
Netlify, 196, 200–202
Node.js and npm, 210, 212, 216
    macOS, 214
    Ubuntu/Debian Linux, 214
    Windows, 214

O

Object destructuring, 253–255, 281
onAddToCart, 280
onClose, 280
One-dimensional layout model, 63, 65, 67, 68

P, Q

package.json, 213, 217
Parcel, 218, 307
PizzaCard component, 237, 239, 292

PizzaCard.css, 247
PizzaCard.jsx, 234
PizzaCustomizer component, 275, 280, 294
Popular bundlers, 218
Portfolio
    images (*see* Images)
    tables (*see* Tables)
    typography (*see* Typography)
    utility classes (*see* Utility classes)
    web page, 80–82
Props, 251
    drilling, 268, 269
    external state, 251, 252
    hardcoding values, 239
    vs. internal state, 252, 253
    JavaScript objects, 233
    passing event handlers, 274–280
    PizzaCard component, 238
    rule, 240
    update Parent State, 268
    work, 234
PropTypes, 306

R

React
    component hierarchy (*see* Component hierarchy)
    event handling (*see* Event handling, React)
React-Bootstrap, 283, 284
    advantages, 285
    benefits and improvements, 303
        accessibility improvements, 303
        bundle size, 303
        component composition, 302
        declarative API, 302

import Bootstrap CSS, 304
integrate with React patterns, 303
use imperative code, 304
vs. Bootstrap, 285
completeness and community, 286
import Bootstrap CSS, 286
install, 286
mix direct Bootstrap class, 303
refactor Header component, 287
- App component, 299
- changes and benefits, 290
- Hero component, 291
- Menu component, 298
- PizzaCard component, 292
- PizzaCustomizer component, 294

React-Bootstrap v2.x, 286
React components, 228, 229, 248
- Bootstrap navbar, 230
- src/App.jsx file, 228

React context API, 307
React development, 249
React Hooks, 307
React project, 222
- CodeSandbox or StackBlitz, 222
- structure, 223
- Vite, 222

React suspense, 308
React web app, 250
Recoil, 306
Redux, 269, 306
removeFromCart function, 272
Rollup, 218, 306
Rows, 49-51

S

SASS/SCSS, 307
Semantic UI, 307

Server components, 308
setTimeout function, 181, 182
Spinners, 133, 179, 182-184
State in React, 251-253

T

Tables
- classes, 100, 107
- portfolio
  - education and certifications, 105-107
  - project timeline, 103-105
  - skill proficiency levels, 101-103

Tabs, 160, 161
- card view, 167
- content, 167
- event delegation, 170
- invoice items section, 161, 162, 164-166
- JavaScript code, 168, 169
- navigation, 167, 170
- parts, 160
- remove button, 170
- synchronization, 168, 169
- works, 167

Tailwind CSS, 307
Testimonials.jsx, 242
Testimonials section, 240
- add testimonials, 243-244
- create testimonial component, 240-241
- create testimonials section component, 242-243

Theme toggle
- implementation, 145-152
- JavaScript to toggle, 144, 145
- light and dark modes, 144

Two-dimensional layout model, 63–65
TypeScript, 306
Typography, 89
   categories, 90, 94, 95
   portfolio
      footer, 94
      header, 90, 91
      projects section, 92, 93
      sidebar, 91, 92
   principles, 89, 90

U

User agent style sheet, 11, 14
User experience, 190, 191
useState, 253, 255, 256
   multiple state variables, 257
   object destructuring, 255
   objects with useState, 258
   update function, 256
Utility classes, 82, 83, 88
   categories, 89
   portfolio
      footer, 87, 88
      header, 83, 84
      projects section, 85–87
      sidebar, 84, 85

V

Vite, 215–216, 218, 222–224, 306

W, X, Y

Web applications, 111, 209, 212
Web design, 59–62, 95
Web layout terms, 67
Webpack, 217, 218, 306
Websites, 80–82, 107, 131, 132
Web UI Patterns, 131–132
Whitespace
     code, 16, 17
   collapsing in HTML, 16
   definition, 14
   HTML element, 17, 18
   html files, 14–16

Z

Zustand, 306

GPSR Compliance
The European Union's (EU) General Product Safety Regulation (GPSR) is a set of rules that requires consumer products to be safe and our obligations to ensure this.

If you have any concerns about our products, you can contact us on

ProductSafety@springernature.com

In case Publisher is established outside the EU, the EU authorized representative is:

Springer Nature Customer Service Center GmbH
Europaplatz 3
69115 Heidelberg, Germany

www.ingramcontent.com/pod-product-compliance
Lightning Source LLC
LaVergne TN
LVHW081537070526
838199LV00056B/3690